Henley Royal Regatta

A Celebration of 150 Years

HENLEY ROYAL REGATTA

A Celebration of 150 Years

RICHARD BURNELL

William Heinemann
in association with
Gieves & Hawkes

Heinemann Kingswood
Michelin House, 81 Fulham Road, London SW3 6RB
LONDON   MELBOURNE   AUCKLAND
Copyright © 1989 Richard Burnell
First published 1989
0 434 98134 6

Printed and bound in Great Britain
by Butler & Tanner Ltd, Frome and London

Contents

Acknowledgements

The illustrations in this book are reproduced by kind permission of the following: Badminton Library no. 25; George Bushell nos. 1, 2, 5, 9, 23, 28, 29, 33, 34, 35, 38, 43, 44, 45; *Daily Telegraph* no. 58; Alan Davidson no. 8; Angus Gillan Album no. 26; Mark Harrison nos. 10, 49, 60; Hulton Picture Library nos. 3, 18, 21, 22, 24, 32; Keystone Press Agency nos. 51, 53, 68; Leander Club no. 27; London News Agency no. 31; Guy Nickalls Album no. 14; Planet News no. 36; Royal Photographic Society no. 20; Nigel Scarlett nos. 55, 56; John Shore nos. 11, 12, 13, 46, 47, 48, 50b, 57, 59, 66, 67, 69, 70, 71; Sport & General nos. 6, 7, 37, 39, 40, 42, 50a, 52, 54; Sybil Reeves Album nos. 15, 16, 17, 19.

We are particularly grateful to Chris Smith for the five photographs (nos. 61–65) which we have called 'Chris Smith looks at Henley'. Seven of the colour illustrations (nos. 5–11 in the colour section) are reproduced by kind permission of Mark Harrison. The two photographs of the new Regatta Headquarters (nos. 12 and 13) are reproduced by permission of Richard Bryant. The maps in the book were specially drawn by Peter Sullivan; and the aerial photograph on page 62 was kindly provided by the Thames Valley Police. The portrait of James Nash is reproduced by permission of the Mayor and Town Council of Henley.

The above acknowledgements fall short of the thanks owed to various people who have given invaluable help in the production of this book, especially Georgina Stonor, Sybil Reeves and John Crocker; also Peter Coni, Richard Goddard and the staff at Regatta Headquarters, who all showed commendable patience in the face of innumerable enquiries and requests; and Jill Fear and Sue Gates who deciphered my hand-writing, always illegible and sometimes, during the past two years, frenetic; and finally of course my wife who had to bear the brunt of my alternating enthusiasm and frustration.

Richard Burnell

Foreword

The fascination of Henley Royal Regatta is not simply the racing, the memorable individuals who have competed and the many good stories that are told about them. It is also the unique way the Regatta has evolved without losing its traditional character so that, after 150 years, it remains very recognizably the Regatta that was so popular in the 19th century.

Richard Burnell has known the Regatta intimately throughout his life. His father was a famous oarsman and a memorable Steward. His family have been closely connected with the Regatta for many years. He was himself an outstanding competitor, and has been a Steward for more than twenty years.

To mark the 150th anniversary of the Regatta, Richard Burnell has written a history which, whilst it remembers highlights of the races and many of the best anecdotes about the characters, concentrates on how the event as a whole has grown and changed. No previous book about the Regatta has examined in detail its changing organization; how its finances have developed; the rationale behind the various races that have been offered; or the changing trends in attendance, with the way those have been affected by such factors as the railway, the motorcar, the houseboat and the hospitality tent. His research covers almost every aspect of the Regatta's development; and he has run to earth a large number of photographs and illustrations which will delight all those who love the Regatta.

There are many who happily admit to being addicted to Henley Royal Regatta. Others find its unchanging appeal something to wonder at, and all will find this book an invaluable work of reference and a most enjoyable history of a very special sporting occasion.

Peter Coni

Chairman,
Committee of Management,
Henley Royal Regatta

Introduction

The problem with history is that it grows longer every year. Indeed, during Henley Regatta it grows longer every five minutes. The historian picks out the historically important races, but in truth every race is important to those taking part. Just 'making it to Henley' may be the high spot in some oarsman's career. One day he will probably tell his grandchildren – and quite rightly so. It is unlikely that his race will be chronicled in this book but no disparagement is intended; it is only one of some 10,000 such.

Many years ago when petrol was still served from hand-operated pumps, a *Punch* cartoonist depicted an exhausted garage attendant appealing to the driver of a petrol-guzzling limousine, 'Please switch off, sir, she's gaining on me.' Henley history has been a little like that.

Recording the first sixty-four Regattas (1839–1902) Herbert Steward described 1,553 races. Sir Theodore Cook covered only twelve Regattas (1903–14) and that added 600 or so more races. Herbert's son, Tom Steward, described another nineteen Regattas (1920–38) and they encompassed 1,548 races which was only five less than his father had covered in sixty-four Regattas. But it was Humphrey Playford, assuming the mantle of Henley historian in 1939, who found himself in the position of that petrol pump attendant. He needed two volumes, running to nearly 1,000 pages and describing 3,220 races, to cover twenty-four Regattas (1939–68); by the time his *magnum*

opus came off the presses there was already a backlog of six Regattas to be written up.

It was at that point, in 1974, that I suggested that *Henley Records* should be produced annually in paperback form, using material available in the programmes. *Henley Records* now appears every five years. They may be less prestigious than the traditionally bound volumes of the past, but at least they keep the *Records*, now covering more than 200 races each year, up to date.

This book is not, and could not possibly be, another book of *Records*, but rather a celebration of 150 years of boat racing at Henley. Hopefully it may render the Royal Regatta more interesting to those who make the annual pilgrimage as *cognoscenti*, and more meaningful to those who come without prior knowledge.

That Henley is a unique phenomenon few will dispute. Like the Grand National and the Oxford and Cambridge Boat Race it has achieved a special status in the British way of life, a Mecca for schoolboys, students, club and international oarsmen, and at the same time a high spot in the social season, and more recently a major venue for corporate entertaining.

I had the good fortune to be born on Remenham Hill. I am told I was carried into the Stewards' Enclosure as a small boy on my father's shoulders and expressed the intention to grow up to be a cricketer, an ambition which I soon shelved when I discovered the hardness of cricket balls. But my first conscious recollection of Henley is of attending as a schoolboy in 1931, and of competing in 1934. I was brought up not so much to believe as to take it for granted that Henley was perfection in all things. Later, when I became a 'consumer', as spectator, competitor, coach, and finally journalist, I discovered that this was not invariably so. I may be prejudiced in favour of Henley, but I believe I have also developed a love-hate relationship because I mind as much about the Regatta's shortcomings – as I see them – as I admire its excellence.

The Committee have paid me the compliment of entrusting to me the task of producing an 'Official' History to celebrate the 150th Anniversary, and have allowed me editorial freedom to criticize as well as to enthuse. So it is only fair to say that the opinions expressed are my own and do not necessarily represent the official view.

March 1989   Richard Burnell

PART ONE

The Management

1 The More It Changes

Henley Regatta may appear unchanging to the casual observer and that is an image which the management have nurtured over the years. In reality of course the Regatta has changed a great deal. Crews have changed, spectators have changed and the environment has changed. Henley's achievement has been to navigate with the changing stream of circumstances, so that it epitomizes the 'golden yesterday' without falling too far behind the 'insistent today'.

Now in its 150th Anniversary year, Henley is governed by an unlimited number of self-electing Stewards who in turn elect a Committee of not more than twelve of their number, 'empowered to manage and exercise control over all matters connected with the Regatta, excepting such as shall involve the alteration of any of the published Rules of the Regatta'. The Stewards are consulted on matters of policy, but have no control over the day-to-day running of the Regatta beyond the ultimate sanction of electing a different Committee, or changing or refusing to change the Rules. The Committee of Management elect their own Chairman and appoint the professional staff.

The Mayor of Henley is a Steward *ex officio* and in recent years the Stewards have also included the Chairman of the Thames Water Authority and at least one serving member of the Town Council for liaison purposes. But of the fifty-two Stewards serving in 1988 forty-six were rowing men elected sometimes in recognition of their standing in the rowing world,

but primarily to carry out the official duties at the Regatta.

It was not at all like that in 1839.

Under dateline 'Henley, March 21, 1839' *Jackson's Oxford Journal* heralded an event which was to shape the future of rowing as an amateur sport in Britain and indeed the world:

> The facilities offered by the fine reach of water here at length seems likely to be made available for the benefit and pleasure of the inhabitants. A public meeting is to be holden at the Town Hall on Tuesday, for the purpose of devising the best means of establishing an annual regatta on a grand and novel scale.

The earliest surviving minute book dates from 1867 and for an account of that first momentous meeting we must rely on *Bell's Life and Chronicle*:

> *Sunday, March 31, 1839*
> A numerous and influential meeting of the town and neighbourhood was held at the Town Hall on Tuesday last, for the purpose of establishing an annual regatta on the beautiful reach of water here, of which Henley has so much cause to be proud though she has so long neglected the advantage which might have been derived from it.
> The Chairman, Thomas Stonor Esq., in

opening the business of the meeting, alluded to the lethargy which had so long prevailed on the subject of aquatics; and said that at last so strong an interest had been manifested in the subject, that, independent of the amusement to be derived from the establishment of a regatta, under judicious management it could not fail to be of great benefit to the town.

Sport being his business, *Bell's* man no doubt had his thoughts focussed elsewhere than on the benefit likely to accrue to the burghers of Henley: '... the gentlemen of the two Universities are likely to become competitors,' he enthused, 'should the crew of the Leander also contend for the open cup ... there will probably be a race of greater interest than any it has been our pleasure to record ... Henley will no longer be under the reproach to which she has been subject ... Like Liverpool and her National Steeple Chace, she will have her National Boat Race, and stand pre-eminent as the centre of attraction to all admirers of the manly exercise of rowing ...'

Such flights of fancy were probably far from the thoughts of those assembled in the Town Hall on that March day. Their priorities lay elsewhere, spelled out by the Chairman, Thomas Stonor, and in the operative paragraph of the resolution shortly to be proposed by W. P. Williams-Freeman Esq: firstly to promote a great benefit to their town, and only secondly to provide some amusement by organizing boat races.

In that context it is hardly surprising that when the inaugural meeting appointed Thomas Stonor, Wm. Williams-Freeman, Wm. Fuller Maitland, Charles Lane, Edward Gardiner and the Mayor of Henley (three to be a quorum) 'to be perpetual Stewards with power to add to their number,' and in addition a Committee of fourteen persons (five to be a quorum) 'to assist the Stewards in preparing rules, receiving subscriptions, and in conducting the general business of the Regatta,' no rowing men were included. It was to be nigh on forty years before any rowing men were involved in the running of the Regatta other than in the capacity of invited umpires.

The duties of the Stewards and Committee were not spelled out, but it is known that the Committee sometimes met separately and made recommendations for consideration in joint session with the Stewards. In effect the Stewards represented the local gentry whilst the Committee represented the town – the distinction seems primarily to have been social. The day-to-day business was in the hands of a triumvirate of officers.

James Nash, to whom, legend has it, the idea of starting a regatta first came as he strolled with a friend in the river meadows, canvassed the support of the neighbourhood and rowing clubs, called the inaugural meeting, and became the first Secretary. If Henley had a single founder it was assuredly Nash. Charles Towsey became Joint Secretary, and P. B. Cooper, whose son John Cooper incidentally held the rudder lines in the *Wave*, first winners of the Town Cup, was Treasurer. At the helm of the Regatta, James Nash remained in charge for fifteen years, after which Towsey carried on alone until his death in 1883, which means that he was in office, either as Joint Secretary or on his own, for all but five years of Henley's first half-century.

As Towsey's long reign neared its conclusion, important changes were afoot. In 1880 a sub-committee was set up to report on the organization and finances of the Regatta. Its main recommendations give us an insight into the problems and their solutions, viz:

REPORT of Sub-Committee appointed to consider and report on the financial and other arrangements of HENLEY REGATTA.

The Sub-Committee having met on several occasions, and duly considered the matters submitted to them, beg to report as follows:

1. At present the managing body of Henley Regatta consists of:

> A President
> The Mayor of Henley
> Twenty-four Stewards
> Twelve Committee

Thirty-eight Members in all, having equal votes.

All these are invited to attend, and have notices from the Secretary of meetings to be held. But only a small proportion of the Members attends regularly. Two consecutive meetings often consist of different persons.

It is evident that, while the whole body is too large for working purposes, it would not be advisable under the circumstances to contract the circle of influence, local or otherwise, which a large body of Stewards ensures.

On the other hand; it is equally evident that, for the conduct of business, and for efficient management, it would be advantageous to have a smaller body, of which all the members would feel the obligation to attend all the meetings, and would be responsible to the larger body for the management of the affairs of the Regatta.

2. We therefore recommend:

(1) That a standing Sub-Committee, or Committee of Management should be elected by the Stewards and Committee, the members not to exceed twelve, with a quorum of five.

(2) That a General Meeting of Stewards and Committee be held once a year, at which the Committee of Management should present their Report and Statement of Accounts for the year.

The Report went on to comment:

5. The Grand Stand is at present erected at the back of the 'Lion Hotel', on the road facing the river, leaving space between it and the river for vehicles, though the thoroughfare is stopped by barriers during the days of the Regatta.

The cost of a ticket for entrance to the Grand Stand and the Lion Garden is 3s. 6d. and from this source the Regatta fund, in the year 1880, received the sum of £122 19s.

The hire of the Grand Stand amounts to £60 per annum, and there is an additional expense of £5 for the ladies' cloakroom, £5 for erecting barriers, use of seats for Lion Garden, housing materials etc. Hence the profit on the Stand to the Regatta Fund is for the year £52 19s. but a few shillings more than that which accrued from the Lion Meadow, viz. £52 7s.

It appears to us, upon consideration, that a much larger sum is paid annually for the Stand, than the original cost of the materials and the labour of erecting it would seem to justify.

6. It is not quite clear that there is any

power to deal with the bridge as a place of vantage for spectators. If in any way this power could be established, we think it would be advisable to assign places for carriages by tickets at a certain rate, and at the same time to provide that foot passengers should not be molested and endangered, as at present is often the case, by the horses being brought to or taken from the carriages.

7. The nett receipts from the Lion Meadow, as above stated, are £52 7s. We think that the meadow might be made much more attractive, and would contribute a much larger sum to the funds of the Regatta if arrangements were made for the convenience of spectators, and especially for ladies.

We would recommend that a portion at least of the meadow should be set apart (as at Ascot and Goodwood) for spectators, and that facilities for obtaining refreshments and other conveniences should be arranged. Space also for carriages, as at present, should be reserved.

11. With regard to the umpire's launch, a question has arisen as to whether it should be allowed to carry any persons besides the umpires and its own proper crew. We think that this question should, for the sake of the Umpires, be settled both as regards their friends and the Press. We propose that the Umpires should be requested to frame certain rules on this point which might be confirmed by the Committee, and remain for the guidance of umpires in future.

The Report was signed by Edmond Warre, R. W. Risley, H. T. Steward, J. G. Chambers, F. Fenner and W. D. Mackenzie in March 1881.

The Report was adopted and in 1881 a Standing Committee was appointed, town and rowing men being equally represented. The old Committee remained in existence until 1885, when a new constitution – if one can describe as 'new' something which appears never to have existed before – was adopted. The original Committee was then disbanded, its members either retiring or becoming Stewards. The new Committee consisted of twelve members elected annually by the Stewards from among their own members and has so remained ever since.

John Cooper, son of the first Treasurer, succeeded Towsey as Secretary, but in different circumstances for there was now a Committee of Management and a Chairman directing policy. Mr J. F. Hodges was elected as the first Chairman, but H. T. Steward was now the power behind the throne, and he succeeded on Hodges's death in 1894.

Herbert Steward was the first rowing man to preside over the Regatta and also, incidentally, the first historian of Henley. With Cooper as his executive officer – the association was a close one – Herbert Steward remained in charge until his death in 1915. Judge C. Gurdon succeeded as wartime caretaker, resigning in 1918. W. A. L. Fletcher was then elected Chairman but died a few days later, a victim of pneumonia and lungs damaged by gas in the war.

If we regard Nash and Towsey as one 'administration', and Herbert Steward and Cooper as another, then these two regimes covered the first ninety years of Henley's history and one begins to see where continuity came from.

In 1919 the pattern changed dramatically, but not the continuity. F. I. Pitman succeeded as Chairman, but did not wish to concern himself directly with the running of the Regatta. He described his position in a letter as 'Chairman of the Board with the particular function of finding the finance if Tom Steward over-reaches himself'. Tom, son of Herbert Steward, became the effective organizer of the Regatta, whilst W. H. Barff, succeeding Cooper as Secretary, has left us his own job specification as he saw it, in a letter addressed to C. T. Steward in 1926: 'I feel that I am primarily secretary of the Stewards' Enclosure Club, though I call meetings and of course draw the cheques for all bills you approve.'

The founding of the Stewards' Enclosure to which Barff referred was reported in *The Field* on 26 April 1919:

> The Stewards of Henley Royal Regatta feel that many people who would like to be annual visitors to the regatta do not attend regularly because adequate provision is not made for their comfort. To overcome this the Stewards have decided to provide a special inclosure to be called the 'The Henley Stewards Inclosure', which will be reserved solely for the use of members and their friends. It is proposed that the original members of this inclosure shall not exceed 300, that they shall be selected on the invitation of the Stewards, and shall not pay any entrance fee.

The Field went on to say that the frontage of the new enclosure would be 300 feet, that a band would play throughout the day and that there would be first-class caterers, a landing stage and a boatman to look after members' boats.

Tom Steward was elected a member of the Committee of Management in 1919 but had been a Steward since 1909, and it was his family connection with the Regatta which helped to bridge the gap consequent on the war years. Fortunately we have the text of a speech which he made at a dinner given by the Committee in his honour on the occasion of his retirement in 1938:

> I think both Bertie [his brother] and I were born with a love of Henley in us . . . undoubtedly we were brought up in the Henley atmosphere. There have been fifty-two regattas since I was born and I have, I believe, been present at forty-seven. [But] my first vivid recollection of anything to do with the Regatta was not until I was about seven or eight.
>
> Father was living at Remenham and he had Colonel Willan and Mr Goldie staying with him, and one morning they put the old wherry into the water, with me in the sitter's seat, and rowed up with three pairs of sculls to superintend the arrangements on the course.
>
> But it was not until about 1902 that I began to get interested in the management side . . . it was not my seeking and it came about because father was rather seedy and not fit to row himself about and superintend the arrangements and so he took me as his boatman and I began to get the hang of how and why things were done.
>
> By degrees father used to send me off to do jobs for him and it was not long before I knew most of the arrangements . . . it was knowledge that proved invaluable when it came to the resuscitation of the Regatta after the war.

I have often wondered how we got through that year 1919. There were two main things for which I considered myself responsible, one was pile driving and the other was tents.

Tom Steward went on to explain that the man who had piled the course in pre-war days let him down, so he persuaded Hobbs & Sons to buy the equipment and take on the workmen who had done the job for years. With occasional changes of personnel they have done it ever since; if the popular story that every pile drops into the same hole in the river-bed each year is not strictly true it is only because booms wear out and have to be shortened, so that the distance between the piles must sometimes be adjusted. But the job he really funked, Steward said, was writing a totally new specification for tents and spectator stands for the new Stewards' Enclosure. He did that too, put it out to tender, and the job went to Edgington's, who, like Hobbs, have been involved with Henley ever since.

Finances are considered elsewhere, but Tom Steward, in his valedictory speech, mentioned that before the 1919 Peace Regatta Henley's funds amounted to £26 in the bank and an investment of £1,600 $3\frac{10}{2}\%$ War Loan. The anticipated expenditure to put the Regatta back on the road was £6,000. In the event it cost £8,000 and there was a profit of £40.

Fred Pitman remained Chairman until 1939, but it was Tom Steward who effectively presided over the twenty years between the two world wars, with Barff in charge of the administration. Barff retired as Secretary after the 1938 Regatta, and L. D. Williams was appointed as Assistant Secretary shortly before that Regatta in order to learn the ropes before taking over responsibility for the Centenary Regatta in 1939. Two months later war once again engulfed Europe, the Regatta Office was requisitioned and the enclosure meadows became a timber dump.

After the war, now quoting from a report by H. R. N. Rickett to a Stewards' meeting in 1958: '... the system changed again, and so did David's [Williams] duties. Under Tarka [later Sir Harcourt] Gold's chairmanship the Committee of Management became the executive body, and the Secretary, now installed in Regatta Headquarters, their principal officer. No longer the spacious days when the Secretary could deal with the Regatta's affairs in his spare time in the summer; no longer was he just Secretary of the Stewards' Enclosure; for the first time one man was expected to know everything about the Regatta, and his office from then on became a full-time occupation all the year round.'

Harcourt Gold resigned as Chairman in 1951, when he was elected President of the Regatta. Harold Rickett succeeded him as Chairman and brought to the Regatta yet another brand of leadership. Of David Williams's Secretaryship Rickett wrote: 'For the last seven years I have been privileged to work intimately with David as colleague and collaborator. His natural stubbornness over matters of principle and his sense of humour naturally endowed him for the task – which he loved. His experience as secretary of a London club during the war enabled him to deal with confident ease with the ever growing correspondence with members of the Stewards'

Enclosure. It was part of David's creed that the impact of Henley depended on a large number of matters of detail, each unimportant perhaps in itself but supremely important in the part it played in the build-up of the whole ... The result of course was that organizing the Regatta became immensely complicated – but also immensely worthwhile.

That was Rickett's verdict on Williams; it could well stand as history's verdict on Rickett himself. For, unlike his predecessors as Chairman, Harold Rickett at once immersed himself in the minutiae of running the Regatta. Everything was researched, planned, written down and checked. The Chairman's dawn patrol of the enclosures became legendary, as also did his midnight sessions at Leander Club where the port flowed and he provoked all and sundry to express their views on all aspects of the Regatta – which most of them probably forgot ere morning but he remembered, pondered, and occasionally implemented. There was certainly no previous Chairman who was so accessible, or who made so many people feel involved.

Williams died in office in 1958, to be replaced by Colonel A. L. Alexander. This was very much the mixture as before until Rickett was forced by ill-health to resign in 1965, when J. L. Garton took over as Chairman. In 1971 Algy Alexander also died in office and P. A. Hannen took over as Secretary, but he too had to resign for health reasons in 1975. It seemed that Henley's tradition of indestructible administrators was failing at last. But the Henley administration was no longer a one-man band, nor even a duet. Hannen was succeeded by R. S. Goddard, the present Secretary, and John Garton, long-versed in Regatta practice, was on hand to initiate him.

Garton was presiding over the Management Committee at a particularly difficult time, and staff changes were perhaps among his lesser worries. The Regatta was expanding against a background of intense economic pressure fuelled by inflation. The cost of mounting a Regatta which had to be built from scratch each year, a dauntingly labour-intensive task, was soaring. Garton's reign is still rather close for a wholly objective assessment. But it may well be that future historians will see his major contribution to have been the consolidation and rationalization of the Regatta's finances. He had perforce to make many economies but achieved this without ever sacrificing the Regatta's traditional style.

Whatever Henley may be accused of it is certainly not democracy. In varying degree it has always been an autocracy. Whether one approves or not, that is undoubtedly one of its strengths. There are no shareholders, no sponsors, no rules laid down by other bodies. Hence unencumbered freedom of action. The Stewards are elected for life and are personally and severally liable for the finances of the Regatta, though probably few of them realize this when they are elected. There are only two perquisites of the job: a Steward's badge in addition to the quota of badges which they receive in common with all other subscribing members of the Stewards' Enclosure, and one free car parking space – on their own property. And they have access to the Committee Lawn and Bar, and to the Stewards' section of the luncheon marquee, both privileges introduced to provide quick service for busy officials.

For five days each year the Stewards are actively engaged in running the Regatta. Apart from that they normally meet only twice a year, on the Saturday before the Regatta when the draw is made, and in December when they elect the Committee, receive the Chairman's report, elect new Stewards and consider changes to the Rules. For practical purposes their power is more apparent than real.

As already remarked the Committee consists of twelve members inclusive of the Chairman and there is no time limit on their tenure, though technically all are elected annually. If there is a weakness in this system it is the lack of any automatic turnover of Committee members. This was evidenced in 1974 when Garton wished to retire as Chairman and found no natural successor, either among the then Committee members or among the Stewards. Uniquely in Henley history a new Steward, P. R. C. Coni, was elected a Steward in 1975, appointed to the Committee in the following year, and made Chairman in 1978. One may say that it was fortunate that there was a suitable candidate for this onerous post, lurking, so to speak, in the wings. But it also says something for Henley's accumulated tradition of continuity that a new leading player could suddenly materialize centre-stage without the audience noticing any material difference.

Generalizations are dangerous but sometimes hard to avoid. Harold Rickett's contribution to Henley was to recreate the gracious, perfectionist, privileged yet popular ambience of the Royal Regatta after the traumatic break of the 1939–45 war, a far longer break be it noted than that caused by the 1914–18 war, and resulting in greater social and economic changes. Rickett's Henley was nevertheless almost indistinguishable from the 1939 version; he was the reviver and conservator of Henley tradition. Having succeeded to a Regatta which was thus outwardly as it always had been, but which below the surface was struggling for survival in the harsh economic climate of the 1970s, John Garton's contribution was to achieve financial stability without sacrificing the essentials of the traditional Royal Regatta. He was the great consolidator.

Peter Coni was cast in quite a different mould. Unlike his predecessors he 'was not brought up in rowing as a child' – his own words. He attended his first Henley at the age of twenty-one as a Cambridge undergraduate competing for St Catharine's College. He had no preconceptions of 'how things have to be because they always have been'. Inheriting a Henley firmly established in the pattern forged by Cooper, Herbert and Tom Steward, and Harcourt Gold, he set out to restructure the Regatta to the needs of a new generation of oarsmen but ever mindful that many spectators were still of an older generation. He was able to take advantage of a growing wave of interest in Henley, almost one might say a 'tidal wave' during the past decade, most especially in the sphere of corporate entertaining, without permitting standards to be eroded.

Conservator – Consolidator – Developer, all are dangerous generalizations of course. But I think they are not unreasonable descriptions of the three Chairmen who have steered Henley's fortunes since 1946 – a period of forty years fully as difficult as the formative years between 1840 and 1880, and surely a period which leaves Henley as prestigious, and more prosperous, than ever before in its hundred and fifty years' history.

2 Royal Henley

Henley Regatta has been 'Royal' since 1851. It was after a meeting of the Town Council in January of that year that the decision was made to seek Royal patronage to boost the ailing finances of the Regatta, and accordingly – quoting from the Stonor House Archives – Mr Brakspear wrote on behalf of the Town of Henley requesting Lord Camoys to seek the patronage of the Prince Consort for the Regatta. Accordingly he wrote to the Prince and received a reply from Colonel Sir Charles Phipps, Treasurer and Private Secretary to the Prince, saying:

> ... the Plan has met with the approbation of his Royal Highness Prince Albert, who has graciously been pleased to contribute (£50).

The Prince's donation was announced in *Bell's Life* on 23 March 1851. *Bell's* later reported: 'Although he has usurped Camoys as chief patron, Prince Albert was not among the throng (at the Regatta). Camoys, now Vice Patron, was not there either, for on finals day at Henley the steam packet *Vivid* arrived at Woolwich bearing Leopold, King of the Belgians and Queen Victoria's uncle, on a visit to the palaces Buckingham and Crystal (where Prince Albert's Great Exhibition was in progress).

Lady Camoys wrote in her diary:

> Now for Henley Royal Regatta – a very wet morning, fine bright afternoon, went to the boat race(s) with all the party except Monica – Hart (Harriet), Viscount Clifden, Car (The Hon. Catherine Stonor) and Margt (Mrs Edward Pereira) (the Stonor daughters) went with us. Lord C. went early, Car and Margt met us at Henley ... returned to Stonor after the race(s) ...

The diary goes on to say that Lord Camoys returned to London that evening on duty as Lord in Waiting and to conduct further Royal visitors, the day after, round the Great Exhibition, so was unable to attend the finals day of the first Royal Regatta.

Prince Albert never visited the Regatta which he honoured with his Royal patronage in 1851. King Edward VII, when he succeeded Queen Victoria, confirmed the Royal patronage which has since been graciously renewed by each Monarch on Accession.

The first visit by a reigning Monarch (but not the reigning Monarch of the United Kingdom, Queen Victoria) came in 1887. Sir Francis Stonor, 4th Lord Camoys, succeeded his grandfather as President of Henley Regatta in 1881. Orphaned in his teens Francis, with his brother Henry and sister Julia (later Marquise d'Hautpoul), had been brought up by the Prince and Princess of Wales (King Edward VII and Queen Alexandra) at Marlborough House. The year 1887 brought many Royal visits to England from the Continent in connection with Queen Victoria's Golden Jubilee celebrations, and it was at Lord Camoys's

HENLEY-ON-THAMES
ROYAL REGATTA
1851.

PATRON.
H. R. H. PRINCE ALBERT.

VICE-PATRON.
THE RIGHT HONORABLE LORD CAMOYS.

STEWARDS.

THE MAYOR OF HENLEY.

THE MOST NOBLE THE MARQUIS OF DOWNSHIRE	THE RIGHT HON. THE EARL OF FALMOUTH
THE RIGHT HON. THE EARL OF MACCLESFIELD	THE RIGHT HON. THE EARL KILMOREY
THE RIGHT HON. THE EARL OF ORKNEY	THE HON. T. STONOR
COLONEL SIR W. R. CLAYTON, Bart.	R. PALMER, Esq. M. P.
SIR GILBERT EAST, Bart.	COLONEL KNOLLYS
W. P. W. FREEMAN, Esq.	S. W. GARDINER, Esq.
C. SCOTT MURRAY, Esq.	G. D. DONKIN, Esq.
C. LANE, Esq.	HENRY BASKERVILLE, Esq.
W. F. MAITLAND, Esq.	G. JACKSON, Esq.
W. H. VANDERSTEGEN, Esq.	J. F. HODGES, Esq.
J. W. BIRCH, Esq.	THOMAS HALL, Esq.
J. WHEBLE, Esq.	J. SIVEWRIGHT, Esq.
W. B. READE, Esq.	

COMMITTEE.

Mr. BRAKSPEAR	Mr. ELSEE	Mr. J. PAGE
„ BROOKS	„ IVE	„ W. PLUMBE
„ P. B. COOPER	„ T. JESTON	„ STUBBS
„ SAMUEL COOPER	„ KINCH	„ TOWSEY
„ JOHN COOPER	„ NASH	„ T. N. WATTS
„ H. CLEMENTS	„ PARTRIDGE	„ E. YOUNG

TREASURER—P. R. COOPER, Esq.   SECRETARY—Mr. NASH.

suggestion that the largest Royal party ever to grace the Regatta came to Henley in July that year. The visit took place on Friday 1 July and *The Times* reported:

The King of Denmark, the King of the Hellenes, the Prince and Princess of Wales, Prince Albert Victor, Prince George, the Princesses Louise, Victoria, and Maud of Wales, the Hereditary Princess of Saxe-Meiningen, the Duke of Sparta, and Prince George of Greece, left Marlborough House and took the special train from Paddington to Henley at 12 o'clock and arrived at Henley at 1.25 pm. There they embarked on Lord Camoys's steam launch, accompanied by other steam launches of the other Stewards to take the royal party to the winning-post. There they moored for a short time.

The party then proceeded down to lunch with Lord Hambleden at Greenlands. They were accompanied by Lady Macclesfield and Colonel Clarke, in Waiting on the foreign visitors, and the suites of the King of Denmark and King of the Hellenes, and the party had been further enlarged by the Princesses Victoria, Sophie and Margaret of Prussia who had joined the train at Paddington.

After lunch the launch again steamed up to the winning-post, where tea was served on board. The Royal party returned to London by train in the late afternoon, accompanied by Lord Camoys. The prizes were afterwards presented to the winners by Lady Camoys on the boat which served as a grandstand.

(The last comment must refer to the following day, Saturday 2 July, when the Regatta was concluded.)

It was in this same steam launch, evidently large enough to cause a considerable disturbance on the river, that two years later Lord Camoys was reprimanded by *The Field*. 'They were exceedingly wroth at the arrogant and unruly behaviour of the very young Lord Camoys, who seemed to think that the popularity of his esteemed grandfather, the old Lord, exempted him, the new Lord, from obeying the regulations and justified his steaming up the course between races until stopped half way by Lieutenant Bell, a check which he met with the remark that "if its President could not do as he liked it was time the Regatta ceased to exist ..."'

For a more formal Royal visit Henley had to wait twenty-five years. *The Times*'s report of that visit, which took place on 12 July 1912, is on the next page.

*   *   *

When the Stewards responded to popular demand to stage a 'Royal Henley' Peace Regatta in 1919 – so named to differentiate it from the regular 'Henley Royal' Regattas – His Majesty King George V graciously presented a trophy for the Allied Services eight-oared event, to be named the King's Cup. It was won by the Australian Army and subsequently became the trophy for the annual Inter-State Championship of Australia. The Duke and Duchess of Connaught attended the 1919 Peace Regatta and the Duchess presented the prizes.

Two years later, in 1921, The Prince of Wales, later to reign briefly as King Edward VIII, came to Henley to present the prizes.

KING & QUEEN AT HENLEY

ENTHUSIASTIC SCENES.

MAGNIFICENT RIVER SPECTACLE.

TWO CUPS GO ABROAD

Henley has had many Royal Regattas, but never before in the long history of the great rowing festival has it had a regatta which so fully justified its proud prefix of "Royal" as that which was brought to a brilliant close on Saturday, when it enjoyed the unique distinction of a visit from Their Majesties, the King and Queen. Henley Regatta, it is true, has before been honoured with the presence of royalty, but it was reserved for the Regatta of 1912 to have conferred upon it so signal a mark of royal favour as that represented by the attendance of the reigning Sovereign and his Queen.

Of Saturday's pageant, with its brilliant series of unrehearsed effects, it is difficult to write so as to convey an adequate idea of its glorious picturesqueness. It was indeed an animated picture of unrivalled beauty—a picture for which nature in her brightest and most joyous mood provided the worthiest of frames. Henley owes much to the Regatta, but on the other hand it is well worthy of remembrance that the Regatta owes much to Henley.

In the forenoon the finely organised train service of the Great Western Railway brought the people from Paddington in thousands ; motor cars arrived from everywhere, as did also practically every other means of conveyance, with the exception, of course, of aeroplanes, which a prudent decision of the authorities did not encourage. By noon the streets of the town were almost impassable, save to those who were—and but few were not—following the route to the river, anxious to secure either on the water itself or on the river banks points of vantage from which to see the marvellously picturesque pageant then in the making.

The prospect, viewed from Henley Bridge, was of surpassing beauty. The central waterway, on either side, was lined with river craft of all descriptions, many of which had taken up positions inside the booms the night before. The banks were thronged with expectant sightseers, and, as far as the eye could reach, from the Bridge to Temple Island, one's gaze travelled through a glorious vista of soft moving colour, with the tree-crowned hills in the distance forming a delightfully fitting background to a truly glorious picture.

THE KING'S ARRIVAL.
CIVIC RECEPTION.

Outside the Railway Station, which was gaily decorated with flags and bunting, a dense crowd had early assembled to witness the arrival of Their Majesties. Swung across the road was a large banner bearing the words "Loyal Henley-on-Thames welcomes their King and Queen," and drawn up in front of it were the school children of the town, to the number of nearly fifteen hundred, dressed in their brightest and best.

THE STATE BARGE.

Pending the arrival of Their Majesties, the spectators assembled in the vicinity of the landing stage found much to delight and interest them in the Royal Barge, which looked quite stately and gorgeous in its immaculate whiteness, with heavy gilding at the prow and a rich curtained canopy at the stern. The eight Royal Watermen also came in for a large share of attention. Clad in their ancient liveries of scarlet with the royal monogram heavily embossed in gold braid at the back, scarlet knee breeches, white stockings, buckled shoes and black velvet peaked jockey caps, they presented a really imposing appearance.

It was indeed a right royal progress. Scenes of indescribable enthusiasm marked the passage of the royal procession as it gracefully moved along the sparkling water between two deep lines of punts, boats and canoes, the occupants of which saluted in the approved fashion, by holding aloft the blades of their sculls, and waved flags, scarves, handkerchiefs, joining their plaudits with the rapturous chorus of welcome of the thousands who lined the river banks. The bells in the tower of the Parish Church also added their joyous greeting.

THE ROYAL PROCESSION.

On their arrival at the landing stage Their Majesties were received by Lord Desborough (chairman of the Thames Conservancy), who presented Sir Robert Buckell, the vice-chairman.

To the accompaniment of resounding cheers from those ashore and afloat, the King and Queen and Princess Mary took their seats in the barge beneath the canopy, the curtains looped to the pillars supporting it being drawn back, so that Their Majesties were visible to all. The Royal Standard was broken from the prow as Their Majesties entered the vessel, and the crowd cheered more heartily than ever. At a word from the King's bargemaster, the King's watermen, who meanwhile had been standing in the barge holding their white oars with glistening scarlet blades at the salute, were seated. Eight oars struck the water simultaneously, and the Royal Barge, preceded and followed by a flotilla of Thames Conservancy guard boats, went on its way, passing under the centre arch of Henley Bridge, and on to the Royal Pavilion, erected next to the Stewards' enclosure, on the river bank.

There were to be four more Royal visits between the wars. Prince Henry of Gloucester attended in 1923; Prince George, Duke of Kent, came in 1928 and presented the prizes; in 1931 Their Royal Highnesses the Duke and Duchess of York (later Their Majesties King George VI and Queen Elizabeth) honoured the Regatta with their presence and the Duchess of York presented the prizes; and the Centenary Regatta in 1939 was graced once more by the Duke of York, who presented the prizes.

Revived after the six-year gap caused by the Second World War, Henley enjoyed a particularly felicitous visit in 1946 by Their Royal Highnesses Princess Elizabeth and Princess Margaret. Before the final of the Grand Challenge Cup the two Princesses processed past the enclosures on board an umpire's launch, escorted by the two finalists, Leander Club and Ruder Club Zurich, Switzerland, paddling side by side ahead of the launch. The Princesses then followed the race, and later Princess Elizabeth presented the prizes, having graciously consented to the trophy for the newly instituted race for schools to be named the Princess Elizabeth Challenge Cup.

After 1946 Henley had to wait eighteen years before the next Royal visit. But when it came, in 1964, it proved to be one of the happiest occasions in the Regatta's history, for Her Majesty Queen Elizabeth the Queen Mother attended the Regatta, attended by H.R.H. Princess Margaret, Countess of Snowdon, and the Earl of Snowdon, and presented commemorative medals to members of the redoubtable Harvard crew of 1914 who were celebrating the fiftieth anniversary of their victory in the Grand Challenge Cup.

His Royal Highness Prince Philip, Duke of Edinburgh, who in 1963 had presented the Prince Philip Challenge Cup for coxed fours, attended the Regatta on the Thursday in 1968, following one of the races and inspecting the boat tents and installations. The 1970s brought two more Royal visits in consecutive years: in 1976, Princess Alexandra, the Hon. Mrs Angus Ogilvy, presented the prizes; and 1977, the Jubilee year of Her Majesty the Queen, Patron of the Regatta, was marked by a visit by H.R.H. Princess Anne, Mrs Mark Phillips. The Princess arrived at the Stewards' Enclosure in a barge manned by past winners of Doggett's Coat and Badge, sixty-nine years after her great-grandparents had similarly arrived by Royal Barge, but on that occasion the crew was made up of King's Watermen.

It would seem that the Royal Regatta has found special favour in recent years, for there have been only two occasions since 1980 when there has not been a visit to Henley by some Royal personage. In 1980 H.R.H. Prince Michael of Kent presented the prizes. And in 1981 there followed the first official visit by foreign royalty, when Her Serene Highness Princess Grace of Monaco, who incidentally was the sister of J. B. Kelly Jr, winner of the Diamond Sculls in 1947 and 1949, came to present the prizes. In the same year H.M. Queen Elizabeth the Queen Mother consented to the trophy for a new event for quadruple sculls to be named the Queen Mother Cup.

In 1984 the prizes were presented once more by Prince Michael of Kent; and in 1985 it was the turn of H.R.H. Prince Andrew to honour the Regatta and to present the prizes. The following year, 1986, was a landmark in Henley history, bringing a royal visit of a different kind, and the first from the reigning Monarch since 1912. In the spring of the year Her Majesty Queen Elizabeth II, accompanied by the Duke of Edinburgh, came to open the new Regatta Headquarters building. The Royal party took this opportunity to make a short cruise along the Henley town waterfront in the Thames Water Authority's flagship *Windrush*.

Prince Michael of Kent attended the Regatta privately in 1987; and in 1988 H.R.H. Princess Anne, now The Princess Royal, presented the prizes and endeared herself to the assembled spectators by braving the worst weather seen at Henley in a quarter of a century, following two finals in the umpire's launch, both contested in torrential rain. After the finals she presented the prizes.

3 The Rules

We take Rules so much for granted today that it is quite hard to visualize a time when they did not even exist. But the fact is that there were no 'Rules for Regattas' nor 'Laws of Boat Racing' in 1839. The colleges at Oxford and Cambridge had evolved their own rules for their peculiar form of Bumping Races. Elsewhere private matches, wagers and sweepstakes were made on whatever terms were mutually agreeable to the parties involved. But a public regatta, with crews entering for advertised challenge cups and prizes, was an innovation. So, on 1 May 1839, Henley produced their 'Rules for the Regulation of the Grand Challenge Cup'. These are reproduced on the next page. There were similar Rules for the Town Cup.

It will be seen that these Rules were organizational. So far as the actual racing was concerned there was really only one rule – 'that no fouling be permitted' – and that was undefined, being left to the judgement of the umpire. Then, as now, a foul implied an actual physical collision between the competing crews. The modern concept of 'interference', when one crew is judged to have impeded the progress of another by trespassing into its water without any collision taking place, did not exist.

There was no marked course, nor any racing 'lanes' in those early days, and a crew's 'proper course' was the course which would lead it most directly to the finish whilst allowing the opposing crew likewise to proceed directly to the finish. But there was one fundamental difference from modern practice in that a crew which crossed ahead of its opponent thereby became entitled to the water which it had taken. So a crew starting on the Bucks station at Henley might gain a lead, cross ahead of the Berks crew and so become entitled to the Berkshire station. If the original Berks crew then sought to regain the lead it could only do so by diverting to the Bucks side.

After 1839 Henley's rules grew piecemeal as problems were identified. In the following year, for example, it was recognized that disqualification of the guilty party in a foul was not always sufficient remedy in a three-crew race. The fouling rule was therefore amended to enable the umpire to order both the innocent crews to race again.

In 1843 a rule was passed to the effect that no substitutes be permitted for oarsmen who had already rowed in a heat and that no one could row for more than one crew in the same event.

Towards the end of 1849 representatives of Oxford and Cambridge and the principal boat clubs in London met together and drafted the first general 'Laws of Boat Racing'. H. T. Steward commented, 'The ... laws had practically been used by the (Henley) umpires since the institution of the Regatta.' Henley formally adopted this code in 1850.

HENLEY REGATTA.

Rules for the Regulation

OF THE

GRAND CHALLENGE CUP.

May 1st, 1839.

RESOLUTION OF THE COMMITTEE.

That a SILVER CUP of the Value of ONE HUNDRED GUINEAS, to be called the "HENLEY REGATTA GRAND CHALLENGE CUP," be rowed for on the Henley Reach, annually, by such Amateur Crews in Eight-Oar'd Boats as may be duly entered and qualified, and be held by the winner on the terms specified in the following rules :—

RULE 1st. That any Crew composed of Members of a College of either of the Universities of Oxford, Cambridge, or London, the Schools of Eton and Westminster, the Officers of the two Brigades of Household Troops, or of Members of a Club established at least one year previous to the time of entering, be considered eligible.

N. B. For the present year all Amateur Clubs established prior to the 1st of May, will be permitted to enter.

2nd. That every Boat shall be steered by an Amateur Member of the Club or Clubs contending for the Cup.

3rd. That all questions of eligibility, qualification, or construction of the Rules, be left to the Stewards, whose decision shall be final.

Another new rule was passed to cater for a new situation when, prior to the 1868 Regatta, W. B. Woodgate announced that the Brasenose College four would race without a coxswain. The rule stated: 'That no eight or four-oar boat would be allowed to compete at the ensuing Regatta without a coxswain, nor will any steering apparatus be allowed in any other boat.' In the following year they introduced an event for coxswainless fours.

A redraft of the Rules in 1869 introduced a minimum weight for coxes linked to the average weight of the crews. This was in order to prevent clubs from employing small boys, not available of course to colleges and universities.

A more important redraft in 1872 sought to define a boat's proper water as '... its straight course, parallel with that of other competing boats from the station assigned to it at starting, to the finish'. This deprived a crew of the right to retain water taken by changing stations. The same redraft abolished the right of the previous year's winner of a Challenge Cup to race only in the final.

Just as the first Committee had to forge rules for racing during the 1840s, so their successors found themselves reluctant pioneers of international sport in the 1870s. When E. Smith of New York made the first foreign entry for the Diamond Sculls in 1872, there were no precedents. Among amateur sports in Britain, only cricket had made overseas contacts previously, and an informal tour of a cricket team in Canada (1859) and Australia (1861) had no lessons for an open sporting meeting which was accepting both crew and individual entries for a range of different events.

The first sizeable foreign invasion of Henley came in 1878, and at once spelled trouble. For it transpired that of two American scullers, G. W. Lee of New Jersey and G. Lee of Boston, one was certainly a professional by Henley reckoning, and the other at best a very doubtful amateur. And the Shoe-wae-cae-mette Boat Club of Monroe, USA, a crew of French-Canadian lumberjacks who entered for the Stewards' Cup, issuing weird battle-cries as they made their way up the sacred Henley reach to the evident alarm of Stewards and journalists, seemed more akin to paid gladiators.

It is not necessary to cry 'cheating', nor to hint at base motives in this story. It was simply that rowing in the United States, outside of the East Coast college fraternity, took place in very different conditions. But that is not to say that contemporary British rowing men did not raise their hands in horror at the idea of such vulgar fellows aspiring to race at Henley.

The immediate result was that in 1879 Henley produced its first formal definition of an amateur:

No person shall be considered an amateur oarsman or sculler, or coxswain:
1. Who has ever competed in any open competition for a stake, money, or entrance fee. (Not to apply to foreign crews.)
2. Who has ever competed with or against a professional for any prize.
3. Who has ever taught, pursued or assisted in the practice of athletic exercises of any kind as a means of gaining a livelihood.
4. Who has been employed in or about boats for money or wages.

5. Who is or has been by trade or employment for wages a mechanic, artisan or labourer.

At the same time the Stewards passed a resolution that 'the entry of any crew out of the United Kingdom must be made on or before March 31, and the entry ... must be accompanied by a declaration ... with regard to the profession of each member of the crew and verifying their amateur status'.

The issue of amateur status was destined to become one of the most controversial in the history of rowing in Britain, but this first attempt by Henley to define an amateur caused scarcely a ripple – and for a good reason. It applied only at Henley, and the clubs, universities, colleges and schools then competing at the Royal Regatta were in general agreement with the new rule.

Genuine professionals were not much concerned either, since they had no intention of competing at Henley. Nor for the time being were the middle-ground men, the aforementioned mechanics, artisans and labourers, who were beginning to take up rowing as a sport and forming what became generically known as 'tradesmen's clubs' throughout the provinces. But that situation was about to change.

There was a distinct possibility at that time that the Stewards of Henley Regatta would take on the role of governing body for the sport of rowing, rather as the Marylebone Cricket Club became the ultimate authority in cricket, and the Royal and Ancient in golf. But this did not happen. In 1879 there came into being the Metropolitan Rowing Association, formed not with any idea of becoming a law-maker but to provide a 'super club', through which crews could be formed to meet the increasing foreign challenge. But in 1882 the Metropolitan Rowing Association, having expanded its membership outside London, changed its name to Amateur Rowing Association, and in 1886 issued General Rules for Regattas, becoming *ipso facto* the governing body of rowing. The ARA did not seek, nor has it ever sought, to assume jurisdiction over the older body of the Stewards of Henley Regatta. But it did adopt the Rules then in force at Henley, so giving them countrywide application. And the 1886 version of the amateur status definition now included a phrase debarring any person 'engaged in any menial duty', so that it was not only restrictive but, to many people's way of thinking, gratuitously offensive.

At once the fat was in the fire because the restrictive amateur definition which had proved acceptable at Henley was anathema elsewhere, where many clubs drew their membership precisely from those social classes banned from racing at Henley. The ARA's rules not only adopted the Henley prohibitions but further stated that only clubs affiliated to the ARA could compete in regattas held under ARA rules, and that ARA-affiliated clubs could not compete under any other rules, nor against crews not affiliated to the ARA.

This meant that, at a stroke of the pen, clubs in the same town which might have different social backgrounds and loyalties but nevertheless were happily competing against each other in local events were now debarred from so doing. There were protests; there were conferences and a great deal of letter-writing to *The Times*, and in 1890 the clubs banned by the Amateur Rowing Association set up a rival National Amateur Rowing Association. More conferences followed in 1891, but neither the ARA nor Henley were willing to change their definition of an amateur.

With the benefit of a hundred years of hindsight the whole episode may seem incredible. One can only conclude, if there were ever any doubt about it, that the Victorians and Edwardians were exceedingly stiff-necked generations.

The particular relevance of the amateur status dispute to the history of the Royal Regatta derives from Henley's status worldwide. Outside the rowing world, and certainly beyond the shores of the British Isles, the Amateur and National Amateur Rowing Associations, between whom the dispute properly lay, were virtually unknown. Henley, then as now, was 'news'. So it was Henley rather than the ARA which bore the brunt of the outrage at the idea that social status had anything to do with professionalism. But, lest we are tempted to sympathize with the Henley Stewards of the day, it must be added that most of the personalities guiding the fortunes of the Regatta were also running the Amateur Rowing Association.

But we have strayed from the strict chronology of Henley's rule-making.

In 1884 amateur status for overseas oarsmen was put on the same basis as for home oarsmen, thus ending the concession on racing for money prizes. In 1893 the Stewards signed their first foreign Agreement, with the French Rowing Union; this enabled French entries to be made up to 1 June, as was the case with home entries, instead of by 31 March. In return

for this concession the French undertook to guarantee that their oarsmen competing at Henley were amateurs under the Henley definition. This set the pattern for future Agreements with other foreign governing bodies.

In 1896 the Amateur Rowing Association called in question the wisdom of accepting foreign entries at all, writing that '... basing ourselves on the opinions strongly expressed for some time past among rowing men ... [the Committee] deprecates the admission of foreign crews to compete at Henley Regatta. The Committee believes that no good result has hitherto come of so-called international races held under conditions prevailing at the Regatta, which, as it appears to the Committee, was instituted for British and not for foreign rowing. In the opinion of the Committee, international boat races should if considered desirable be held only by means of private matches carefully arranged to suit the peculiar exigencies of such an event'. The Stewards, apparently less insular, or perhaps just mindful of the value of their foreign entries, resolved: 'That in the opinion of the Stewards of Henley Regatta the present time is not an opportune one to discuss the question of the admission of foreign crews to compete at the Regatta'.

But, before long, discuss it they did, for in 1901 W. F. Grenfell (later Lord Desborough) moved, and Dr Warre seconded, a motion that Henley should be restricted to home crews. T. C. Edwards-Moss refused to become a Steward over this issue, which was again rejected. Cooper made an interesting point in his memoirs, which would probably not occur to most of us today, namely that Americans and Canadians, in the early days of foreign entries, needed to take two months leave to come to Henley, whilst Australians, allowing a few weeks for their training in England, needed six months to make the return trip by sea. So it is remarkable that so many were able to come.

The employment of professional coaches, other than by scullers, within four weeks of the Regatta, was banned in 1903. This move seems to have been prompted by friction with the professional coaches of some of the American crews.

Cooper recalls that this rule, which was borrowed from the A R A code, was widely ignored, but explains the strong feeling against allowing professionals to coach at Henley. 'Was it not Biffen the Waterman who greased the seats of the boat of the Bedford School four so that the boys could slide, giving them an unfair advantage? And was it not a professional coach who would not allow Cornell to accept the hospitality of other crews for fear their food might be doctored, and insisted on keeping their boat in a private boathouse under lock and key for fear a hole might be bored in it by some of the other competitors?' The suspicion against 'professionals', and particularly 'American professionals', ran high in those days.

A more serious trans-Atlantic clash came two years later. After the 1905 Regatta there were rumours that some members of the Vesper Boat Club of Philadelphia, competing in the Grand Challenge Cup, were not amateurs. Their entry had been supported by the National Association of American Oarsmen, whose secretary, Mr Fortmeyer, had written on 21 March 1905, stating: 'We have carefully considered the amateur standing of each member of the crew as to whether he is qualified under your and

our own rules, and we unhesitatingly indorse them ...' The grumblings at Henley might have died down, but early in 1906 an announcement appeared in the London press, from Laffan's Agency, that an investigation into these allegations had begun in the United States.

Henley then wrote to the N A A O enquiring about this report, and Mr Fortmeyer duly replied, enclosing a copy of the findings of the investigation. On 30 June 1906, *The Field* reported:

> The Committee of Management of Henley Regatta ... have unanimously come to the following conclusion: that the cost of sending the Vesper crew to Henley was mainly defrayed by public subscription; that all members of the Vesper crew accepted money; and that sworn declarations of some members of the Vesper crew, made before a notary public, were in some particulars untrue.
>
> The Committee of Henley Regatta thereupon unanimously agreed that no entry of the Vesper Boat Club of Philadelphia, or any entry comprising any member of that club's crew of 1905, be accepted in future ...

Even that statement was not strong enough for all. Mr W. A. L. Fletcher proposed, 'That in future no entry from the United States be accepted'. But in this he was defeated.

Still on the witch-hunt for professionals, or 'non-amateurs' as some might say, the Stewards next ruled, in 1907, that an amateur could receive no contribution towards his expenses in competing at the Regatta except from his own club.

In the same year Henley came under fire from a different quarter. In 1906, and again in 1907, the Grand Challenge Cup had been won respectively by the Club Nautique and Sport Nautique de Gand, Belgium, the first foreign victors in Henley's premier event. Inevitably great public interest was aroused by what some saw as the humbling of the British 'rowing establishment'. Then, before the 1907 Regatta, though Henley's critics seem not to have noticed the occurrence until later, the Stewards announced that because the Olympic Regatta was scheduled to take place on the Henley course in mid-July, overseas entries would not be accepted at the 1908 Royal Regatta, taking place only two weeks before the Olympics.

When the implications of this temporary rule-change were appreciated, a storm of protest broke out, both in the British press and in the United States, where criticism of Henley was endemic. Typical of the accusations was an article in the *New York Herald*:

HENLEY STEWARDS CONDEMNED FOR TREATMENT OF BELGIAN CREW.

> Captain Beddington says Decision not to allow Cup Winners to defend Title is Unprecedented.

... in every quarter the action of the Henley stewards is condemned. I can most emphatically state that the universal opinion in Great Britain is that the Belgians should be permitted to defend the Cup ... The following stewards of the Henley Regatta Committee are responsible, for they passed the resolution the effect of which is that the

holders of the Grand Challenge Cup may not defend their title: Lord Desborough, Mr. Lehmann, Mr. Steward, the Hon. W. F. D. Smith, M.P., Messrs. Pitman, Fletcher, Gridley, Bradshaw, Eyre and Gurdon. It appears to me that these ten gentlemen must either climb down and revoke their decision, or retire from the committee ... The Grand Challenge Cup is a perpetual challenge cup. No one in this world can for a moment suggest that the holders of a perpetual challenge cup have not the moral right to defend it ...

It probably would not have occurred to a man of Beddington's ilk that the Belgians themselves might not wish to compete at Henley two weeks before the Olympic Regatta.

Herbert Steward wrote to *The Times* in December explaining that the decision had been made and announced, after consultation with the Belgians, before the 1907 Regatta. He quoted from a letter written by the President of the Belgian Rowing Federation to *La Vie Sportive*, Brussels, and *La Flandre Libre*, Ghent:

> As you ask my views on the decision of the Henley Committee ... I tell you frankly that, in my opinion, the English are perfectly right. In a year like 1908, which will see the Olympic Regatta take place at Henley ... it is not reasonable to hold an international regatta 15 days previously ... the Belgian holders of the Grand Challenge Cup would not have any object in going to defend it in 1908 ...
>
> OSCAR GREGOIRE

In the meantime the amateur status dispute

was temporarily quiescent, overshadowed by Olympic euphoria but still rumbling beneath the surface like a sleeping volcano. During the war years 1914–18 it was no doubt forgotten. But in 1919 there came a sudden eruption; to say the least the circumstances were unfortunate.

In this first year after the end of the First World War the Stewards decided that it was not possible to revive the Royal Regatta. But in response to widespread demand they agreed to stage a Peace Regatta. Originally planned for two days it proved so popular that it was extended to four days, and the main eight-oar event was offered for 'any crew of amateur oarsmen who, previous to November 11th, 1918, served in the Army, Navy or Air Force of any country which fought for the Allied cause'. A special trophy was presented by King George V, to be named the King's Cup. And since they were dealing with crews from a number of different countries the Stewards stipulated that the definition of 'amateur' on this particular occasion should be that which prevailed on 4 August 1914, in the country of each competing crew. Most reasonable, one might say. But one of the entries received came from the National Amateur Rowing Association, certifying their crew as amateurs according to the NARA definition. The Stewards indicated that whilst they did not recognize the NARA as the competent governing body of rowing in the United Kingdom, they would nevertheless accept the entry, providing the NARA would certify that the oarsmen were individually amateurs in accordance with the ARA definition. This the NARA declined to do.

One may think today that in dealing with an *ad hoc* regatta in the unique circumstances of 1919 the Stewards would have been well advised to overlook the fact that one of the entries came from an Association which they did not recognize. But the Stewards in those days were not disposed to sidestep their principles, even to get themselves off an awkward hook. They declared that it was not possible to alter the amateur status requirements after the rules had been published and the entries accepted. So they had to face a storm of protest at what many regarded as the deplorable spectacle of Henley rejecting an entry by a crew of servicemen, for a trophy donated by the King to celebrate the end of the hostilities.

In his *History of Rowing* (Herbert Jenkins, 1950) Hylton Cleaver remarked that the King himself was most displeased, and indicated that he would not again grace Henley with his presence until the offending rule had been rescinded. Whether that story is true or apocryphal – and of course the conditions for this competition had been published before the King agreed to present his trophy – one might again think that the events of 1919 were sufficiently embarrassing to warrant a change. But not so. Henley, and presumably the clubs represented by the Amateur Rowing Association, took the view that whilst it would have been reasonable to permit an NARA crew to compete in the Peace Regatta, it was not reasonable for them to refuse to accept the conditions under which the prizes had been offered.

So the rules remained unchanged and it was only twelve months before the Committee were again embroiled in controversy. The minutes for 3 June 1920 read:

> The list of entries ... outside of the United Kingdom under Rule iv was presented ... and received with the exception of Mr J. B. Kelly of the Vesper Boat Club to compete in the Diamond Sculls, which was refused under the resolution passed by the Committee on 7th June, 1906 'viz' 'That no entry from the Vesper Boat Club of Philadelphia, or from any member of their 1905 crew be accepted in future': Mr Kelly was also not qualified under Rule I (e) of the General Rules (manual labour).

The Kelly affair was manna from heaven for the press on both sides of the Atlantic, and especially in Philadelphia and New York, where Henley's rejection of Kelly was seen as an attempt to prevent an American sculler from winning the Diamonds. That it probably did, for Kelly went on to win the Olympic single sculls title from Jack Beresford, the Diamonds winner.

Later Kelly and Beresford became close friends, but Kelly always like to encourage the story that he was banned from Henley because he was too strong for the English, having served an apprenticeship as a bricklayer in his youth. He also claimed at the time that several individual Stewards had indicated that his entry would be acceptable, and that his boat had actually been packed for shipment to England before he was told that his entry had been rejected. The Stewards declared that they had advised the American Rowing Association as soon as the entry was processed, and that it was

not their fault if the information was not passed on.

Two things one can say with certainty. The first is that the 'Vesper Resolution' was undoubtedly 'on the book'; the second is that under the rules as they then were, Kelly was certainly not eligible, for Rule I (e) read: '... who is or *ever has been* ... by trade or employment for wages a mechanic, artisan or labourer'. Why then, one may speculate, did Henley cite both reasons for rejecting his entry? Perhaps they wished to make the point about the Vesper Resolution, but recognized that it was not part of the formal Rules to which the NAAO had subscribed, and so added the rider about Kelly's non-eligibility, because, of course, the NAAO must once again have been in contravention of their Agreement with the Regatta by endorsing the entry of a manual worker.

In 1921 the Stewards changed the rules to forbid substitutions unless 'the original competitor is prevented from rowing by circumstances which are outside his control, and are not attributable to his having rowed in the Regatta'. This attempt to regularize substitutions may appear a small matter, but must surely have caused anguish to many oarsmen over the years, for it made it well nigh impossible to obtain permission for substitutions for oarsmen suffering from muscular injuries once they had rowed a race, since even if the condition had existed before the Regatta it was likely to have been aggravated by rowing a race.

The Regatta's popularity was growing apace in the early 1920s, and in 1924 C. T. Steward wrote, 'Owing to the excessive number of entries it was decided to restrict clubs to one crew for any eight-oared or four-oared event.'

This seems a strange decision at that particular moment, for the entries reveal only two cases of a club (Thames Rowing Club) entering 'A' and 'B' crews for the same event during the preceding five Regattas. In 1928 the Stewards moved a step further on the same road when they barred double entries in the Ladies' Plate and the Thames Cup. At the same time the number of crews permitted to compete during the Regatta was limited to thirty-two for the Thames Cup and to sixteen for all other events. Eliminating Races on the Saturday before the Regatta were introduced where necessary.

This arrangement of course meant that crews which were eliminated did not take part in the Regatta proper, nor even appear in the programme. Predictably this was unpopular and nowhere more so than among the public schools, which regarded the label of 'Henley School' as important to their status. And school entries were important to the Regatta, not only because at that time they were providing more than half of the entries for the Ladies' Plate, but also because they brought along a great many parents and supporters, so that the opening day of the Regatta was widely referred to as 'Schools Day'. In 1933 the Stewards yielded to popular demand and withdrew the limit on the number of entries, in all events except the Diamond Sculls. The corollary of that decision was that it became necessary to row two rounds of the oversubscribed events on one day, which initially was the opening day.

In 1936 the amateur status controversy surfaced once more, and this time the shock administered to Henley was impossible to ignore. An Australian eight, bound for the Olympic Games in Berlin, sought to enter for the Grand Challenge Cup as part of its training preparations. A most welcome occurrence, one might think, for it was not often that crews from Britain's far-flung Dominions were able to come to Henley. But, alas, this crew was composed of policemen, *ergo* 'manual workers' by Henley reckoning. Their entry was refused and they went on their way to Berlin, perplexed and in considerable dudgeon.

The proposition that a crew from Australia, competing in the Olympic Games, could be unacceptable at Henley Regatta was so grotesque that even the moguls of Henley and the Amateur Rowing Association at last realized that they could not remain for ever out of step with the rest of the world. At a meeting in April 1937, the ARA resolved 'that the time has arrived when the Association's amateur definition should be reviewed' – surely one of the more remarkable understatements in the history of rowing. Revised it was, at a Special Meeting on 9 June, which duly deleted the offending references to manual labourers, mechanics, artisans and menial duties. On the following day the Henley Stewards reached the same decision and the two bodies issued a joint statement. The amended rule applied immediately to regattas under the ARA jurisdiction, but could not come into effect at Henley until the 1938 Regatta.

In the meantime the rule barring the employment of professional coaches was rescinded, and the Stewards had been having second thoughts about the Ladies' Plate, concluding that it was unfair to make school crews race twice in one day if the second race was against a college crew. A scheme was therefore devised by which schools and colleges were kept apart through the first two rounds which took place on the opening day. This system was introduced in 1938.

Immediately after the 1938 Regatta plans were put in motion to celebrate the Centenary Regatta the following year. This is perhaps not relevant to the Rules, but does concern the organization. For the first time the Stewards, who had never been enthusiastic about encouraging overseas entries, acknowledged Henley's growing international standing, and issued invitations, first to all the Dominions and then to all Foreign Associations with which the Committee of Management had Agreements. And a special event was announced for Double Sculls in recognition of the fact that this was the only Olympic title which Great Britain had won in Berlin.

The Centenary was suitably celebrated, both on and off, and after some of the festivities in, the river; there was a dinner in the Stewards' Enclosure in honour of the visiting crews, and a tour of Windsor Castle. But the storm clouds were gathering over Europe, and in September war broke out.

At the December meeting of the Stewards the existing Committee were re-elected, for the duration or until the next Regatta should be held. As already mentioned, the Regatta Office and enclosures were requisitioned during the war years. Arrangements were made jointly with Marlow Regatta Committee to organize at least one day's racing for schools at Henley in the late spring of 1940, but with the war situation deteriorating these were cancelled. In 1941 facilities were granted to Eton College to arrange one day of racing on the Henley course

which duly took place, over a short course, each year between 1941 and 1944. The only other rowing activities during the war years were contests between Oxford and Cambridge Universities in 1940 and 1941.

A Peace Regatta with special events was staged in 1945 within two months of the cessation of hostilities in Europe, and whilst the war against Japan was still being waged. In the autumn of that year Herbert Steward proposed to the Committee the introduction of a new event for schools, for 1946.[*] The idea behind this was that whilst there had been regular entries from some ten schools before the war, the Ladies' Plate entries had become so numerous, and the standard so competitive, that only two or three of these schools had any realistic chance of surviving the opening round. The proposal was agreed, and Her Royal Highness Princess Elizabeth graciously consented to her name being given to the new event which was instituted in 1946, on an experimental basis, with races over a shortened course from the Barrier, starting on the Friday, the Regatta then ending on the Saturday. Schools were permitted to enter for both the Ladies' Plate and the new event, with a proviso that a crew qualifying for the final of the Ladies' Plate must scratch from the Princess Elizabeth Cup, whilst a school losing a Ladies' Plate semi-final would be given a bye in the first round of the Princess Elizabeth Cup.

Other innovations in 1946 were the admission of ladies to membership of the Stewards' Enclosure, the publication of the first mem-

[*] Dr Susman had suggested a special event for public schools in 1929, for which the Henley Town Council would present a cup, but nothing came of this proposal.

bership list, the first BBC radio commentary on Henley racing, and the first public address commentary in the enclosures. And the Double Sculls, introduced as a special event in the 1939 Centenary Regatta, became a permanent feature. All in all the Stewards were declaring to the world that Henley Royal Regatta was back in business and ready to expand both racing and spectator facilities.

In 1948 the Princess Elizabeth Cup was confirmed as a permanent event in the programme, to be rowed over the full distance. The concession to schools entering for both the Ladies' Plate and the Princess Elizabeth Cup was withdrawn. The hope at the time was that some of the stronger schools would continue to enter for the Ladies' Plate, perhaps sending their second eights for the Princess Elizabeth Cup. In 1947 six schools had tried the new event and five stayed with the Ladies' Plate.

The Olympic Games were revived in 1948 and allotted to London, with the Olympic Regatta at Henley, which thus became the first rowing course in the world to host an Olympic Regatta twice. In order to allow crews to use the Royal Regatta as a trial for the Olympics the rules were amended, as they had been in 1908, to permit composite crews to compete, for 1948 only, in the Grand and Stewards' Challenge Cups. And as a concession to changing fashions the old rule that oarsmen's clothing must extend from elbows to knees was replaced with a rule, which the Victorians would no doubt have considered rather shocking, that 'every competitor's clothing must consist of a vest and shorts as a minimum'. Progress indeed.

At the December meeting in 1948 the Stewards voted by 24:1 against the introduction of an event for coxed fours. They had been invited to study the Olympic Coxed Fours and were apparently unimpressed. At the same meeting the Princess Elizabeth Cup was accepted as a permanent Regatta event.

In 1949 there was another change in the amateur status definition, deleting the reference to employment 'in or about boats for money or wages'. At last, after seventy years, professional status in rowing was confined to those actually racing for money, or earning their livelihood by coaching.

By 1950 Regatta entries had risen to 165, from 117 in 1946, an increase of forty-eight which in itself was both healthy and manageable. The distribution, however, was giving cause for concern. The Ladies' Plate entry had fallen by six, the Thames, Wyfold and Visitors' Cups had together increased by forty-seven. One result of this was that there was an increasing number of weak crews, and therefore ill matched races in those events. The Committee considered introducing a seeding system, but rejected the idea because they could see no practical way of assessing the quality of the crews. However, they did modify the Rules to allow themselves the option of holding eliminating races before the draw, which they believed would have a deterrent effect on the weaker entries.

The Rules were again amended in 1952, when the Olympic Regatta was held in Helsinki, to permit Olympic Trial Eights and Fours to compete in the Grand and Stewards' Cup for that year only.

At the December Stewards' meeting in 1952 the Chairman was reporting on another problem which was fundamental to the Qualification Rules, that of 'excess entries'. This problem was discussed in *The Times* on 24 June 1953:

QUALIFICATIONS FOR HENLEY

PROBLEMS TO BE FACED

FROM OUR ROWING CORRESPONDENT

Though it might appear otherwise, the Royal Regatta at Henley has always been subject to change, in all its aspects; but it may well be that recent developments are pointing the way to further changes, of a more obvious and far-reaching nature, than any in the present century.

Of the three main eight-oar events at Henley, the entry for the Grand Challenge Cup, being naturally limited by its high standard, presents no special problems. The Ladies' Plate was first offered in 1845 as " a new challenge cup for eight-oar boats, open to colleges and other amateur boat clubs, except University clubs, Subscription Rooms, and clubs similarly constituted." In 1857 the qualification was altered to admit only college clubs of Oxford and Cambridge, and the schools of Eton and Westminster. Since then the only specific change has been the inclusion of all public schools of the United Kingdom, of Trinity College, Dublin, and of the boat clubs of the military academies. But, indirectly, the institution of the Princess Elizabeth Cup in 1946, and the new regulations for the General Certificate, have had the effect of drawing off almost the whole of the school entry, while the decision, made in 1949, to limit the number of crews to 16, has encouraged many colleges to see in the Thames Cup a better prospect of gaining racing experience.

LOST PRESTIGE

Nominally, the Ladies' Plate remains the " second senior " eight-oar event at Henley, and generally, though not invariably, it produces a faster winning time than the Thames Cup. But its prestige has suffered sadly, both from the dwindling entries and from the loss of the schools. This year it has attracted only 11 crews, including two schools. This is the smallest entry since 1913, and a clear indication that action is needed at once. Apart from other aspects, the exodus of colleges to the Thames Cup means that this year at least 10 crews in the Thames Cup are forced, quite unnecessarily, to row in eliminating races before the regatta begins.

The Thames Cup, which in many ways is the key to the present problem, was instituted in 1868, and has had, for many years now, the same qualifications as the Grand, except than no one can compete who is also competing in the Grand, the Ladies', or the Stewards' Challenge Cup, while before 1951 no one could row who had ever won the Grand or the Stewards'. The real difficulty can be immediately appreciated if one studies the list of winners of the Thames Cup. With the exception of 1946, when there were no foreign challengers, the event has been won 10 times in succession by an American school, or university light-weight crew; and on many occasions the runner up, actual or moral, has come from the same source.

These American crews, notably Kent School, Tabor Academy, and Princeton and Pennsylvania, have become old friends at Henley, and it is in no spirit of jealousy that we seek a means of preventing them from continuing to win the Thames Cup. Rather is it that we should like to enable them to compete for an event more appropriate to their high standard. Yet they cannot reasonably be expected to try for the Grand, and are ineligible for the Ladies' Plate. This is a problem which is not really affected by the fact that this year we may ourselves have one or two crews of unusual quality in the Thames Cup. It is true that one possible solution to the problem would be to attempt to raise the standard of British entries in the Thames Cup, for example, by admitting past winners of the Grand, as has now been done. But in the long run this might merely substitute the Thames Cup for the Ladies' Plate as the second eight-oar event, and it would certainly not encourage the rank and file of British clubs, whose hopes lie traditionally in the Thames Cup.

A POSSIBLE SOLUTION

A second possibility, and the one which has perhaps received the most canvassing so far, is to open the Ladies' Plate to the Americans. This is an attractive proposition, whose possible consequences are seldom considered. Are we, for example, to name a few crews whom we look on as " regulars," and to invite them alone to try their luck in the Ladies' ? If so, what logical answer have we when some other American school or university wishes to enter ? It would hardly be satisfactory to relegate them to the Thames Cup until they too had built up a reputation as " regular " winners. And what of schools and universities from other countries, including, be it remembered, our own universities and university colleges ? With the steady improvement of such universities as London and Reading this may soon be a serious consideration.

There is a third possibility, which appears to entail the most sweeping change of all, but which, in the long run, might prove the easiest to work. This is simply to remove all remaining restrictions on all three events, so that there would be, in effect, three " classes " of eights, Grand, Ladies', and Thames Cup. There seems to be no reason why the various competitors should not then find their proper level.

Finally, we must remember that Henley cannot be considered solely in terms of particular events. A change in the qualifications for the eight-oar events, as above envisaged, would almost certainly have its counterpart in the qualifications for the four-oar events. And indirectly the standard of four-oar and pair-oar rowing, both traditional strongholds of British rowing, and both providing some of the greatest pleasure at Henley, might be adversely affected. For, if the scope of the Ladies' Plate were widened, its entry could hardly continue to be limited to 16 crews. That in turn would entail two rounds, probably final and semi-final, on the same day, so that fours and pairs would have to face the possibility of racing three times on the final day ; of the 42 fours in the Visitors' and Wyfolds this year, 16 are drawn from college eights. So we must at least consider the effect on the small boat races of any changes in the eight-oar events.

In 1953 *The Times* still maintained its traditional anonymity of writers. Their Rowing
Correspondent was in fact the author of this
book, who, it may be seen, was recommending
a solution which the Stewards finally adopted
in 1986.

Harold Rickett, Chairman of the Management Committee, referred to the recent
Times article at the June meeting, commenting
that there was a great diversity of opinion
amongst oarsmen.

At the subsequent December meeting
Rickett pointed out some of the problems. Most
people, he suggested, would welcome the
admission of American school crews into the
Ladies' Plate, but it might be difficult to do
this without also admitting American 150-lb
college crews, and possibly some British university crews. He quoted an anonymous poem
received after the 1953 Regatta:

Robust and amusing discussions
So far do conclusively tell
That a change of conditions of races
Is by no means agreeable to all.

So until there is general agreement
As to what is required to be done,
It seems better to go a bit steady
And not to start off at a run.

But what has come out of the chatter
Is that the Stewards aren't really old fools.
They've run the Regatta for ages
And are always revising the rules.

So let us all trust the old Stewards,
Who are always abreast of the times;
And as soon as they're sure what is wanted,
You can trust them to do it – they're Wise!

Harold Rickett concluded his report to the
Committee by remarking that his personal forecast was that the time would probably come
when, 'in order to maintain the Ladies' Plate
as the second-best event, some widening of the
qualifications would be generally desired'. But
for the present he thought the Stewards would
endorse the poet's conclusion that 'It seems
better to go a bit steady'.

It was significant that Rickett's concern was
not that the racing in the Thames Cup was
becoming uneven, but that the traditional prestige of the Ladies' Plate, as the Regatta's second
eight-oar event, was under threat.

The qualification rules for all Henley's
events are dealt with elsewhere (see Chapter 7)
but it may be helpful to say something here
about the *mystique* of the Ladies' Plate. It was
indeed the 'second-best' eight-oar event after
the Grand Challenge Cup, not only historically
but also in quality. It had been tailored for
Oxford and Cambridge college crews, and later
for the public schools, and, up to 1939 at least,
the colleges were the source of most of Britain's
first-class oarsmen. The strongest colleges often
entered their first crew for the Grand and their
second crew for the Ladies' Plate; or they might
enter the first crew for the Ladies' and the
second for the Thames Cup. During the 1930s
the Thames Cup began to change its nature as
it attracted an increasing number of American
school and lightweight university crews. In the
1950s the situation changed even faster as some
of the best British club and university crews
began to go for the Thames Cup, feeling themselves squeezed out of the Grand by composite
international crews. At the same time Oxbridge
college rowing was falling into decline as a

result of academic and social pressures at the universities.

Unfortunately – and this is a statement of personal opinion with which the Henley establishment of the day would surely not have agreed – the status of the Ladies' Plate and the assumed benefit of having an event catering specifically for Oxford and Cambridge college rowing, had become so much an article of faith among members of the Committee and the senior Stewards, themselves overwhelmingly Oxbridge men, that they were loath to accept the fact that the twin objectives of upgrading the standing of the Ladies' Plate, and at the same time retaining it as a closed student event, were incompatible.

In 1960 the Presidents of the Oxford and Cambridge Boat Clubs actually requested the Stewards to make the Ladies' Plate and Visitors' Cup into open events. In his December report in that year the Chairman remarked, 'the relative status of the two [Ladies' and Thames] events can be altered only if all the best competitors now in the Thames Cup – whether from home or overseas – are admitted to the Ladies' Plate; and that means making the Ladies' an open race'. The Committee nevertheless recommended that the Ladies' and Visitors' should remain closed student events. At the December meeting the Ladies', but not the Visitors', was opened to non-collegiate boat clubs of Oxford and Cambridge, and to the various clubs of London University.

Thus the Stewards had proceeded 'steady', as the anonymous poet had put it, for seven years before admitting composite Oxbridge crews and crews from London University. It was another six years before foreign student crews were accepted, and yet another nineteen years to the day when the Ladies' Plate became truly open, and resumed its historic position as Henley's 'second' eight-oar event.

In 1954 there occurred one of the very rare interventions by the International Rowing Federation at Henley. In the final of the Diamond Sculls P. Vlasic, of Yugoslavia, encroached on the water of A. Colomb, of Switzerland, due to exhaustion rather than to any intent to impede. Vlasic got home with only six feet to spare – 'a foul imminent, which, had it occurred, could only have resulted in his disqualification' (Richard Burnell's *Henley Regatta – A History*). FISA subsequently suggested that Henley should introduce an 'Interference Rule' in accordance with the international code. The Committee did not immediately concur.

Two years later, in 1956, the Stewards relented a little in their hard line on sub-standard entries, allowing the names of crews which had been eliminated before the draw to appear in the programme. Also in 1956 Henley received an unwelcome letter from Berkshire County Council claiming the towpath in front of the enclosures as an unrestricted right of way. This was hotly disputed because the loss of the river frontage would have spelled ruin for the Regatta. Fortunately, after hearing evidence from Colonel Burnell, one of the senior Stewards, that to his personal knowledge sections of the towpath had been closed during every Regatta since 1892 the Quarter Sessions in June 1957 declared the right of way to be conditional upon the right of the Stewards to close the towpath along the frontage of their enclosures for Regattas.

Once again, in 1956, the rules were temporarily varied to permit composite crews to enter for the Grand and Stewards' Cups for the purpose of assisting the Amateur Rowing Association's selections for the forthcoming Olympic Regatta.

In 1957 there were two rule changes of some importance. The first brought Henley into line with the international rule on 'Interference', as FISA had suggested three years earlier. This meant that a crew could be disqualified for impeding its opponents even though no collision had taken place. The second change was an amendment to the rule on substitutions, which removed the proviso that a substitution could only be made if the incapacity of the original competitor was not attributable to his having rowed in a race. No longer were coaches and captains faced with the choice between rowing an unfit man or scratching from the competition.

In 1960 Henley obtained a ruling that boats were not entitled to moor along the bank without the permission of the riparian owner. This confirmed the possibilities of earning revenue from letting launch moorings outside the Regatta period. The rules for the Princess Elizabeth Cup were altered to admit thirty-two instead of sixteen crews to compete; and three years later, in 1963, the event was thrown open to foreign crews. At the same time the rules for all foreign entries were altered so that they could be made by the same date as domestic entries. This was effectively a vote of confidence in the guarantees of amateur status given by the National Associations of countries which had signed the 'Henley Agreement'.

The unpopular 'Eliminating Races' became 'Qualifying Races' in 1964. It was thought there would be a psychological advantage in 'making it clear that it is for crews themselves to qualify rather than for the Stewards to eliminate', surely a differentiation of some subtlety.

In 1966 foreign student crews were admitted to the Ladies' Plate, and to help home crews to meet this challenge any number of UK colleges within the same university were permitted to combine in composite crews.

The minutes record that 'The Committee had investigated a large number of suggestions for raising the standard of the Ladies' Plate, and found itself completely unanimous that it was in the best interests of the Regatta and rowing generally to retain an academic qualification for this event'. Such emphatic wording may suggest a closing of the ranks in the face of outside criticism. The proposition that it is inherently beneficial to student oarsmen to be segregated from competition against non-student oarsmen of like standard is not overwhelmingly self-evident.

The problem of too many entries for the Princess Elizabeth Cup took a new turn in 1966, when it became evident that changes in the dates of the Oxford and Cambridge Schools Examination Board's 'O' and 'A' level examinations would clash with the normal date of the Regatta. School headmasters issued what looked like an ultimatum that unless Henley could be postponed for four weeks in 1967, their schools would not enter. A four-week postponement was not possible because it would have clashed with the newly initiated

National Championships. A proposal for a two-week postponement was also ruled out on administrative and economic grounds. In the end the change of date for the examinations was put off until 1968, in which year the Regatta was held one week later than usual. In the words of Humphrey Playford (*Henley Royal Regatta 1939–1968*) this 'pleased the schools but nobody else'. It resulted in Henley clashing with Lucerne Regatta to the considerable detriment of Henley's foreign entry. It was subsequently made clear that the Royal Regatta would lose its place in the international calendar if it continued to clash with Lucerne. But even without this threat the conclusion was inescapable; Henley Royal Regatta could not change its traditional date simply to suit the school entries.

The desirability of seeding the draw had often been discussed, and rejected on the grounds that there was no reliable way of picking out the fastest crews. Nevertheless a 'selective draw' system was introduced in 1969. Henley insisted that 'selection' is not the same as 'seeding', but the result is similar. The main difference is that there is no 'rank order' as is usually the case, for example, in a tennis tournament. Often there are no 'selections' at all. But if it is apparent that there are a number of outstanding crews, they will be 'selected' and drawn separately from the rest of the entries, to occupy pre-determined positions in the draw chart.

Composite crews were admitted to the open events in 1970, and schools were permitted to enter composites in the Ladies' Plate, but not in the Princess Elizabeth Cup. At the same time the Visitors' Cup was thrown open to foreign crews on the same basis as the Ladies' Plate.

There was a suggestion in 1971 for a special race for the benefit of schools which were prevented by examinations from entering for the Princess Elizabeth Cup, but this idea was not welcomed.

Administratively 1972 was an active year in which the most important decision was to move the Regatta back a day, to start on Thursday and finish on Sunday, the change to come into force in 1974. The traditional big crowd attracted by what used to be known as 'schools day', the opening Wednesday, had dwindled with the exodus of school crews from the Princess Elizabeth Cup. It was reckoned, correctly as it proved, that holding finals on the Sunday would be profitable.

More immediately in 1972 the Ladies' Plate entry quota was increased to thirty-two, the first anti-doping rules were introduced, and, to come into line with international practice, automatic disqualification was introduced for crews guilty of causing two false starts.

In December a bad rule was rescinded, triggered by an unhappy occurrence in the Princess Elizabeth Cup when Ridley College, Canada, lost a man overboard near the Barrier whilst easily winning a semi-final heat; and despite finishing first with a depleted crew were adjudged not to have completed the course. The story of this rule dated back nearly twenty years, to 1955, when A. D. Lee was forced to withdraw from a First and Third Trinity crew due to a back injury. A substitute was not permissible under the rules then in force; Trinity wished to race with seven men, but the

Committee ruled that a crew must be 'complete' from start to finish.

The rule at that time read: 'The whole course must be completed by a competitor before he can be held to have won ...' The question for sea lawyers was whether this meant that every individual in a crew must be 'on board' from start to finish. The Committee's ruling on the Trinity affair inferred that this was so. But as it happened, on the very day before this occurrence, Methodist College, Belfast, had lost a man overboard, almost on the finishing line. They passed the post with only seven oarsmen, a canvas behind King's School, Chester, and the verdict was that Chester had won by 'a canvas'. But it is not possible for a crew to win by a canvas if its opponent is deemed not to have completed the course for the purpose of being placed second – the routine verdict in such circumstances is 'not rowed out'. So strictly these two verdicts were contradictory.

Two years later the rule was changed to read: 'The whole course must be completed by a full crew before a crew can be held to have won the race ...'

Under that ruling there was no disputing the disqualification of Ridley College in 1972. But it was unpopular, and many thought unreasonable. And there was the further point that, if Ridley's accident had occurred where Methodist College's accident had occurred, there would have been ample time for their missing crew member to cross the finish line, either swimming or holding on to the boat. One wonders what the ruling might have been in that case. The rule since 1972 has been that a crew must start the race with its full complement, and

completes the course when its bow reaches the finishing line. Only the coxswain must remain so to speak *in situ*, for obvious reasons.

Nottinghamshire International Regatta was held on the multi-lane course at Holme Pierrepoint for the first time in 1973, on the Saturday preceding Henley. The Henley Committee were opposed to this arrangement, on the grounds that it would interfere with the Henley draw and build-up for the Royal Regatta. It did in fact cause some problems due to the sudden influx of boats and competitors on the Monday. But on the credit side the new fixture boosted Henley's entries from the United States.

With many schools still handicapped by examination dates, the Special Race for Schools was introduced in 1974, over a short course starting at the Barrier, and with racing taking place only on the Saturday and Sunday. The Special Race was not recognized as an official 'Henley Event', and has not been since, despite pressure from some of the schools involved.

The number of Qualifying Races on the Friday and Saturday before the draw rose to fifty this year, and in order to improve the standards in the Wyfold and Britannia Cups a rule was introduced requiring that at least half the oarsmen in competing crews, in these events, must either be previous Henley winners, or have won at Senior 'A' level elsewhere during the preceding five years.

The Sunday racing, introduced this year, proved to be financially beneficial, but had an unfortunate side-effect in that it destroyed the traditional closing celebrations on the Saturday night, since all the finalists, and many semi-finalists, were still in training.

In 1975 Qualifying Races took the form of timed races so that all could be completed on the Friday evening before the draw. There have been periodic complaints that this method is unfair because of variable wind conditions. But for this particular purpose time trials are often fairer than side-by-side racing. If, for example, it is necessary to eliminate ten crews, then twenty crews must be drawn in side-by-side races and some of the faster crews may go out. In a time trial only one or two of the marginal crews will be at the mercy of wind conditions.

The 1976 Regatta saw a unique variation, if not of the Rules then of Henley custom. With the temperature rising above 90°F, with high humidity, the requirement that gentlemen should wear jackets in the Stewards' Enclosure was suspended. Elsewhere there was great difficulty in keeping swimmers off the course. There was much discussion at this time about the introduction of events for women. The dilemma was similar to that which faced the Committee concerning coxed fours a decade earlier. On the one hand it was argued that women's rowing would never flourish whilst there were no women's events at Britain's premier regatta; on the other hand it was clear that open women's events would be dominated by foreign competitors, whilst events closed to foreign competitors would not serve the desired purpose.

In 1979 the Committee came up with a compromise, announcing that there would be exhibition events for women in 1981, with entries by invitation only.

A sad event occurred in 1983 when Henley imposed a ban on the use of the 'sliding rigger'.

Sad because Henley had never before departed from the principle that there should be no restriction on the design of racing boats. Indeed for many years racing boats were known as 'best boats' precisely because they were 'the best that could be designed'. Perhaps the Stewards had no option but to follow the ruling already imposed by the International Rowing Federation, which banned this device, in which the outrigger and stretcher assembly moved up and down the boat instead of the conventional 'sliding seat', on the somewhat doubtful grounds of cost. Inevitably the first sliding rigger boats were expensive, because they were all individual prototypes. But by the time the ban was imposed there was already at least one British boat builder who was offering a sliding rigger as an optional alternative to a sliding seat, at no extra cost. There is an argument, of course, that racing should be between people, not between boats, equipment, or money. If our forebears had followed that principle we would presumably still be using clinker-built boats without sliding seats or outriggers.

A happier event in the same year was the gift to the Regatta by George Bushell and Son, the local photographers, of their stock of photographic negatives covering every race at the Regatta since 1946, and many older negatives of great historical interest. And in the week following the 1983 Regatta the first Henley Arts Festival was held in the enclosures.

The Qualification Rules for the Ladies' Plate and Thames Cup have been mentioned several times before. In 1984 the Stewards at last came to terms with the fact that the success of any event must depend upon its attracting an entry of crews of comparable standard. Over a long period of years adjustments to the qualifications for the Ladies' Plate, the presence of student crews and the increasing number of crews, both club and student, competing at the Regatta, had resulted in an excessive spread in the quality of crews in both events, so that the weakest were many lengths slower than the strongest, whilst the overall standard of the two events was almost identical. This problem is discussed in Chapter 7.

4 Finances

In its 150th Anniversary year Henley may be regarded as a wealthy institution. Certainly in recent years the balance sheet has made encouraging reading for the Stewards at their Annual Meetings in December. But, only twenty years since, the financial outlook was distinctly bleak. Over a century and a half the Regatta's fortunes have ebbed and flowed. And today's relative affluence cannot be, and certainly is not, taken for granted.

The sport of rowing has always suffered one inherent problem which does not face most other sports. With the exception of a handful of purpose-built courses, regattas take place on rivers or lakes to the banks of which the public enjoy free access. Areas may be fenced off as enclosures; but it is not possible to exclude non-paying spectators, either from the banks, or in many cases, including Henley, from going in boats on the water itself. It is rather as though the tennis courts at Wimbledon, or the football pitch at Wembley, were sited in the middle of common land.

One might indeed say that there are two inherent problems rather than one. For Henley, in common with most other regattas, is not permitted to build permanent grandstands on the bank – despite owning the land. Nor can the piles and booms which mark the course, or any of the other installations, be left on site.

Thus on the one hand an elaborate and extensive complex, ranging from nearly one and a half miles of booms, signal boxes, boat rafts, grandstands, luncheon marquees and boat tents, down to the humblest clump of forget-me-nots in the flower beds in the Stewards' Enclosure, must be put in and taken out each year, at huge cost. And on the other hand many thousands of spectators are able to watch the Regatta without contributing one penny towards its cost.

The history of the past hundred and fifty years is as much about the ways in which the management of the Royal Regatta has striven to solve these problems, as it is about the boat racing.

We have already seen how the townsfolk of Henley founded their Regatta in 1839, with the objective of benefiting the town rather than to foster the art or sport of rowing. One might say that the 'launch' was most encouraging. *Jackson's Oxford Journal* on 18 April 1839, reported:

> The success of this undertaking far exceeds the most sanguine expectations of its originators, both in the amount of subscriptions, which already reach 180 guineas, and also in the distinguished support which it receives from the neighbouring nobility and gentry. The Earl of Macclesfield has, within the last few days, enobled his name as Patron . . .

It takes more than a noble name to establish a Regatta, and the success of the undertaking, as we shall see, was not immediately destined to exceed the sanguine expectations of its originators. They had a long furrow to plough.

The earliest accounts, covering the first six Regattas, speak for themselves:

A Statement of the Annual Receipts and Disbursements of the REGATTA COMMIT-TEE, from its establishment in 1839.

	RECEIPTS.	£	s.	d.		DISBURSEMENTS.	£	s.	d.
1839	To Amount of Subscriptions	220	19	7	1839	By GRAND CHALLENGE CUP	105	0	0
	„ Amount of Entrances	39	7	6		„ Town Cup	31	10	0
						„ Medal Dies	30	0	0
						„ Medals	17	18	0
						„ Umpire's Expences (gratis)			
						„ Advertisements, Printing, &c.	16	8	0
						„ Subscriptions for Fire Works	5	0	0
						„ Ringers	3	3	0
						„ Stewards & Committee Stand, Watermen, Boat-hire, Band, Constables, and minor incidental expences	43	5	3
						Balance in hand	8	2	4
		£260	7	1			£260	7	1
1840	To Balance brought forward	8	2	4	1840	By District Cup	52	10	0
	„ Amount of Subscriptions	111	4	0		„ Medals and Engraving Cups	20	4	0
	„ Amount of Entrances	67	9	6		„ Umpire's Expences	17	10	0
						„ Advertisements, Printing, &c.	29	6	6
						„ Ringers	4	4	0
						„ Expences incurred by Public Dinner	24	9	6
						„ Stewards & Committee Stand, Watermen, Boat-hire, minor Prizes, &c. &c.	35	5	4
						Balance in hand	3	6	6
		£186	15	10			£186	15	10
1841	To Balance brought forward	3	6	6	1841	By Cost of Medal Dies, Medals and Engraving Cups	68	12	10
	„ Amount of Subscriptions	78	1	6		„ Umpire's Expences & Balance of last year's Account	23	3	0
	„ Amount of Entrances	50	8	6		„ Advertisements, Printing, &c.	20	1	5
	„ Balance due to Treasurer	22	11	6		„ Ringers	3	3	0
						„ Stewards & Committee Stand Watermen, Boat-hire, minor Prizes, &c. &c.	39	7	9
		£154	8	0			£154	8	0
1842	To Amount of Subscriptions	92	5	6	1842	By Balance due to Treasurer, 1841	22	11	6
	„ Amount of Entrances	69	11	6		„ Medals and Engraving Cups	44	0	8
	„ Balance due to Treasurer	83	5	0		„ STEWARDS CUP	77	5	0
						„ Umpire's Expences	20	0	0
						„ Advertisements, Printing, &c.	36	17	9
						„ Ringers	3	3	0
						„ Stewards & Committee Stand, Watermen, Bands, Boat-hire, minor Prizes, &c. &c.	41	4	1
		£245	2	0			£245	2	0

1843	To Amount of Subscriptions	96	16	6
	,, Amount of Entrances ..	46	15	0
	,, Balance due to Treasurer	50	12	11
		£194	4	5

1843	By Balance due to Treasurer, 1842	83	5	0
	,, Medals and Engraving Cups	32	7	10
	,, Umpire's Expences	20	0	0
	,, Advertisements, Printing, &c	23	4	6
	,, Ringers	3	3	0
	,, Stewards & Committee Stand, Watermen, Bands, Boat hire, minor Prizes, &c. &c	32	4	1
		£194	4	5

1844	To Amount of Subscriptions	109	4	6
	,, Amount of Entrances .	59	8	0
	,, Balance due to Treasurer	26	8	8
		£195	1	2

1844	By Balance due to Treasurer, 1843	50	12	11
	,, DIAMOND SCULLS	12	12	0
	,, COAT AND BADGE, &c. ..	6	15	0
	,, Medals and Engraving Cups	34	11	8
	,, Umpire's Expences	20	0	0
	,, Advertisements, Printing, &c.	27	16	7
	,, Subscription to Purse for London Watermen	5	0	0
	,, Ringers	3	3	0
	,, Stewards & Committee Stand, Watermen, Bands, Boat hire, minor Prizes, &c. &c.	34	10	0
		£195	1	2

It is tempting to take items from these early balance sheets to compare with today's figures. Tempting but unprofitable because in most instances it would not be comparing like with like. We know that the original Grand Challenge Cup cost 100 guineas, and the Town Cup 30 guineas, and that those two items together accounted for half the cost of staging the 1839 Regatta. Today a silver cup similar to the Grand would cost many thousands of pounds, even without the addition of the pedestal, which was added later, and the inscribing of a hundred and fifty years of winners' names. But one can hardly envisage that an umpire today would claim expenses equal to half the cost of building the Stewards' stand, hiring the band, and paying for '... watermen, boatmen and minor Prizes etc ...'

The first Regattas produced modest profits. But in 1841 the balance sheet moved into the red, in the form of a balance due to the Treasurer, Mr Cooper. Henley remained indebted to Mr Cooper for several years, though the substantial deficit of £83 in 1842 was down to £26 in 1844. Probably there was no undue concern about the finances at that time, as it was common practice in organizations such as rowing 'subscription rooms', for members to pay off their corporate debts *post facto*, and no doubt the Stewards would have expected to do likewise if needs be.

What caused more concern than modest cash deficits was the fact that the Regatta itself was showing no sign of expansion. By 1844 the number of events had increased from two to five; but entries for the Grand Challenge Cup had fallen from four in the inaugural year, to two, and, of a total of twenty entries in 1844, ten were from scullers. Four more events were added to the programme in the next three years, all probing for new entries, but with little effect.

Access for spectators improved in 1843, when the Great Western Railway reached Twyford, linked to Henley by a four-horse 'omnibus' in time for the 1844 Regatta. The first proposal for a line which would have passed through Henley came from the Tring, Reading and Basingstoke Railway as early as 1832. By the time that scheme reached Parliament for approval, in 1845, there were also rival bids from the South Midlands and Southampton, and Midland Grand Junction Railways, for routes traversing the town, and from the Great Western for a branch line from Twyford. An amended GWR plan was finally accepted in 1847, but it was to be another ten years before the line opened. Supervised by, if not actually from the pen of, the great Isambard Kingdom Brunel, the original plans provided for a station in Friday Street. There was an alternative proposal for a station in the market place. But in the end the present site was chosen, which was then well outside the town.

But that good news was still in the unforeseeable future when the correspondent of the *Illustrated London News* wrote, on 29 June 1844: '... about the time the sports commenced, the bridge was covered with handsome equipages, and hundreds of fashionably dressed persons had congregated on the stands erected for visitors on the towing path, and in the meadows on the Berks shore. In the grandstand we observed Lord Camoys, the Earl of Falmouth, Sir George and Lady Napier, Lady Dungarvon, Lady Caroline Pechell, Sir E. C. East, and others of the nobility and gentry.'

So we know that there were spectator stands on the Berkshire shore, as well as the Stewards' and Committee's own stand on the roadway outside the Red Lion hotel. But the accounts show no receipts from these facilities and it may be that they were put up by private enterprise. The 'handsome equipages' parked on Henley bridge might have paid something to the Bridge Commissioners, but not to the Regatta, for there is a note in the Corporation minutes, much later in 1881, to the effect that an application from the Regatta Committee to place carriages on the bridge 'made as stands and sublet' was refused.

No minute books survive from the early days of the Regatta so we can only surmise that some voices were to be heard at that time suggesting that the considerable effort of running the Regatta was not worthwhile. But the local inhabitants clearly thought otherwise. On 15 June 1849, they sent an Address to the Stewards exhorting them to persevere, an Address which is reproduced on the opposite page.

Besides the sentiments it expresses, the Address offers an insight into the local community at that time. The list includes no less than twenty-five publicans and innkeepers, and four brewers or brewery workers, all no doubt dodging the attentions of the two excise men. There were three druggists and one chemist to mix potions for those who over-indulged. But perhaps the most interesting feature of the list lies in the number and diversity of tradesmen who thus identified themselves with the benefits stemming from the Regatta; carpenters, milkmen, shoemakers, bricklayers, a clutch of painters, one 'Elizabeth Alleway', and wharfingers, per-

HENLEY-ON-THAMES
GRAND REGATTA.

EXTRACT FROM THE MINUTES OF THE REGATTA COMMITTEE.

"Henley, July 5th, 1849."

At a Meeting of the Stewards and Committee of the Henley Regatta, held this day, the Right Hon. LORD CAMOYS in the Chair; the Secretary read an Address received from Lieut. H. A. D. THORNTON, R. N. as follows;"—

"TO THE PATRON AND STEWARDS OF THE HENLEY GRAND REGATTA,"

"We the undersigned Tradesmen, and Inhabitants of Henley, respectfully avail ourselves of this mode of tendering our best thanks to the Patron and Stewards of the HENLEY GRAND REGATTA, for their kind, disinterested, and unceasing exertions during the last TEN YEARS, in promoting the interests of our town by the establishment and continuance of its Regatta, which from its superior attractions has introduced the Town of HENLEY to the notice of thousands, and causes so great an influx of visitors during a considerable portion of the year, which may in a degree compensate for the injury the trade of the town has sustained from various causes, and we earnestly hope that the PATRON and STEWARDS will not cease to give it their countenance and support, affording as it unquestionably does amusement to many, and benefit either directly or indirectly to the tradesmen of the town generally."

Charles Norton, *Gentleman*
James H. Brooks, *Surgeon*
Joseph Lawrence, *Gentleman*
George Shelton, *Silk Throwster*
William H. Brakspear, *Brewer*
Edward Johnson, *Boatbuilder, &c.*
Thomas Carter, *Grocer*
Charles Palmer, *Jeweller, &c.*
Charles Towsey, *Wine Merchant*
J. F. Hearne, *Schoolmaster*
James Bennett, *Gentleman*
John Dobson, *Corn Dealer*
Charles Kinch, *Druggist*
Elizabeth Williams, *Innkeeper*
James Farley, *White Hart Inn*
Nicholas Mercer, *Solicitor*
Samuel Cooper, *Solicitor*
John Drewett, *Innkeeper*
Samuel Lench, *Gentleman*
Henry Hughes, *Schoolmaster*
Thomas Rose, *Currier*
John T. Mattingley, *Upholsterer*
George Long, *Grocer*
William H. Tanner, *Town Sergeant*
Charles Sandy, *Upholsterer*
George Paulin, *Hair Dresser*
John Cottrell, *Coach Builder*
J. H. Dimblebee, *Confectioner*
John Carter, *Broker*
Charles Poynder, *Gentleman*
John S. Plumbe, *Gentleman*
George Wright, *Brewery*
Henry Thornton, *Lieut. R N.*
Robert Marsh, *Brewery*
Thomas Jeston, *Surgeon*
John Casey, *Butcher*
William Hickman, *Stationer*
Thomas Reeves, *Cooper*
John Dew, *Draper*
Henry Clements, *Perfumer*
John Cooper, *Solicitor*
Charles Coster, *Watchmaker*
William Grayson, *Jeweller*
John Williams, *Wheel Inn*
Thomas Briant, *Baker*
Mary Rogerson, *Angel Inn*
George Avery, *Carpenter*
Henry Sargeant, *Bricklayer*
Frederick R. Sandy, *Butcher*
Richard Potter, *King's Arms Inn*

George S. Avery, *Hair Dresser*
William Herbert, *Corn Dealer*
Thomas Hews, *Estate Agent*
John Kirk, *Steward*
E. Rickford, *Grocer*
T Marshall, *Publican*
George Collins, *Exciseman*
Joseph Sharp, Jun. *Grocer*
Thomas W Jeston, *Surgeon*
T. K. Chittenden, *The Rev*
William Plumbe, *Draper*
Edward Young, *Surgeon*
Samuel White, *Grocer*
Thomas Mellett, *Veterinary Surgeon*
William Leaver, *Parish Clerk*
Daniel Reeves, *Publican*
Thomas H. Crouch, *Grocer*
William Powell, *Saddler*
James Allday, *Chemist*
Joseph Bisley, *Tailor*
James Thomas, *Fishmonger*
John Pescud, *Ironmonger*
James Wheeler, *Wharfinger*
John King, *Coach Builder*
Joseph Partridge, *Gentleman*
Joshua Watts, *Tailor*
Arthur Eaton, *Publican*
Alfred Ive, *Wine Merchant*
John Page, *Savings Bank*
Robert Owthwaite, *Builder*
James Wallace, *Exciseman*
Caroline Long, *Grocer*
Richard Massey, *Glover*
William Cobb, *Corn Dealer*
William Bevan, *Cabinet Maker*
Joseph H. Cooper, *Turner*
George H. Robson, *Surgeon*
Samuel Cobley, *Gentleman*
Elizabeth Alleway, *Painter*
Joseph Dance, *Watchmaker*
George Vaughan, *Publican*
William Lovegrove, *Shoemaker*
Joseph Wilder, *Iron Founder*
Thomas Gunne, *Gentleman*
Ann Collins, *Bull Inn*
Job Gonnell, *Shoemaker*
William Wright, *Publican*
Charles Lewis, *Exciseman*
William Horsley, *Grocer*
William Talbot, *Tailor*

Edward Blackall, *Publican*
John T. Marlow, *Feathers Inn*
Samuel Cripps, *Grocer*
Mary Hyatt, *China & Glass Warehouse*
Mark Woodbridge, *Saddler*
John Lewington, *Butcher*
Edmund Chamberlain, *Baker*
A Brown, *Publican*
M. Jefferis, *Tanner*
James Wilder, *Publican*
George Spearing, *Ironmonger*
Frederick Tagg, *Ironmonger*
D. Prior, *Publican*
John Castle, *Baker*
William Spicer
Henry Stubbs, *Grocer*
Samuel Goff, *Draper*
William Stevens, *Saddler*
Joseph Sharp, *Pork Butcher*
Charles Cooper, *Painter*
Thomas N. Watts, *Tailor*
Samuel Clements, *Hair Dresser*
Jeremiah Heath, *Publican*
R. C. Archer, *Baker*
Thomas Giles, *Broker*
Thomas C. Binfield, *Butcher*
C. B. Judson, *Gentleman*
James Blackall, *Butcher*
David Toomer, *Gentleman*
J. T. Swallow, *Baker*
Richard Blackall, *Publican*
A Adams, *Publican*
Daniel Plumby, *Publican*
C Giles, *Tailor*
John Brown, *Publican*
J Barnett, *Brewery*
Thomas Parker, *Gentleman*
C. H. Godby, *The Rev. Head Master of the Royal Grammar School*
William Johnson, *Green Grocer*
James Aveil, *Horsekeeper*
William Manstone, *Shoemaker*
W. O. Newport, *Shoemaker*
William Tucker, *Publican*
W. H. Reeks, *Farmer*
James Lawson, *Precentor*
H. Wethecell, *Publican*
Matthew Wells, *Iron Founder*
John House, *Tailor*
Edward Freebody, *Publican*

Thomas Saywell, *Baker*
William R. Reade, *Gentleman*
William Ibbs, *Publican*
George Dunn, *Publican*
Sarah Ballard, *Dressmaker*
Daniel Brown, *Publican*
George Thompson, *Carrier*
Robert Irving, *Broad Gates Inn*
Robert Wichellow, *Publican*
Thomas Bowling, *Veterinary Surgeon*
William Horsely, Jun. *Grocer*
Mary Cooper, *China & Glass Warehouse*
E. J Giles, *Publican*
A. Newton, *Baker*
William White, *Publican*
E. Peacy, *Shoemaker*
E. Fitzgerald, *Shoemaker*
Byles and Son, *Brewers*
Charles House, *Tailor*
Richard Cox, *Brewer*
F. Paulin
William Paul, *Publican*
Richard Tayler, *Gentleman*
James Iverinee, *Bricklayer*
James Slater, *Bricklayer*

Sarah Gore, *Publican*
Richard Slater, *Exciseman*
Francis Norris, *Ropemaker*
Frederick Spiers, *Saddler*
Zachary Allnutt, *Attorney*
William Saunders, *Baker*
V. W. Bate, *Druggist*
Henry Hart, *Gunsmith*
George Strange, *Farmer*
John Clinch, *Coachman*
Harriet Jones, *School Mistress*
William Noel, *Waterman*
Samuel Kile, *Accountant*
Abraham Richards, *Coach Smith*
Mary Bizzle, *Baker*
Henry S. Williams, *Upholsterer*
Edmund Butler, *Publican*
James Thackary, *Hair Dresser*
Charles Francis, *Painter*
Henry Lawrence, *Bricklayer*
Richard Brown, *Barge Master*
William Parker, *Gentleman*
William Neville, *Baker*
Thomas Binfield, Jun. *Butcher*

Thomas Sadler, *Milkman*
Benjamin Allum *Publican*
Charles Lambourne, *Waterman*
Henry King, *Waterman*
William Jones, *Saddler*
John Shaw, *Broker*
John Ashby, *Carpenter*
John Adnains, *Carpenter*
William Jones, *Bricklayer*
Thomas J. Bainsey, *Gas Fitter*
Peter Soundy, *Printer*
Richard Henwood, *Poulterer*
John Farley, *Carpenters' Arms*
William Woodley, *Fisherman*
W. H. Godfrey, *Carpenter*
Richard Reeves, *Carpenter*
Charles Dawson, *Gentleman*
Thomas Glanville, *Surgeon*
George Deacon, *Sadler*
Thomas Usher, *Publican*
William New, *Druggist*
William Hickman, *Publican*
William Neal, *Waterman*
William Jones, *Carpenter*

" *Henley Oxon, June 15th, 1849.*"

fumers, glovers and ropemakers, all reminding us that ten years into Victoria's reign local communities were still of necessity self-sufficient. George III might have been able, some seventy years earlier, to breakfast at nearby Culham Court on hot rolls brought down from Gunter's in London by relays of horsemen, but in Henley Town the necessities, and most of the luxuries, had to be produced locally.

One also notes on the list that Charles Towsey, Joint Secretary of the Regatta, was addressing himself! William H. Brakspear's brewery still overlooks the Regatta finish today. Zachary Allnutt and John Cooper had both been members of the *Wave* crew which had won the Town Cup in 1839; Peter Allnutt, a descendant of Zachary's, sculled in the Diamonds in 1939, is a member of Leander Club and resides locally; John Cooper's firm are still the local solicitors. There are no Coopers in the business today, but when I was rowing for Leander in 1949 our crews regularly stayed in the Cooper house behind the Town Hall; and I well remember the two Miss Coopers double-sculling a skiff before 1939, and reminiscing about their earliest memory of the Regatta, watching from a carriage on Henley Bridge, which must have been in 1885 or earlier. And I cannot but mention that 'James Bennett, Gentleman' was the great-grandfather of Miss Sybil Reeves who has provided some of the oldest photographs in this book from her family albums. Miss Reeves also gave the Regatta a handsome clock which now adorns the wall of the Committee Room. I would like to believe that it once graced Mr Bennett's house in Henley but that is sheer romanticism.

On 5 July 1849, the Stewards responded to the Address:

That the following reply to the Address be adopted, and that the Secretary be requested to forward the same to Lieut. THORNTON.

"GENTLEMEN,
The Patron and Stewards of the Henley Regatta have received with the greatest satisfaction the Address to them from the tradesmen and inhabitants of Henley.

It is peculiarly gratifying to find, that while the exertions of those to whom is entrusted the management of the Regatta, have been successful in affording the great amusement which the aquatic contests have invariably given, those same exertions have also promoted the prosperity of the trade and the interests generally of the inhabitants of Henley; – to continue such results and still further to merit the approbation and support of the town and neighbourhood, the Patron and Stewards with the assistance of the Committee of the Henley Regatta, will not cease their exertions to render if possible, more attractive and serviceable, that annual festivity, the happy consequences of which have called forth an Address to them so numerously and respectably signed.

CAMOYS."

"To Lieut. H. A. D. THORNTON, R.N.
and the other Subscribers to the above
mentioned Address."

"Resolved,
That the Address and Reply be printed,
and forwarded to each of the Stewards and
Committee."

J. NASH,
Secretary.

Perhaps it was as well that the Stewards
received local encouragement, for they faced
difficult times. We have no records of the
accounts during the ensuing years, but the
entry lists remained very thin, reaching their
nadir in 1850 when there were only six races,
and one day of the two-day Regatta had to be
abandoned.

The grant of Royal Patronage in 1851 must
have boosted morale, but it had no significant
effect on the entries. Without doubt the limiting
factor was logistics. Henley at that time was a
flourishing market town, well served by coaches
from Holyhead, Shrewsbury, Worcester,
Gloucester, Cheltenham, Stroud, Faringdon,
Wantage, and Oxford en route to Maidenhead
and London. And of course there was the
omnibus connecting with the Great Western
station at Twyford. But bringing boats to
Henley was another matter altogether. From
other towns on the river they could be rowed
to Henley or conveyed by horse-drawn barge,
a slow business. But from elsewhere they had
to come by horse and cart. In retrospect one
can see that running a Regatta at Henley in the
mid-19th century was a daunting task.

In 1854 *Jackson's Oxford Journal* was again
reporting: '... entries not very numerous ...

bridge well covered with carriages ... river gay
with boats of all sizes, amongst others an Eton
eight-oar in elegant blue uniform, sometimes
rowing an impromptu race with the umpire's
crew of London watermen ...'

In 1857, as we have already learned, the
branch line from Twyford reached Henley. On
5 July *Jackson's* commented: 'The railway
[recently opened] brought a large number of
passengers; the great facility of access, combined with cheapness and certainty of conveyance which it offers, will undoubtedly
increase the number of visitors on all future
occasions.'

In the same year the Regatta days were
changed from Monday and Tuesday to Friday
and Saturday, 'not quite as convenient for many
of the pleasure seekers', according to *Jackson's*
man, '... but the Stewards, ever anxious to
meet the wishes of those gentlemen most deeply
interested, namely the competitors, acceded to
the request to fix it for Friday and Saturday'.

Just why the end of the week should have
been less convenient for the pleasure-seekers is
not obvious. Perhaps it was because Thursday,
when the locals would have wished to be watching the crews preparing for the great event, was
market day, or the fact that the festivities after
the end of the Regatta on Saturday night would
have made it impossible for many people to get
home in time for Sunday morning church. The
popular story however is that the Stewards had
been loath to hold races on Saturday for fear
of preventing the clergy from writing their
sermons.

In the mid-1860s general support for the
Regatta was at last beginning to increase. Not
all the newcomers were welcome, and in 1893

Jackson's was reporting, 'James Sullivan, of no fixed abode, was charged with having been at Henley Regatta on the previous day, for the purpose of committing a felony – a gold watch and eleven shillings were found on his person; committed for three months to hard labour.'

But generally speaking the influx of new spectators, and increasing entries, were welcome, and had to be encouraged. On 17 June 1864, *Jackson's Journal* was reporting, '... an entirely new, elegant, and capacious stand, which will be erected as heretofore near Red Lion Hotel, a site which cannot be surpassed. Another great desideratum has this year been supplied by the same authorities, which, although not immediately affecting the general public, is already hailed as a great boon by the class for whose accommodation it is intended. For many years past the rowing men have been much inconvenienced by the want of a place in which to store their elegant and fragile craft. On the Berks shore, above the bridge, has been erected a spacious and permanent boathouse, for the free use of all crews bringing boats to contend at the Regatta; the interior arrangements are such that it is supposed there will be ample space for the largest number of boats that may possibly ever be required ... the building itself forms a prominent and pleasing object in the locality of the bridge.' This was Henley Regatta's first property acquisition.

We have detailed accounts again for 1878 (see the next page), which reflect an altogether more sophisticated operation, but not really a stronger financial position. In 1878 the credit balance after the Regatta stood at £22 0s. 9d.; in 1844, allowing for the monies outstanding to the Secretary, it had been £24 4s. 3d. Sub-

scriptions were up by about £100, and there was a profit of some £80 on the provision of stands and enclosures. Instead of acting as unofficial banker to the Regatta, the Secretary was now drawing a modest salary. Music had become more expensive, but the umpires were making do with free lunch instead of claiming expenses. And the press were enjoying lunch at the expense of the Regatta, too; in the early days, Mr O'Grady had been entertained by individual members of the Committee (see page 89). The Thames Conservancy had an official presence, and it was costing £21 17s. 6d., including a 'donation' of £5 to Mr Lord.

One item, however, showed no inflation. 'Ringers' cost three guineas in 1844, and still cost three guineas in 1878. 'Ringers', I am told by Mr John Crocker, who has forgotten more about the history of Henley Town than the rest of us put together are ever likely to learn, probably refers to the bell-ringers of Henley church.

The 1878 accounts showed expenditure of £588. Twenty years later the figure had risen to £785. Today it may seem incredible that the cost of running a Regatta which, without question, was expanding rapidly at that time, could increase by only £200 in twenty years.

STATEMENT OF ACCOUNT, 1878.

RECEIPTS.

	£	s.	d.
Balance	26	11	7
Amount of Subscriptions received	207	18	0
Amount received for Housing Boats in Boathouse	16	0	0
Amount received for Entrance Fees	111	18	0
Amount received from Stand, Lawn and Meadow	192	1	6
	£588	12	1

EXPENDITURE.

	£	s.	d.
By paid Secretary One Year's salary due July 1st, 1878.	50	0	0
Watts, Hire of Stewards' Stand	60	0	0
Ditto Stand on Lawn	5	0	0
Ditto, Ladies Cloak Room	5	0	0
Erecting and removing Barriers, Housing materials, use of Seats for Lawn, &c.	46	0	0
Band, Two days	7	0	0
Plumbe, Flags, Ribbons, &c.	1	4	6
Young and Son, Hire of Tent for Boats	7	0	0
Robertson, Balance due on 1877 Account	24	7	0
Cups, Medals, &c. 1878.	102	9	7
Police Constables, Berks and Oxon	15	9	7
Parrott, putting down and removing Rafts and other work	14	10	3
Use of Lion Meadow	30	0	0
Hotel Bill—Luncheons for Stewards and Umpires	7	15	0
Ditto for Reporters	2	14	0
Ditto for Mr. Lord	1	10	6
Desvignes and Charmant, Hire of Umpires' Launch	20	0	0
Thames Conservancy, Mr. Lord, Boat Hire and Men	15	7	0
Donation, Mr. Lord	5	0	0
Henley Bridge Trustees, Use of Lion Lawn	6	0	0
Rent of Boat House, one Year to Midsummer	5	0	0
Insurance, Boat House	1	1	6
Bills for Advertising, Newspapers, &c., including part of 1877	24	6	0
Printing, Stationery, Stamps, &c.	19	7	4
Hire of Boats, West, 1877	3	0	0
Men employed at Regatta in Guard Boats, Porters, Messengers, &c.	21	16	0
Boat House Keeper, one Year	6	10	0
Donation, to ditto 1877 and 1878	2	0	0
Weyman, Repairs at Boat House, Stools for Bath, erecting and removing Bath, &c.	10	6	2
Ball, painting Boat House	6	7	9
Employés, at Boat House, during Regatta	7	7	9
Man, guarding Tent Eight days and nights	3	0	0
Owthwaite, Hire of Ground, for Tent	3	3	0
Ringers,	1	0	0
Use of Town Hall and Attendance	2	2	0
Time Keeper (Benson)	2	2	0
Journies to London, on account of American Entry	0	19	2
Webb, Timber for Rafts, &c.	3	11	3
McBean, Iron Work, Bags for Raft, Hire of Scales, &c.	2	7	6
Sundry Payments, Rates, Taxes, Postage, &c.	11	19	3
	£566	11	4
Balance	22	0	9
	£588	12	1

Audited 12th November, 1878.

JOHN PAGE.
Wm. HUMBY. } Auditors.

(Signed), CANOFS, Chairman.

Oh for a return to the Gold Standard we may say!

This period at the turn of the century was the golden age of the houseboat. John Cooper wrote at some length about houseboats at Henley in his memoirs:

It is not very easy to say which was the first houseboat at Henley Regatta. It would be about the beginning of the seventies. I believe it was a little houseboat rather of the Ark type owned by a man named Atkinson who resided on Remenham Hill, drove a four-in-hand and was supposed to be the proprietor of 'Atkinson's Bear's Grease'. He was locally called Major Atkinson presumably because he wore a long moustache but so far as I have ever heard the majority of his military duties were performed in Bond Street. Mr. (afterwards Sir) W. H. Weldon's *Athena* was the first big houseboat that came to Henley somewhere about 1880. J. Ashby Sterry, the bard of the Upper Thames, used to sing of this boat:

'I fly to the cheery *Athena* for shelter
'The pâté is perfect the Giesler is dry.
'And think while I gaze undismayed at the pelter
'That Henley's still joyous in dripping July.'

After the year 1880 houseboats began to increase rapidly in number and in size, and by 1884 there was quite a fleet of them. I particularly remember that year because assisted by the late Pat Labat I tried to collect some subscriptions from them towards the Regatta Fund. We were not very successful as £27 was all we got and that somewhat grudgingly given. The next year we got £80 odd. In 1886 it rose to £170 and then rapidly increased so that by 1897 we were getting roughly £1,000 a year from houseboats and launches and might have done better still if the Conservancy had been more pliable. Our methods with that body savoured too much of the '*suabiter in modo*'. A little more of the '*fortiter in re*' with a threat of a letter to *The Times* or *The Field* would soon have brought them to their senses for the public would not have stood Henley Regatta being in any way interfered with by the Conservators. They always insisted on placing the houseboats and would never allow us to do so alleging legal difficulties!! It is comic however to think that the Marlow Committee were allowed to allot places to houseboats and launches at their Regatta – Henley could not – '*de minimis non curat lex*', as translated by the Conservators 'legal difficulties do not apply to little regattas'. We were merely used as a lever to collect houseboat and launch dues because under the regulations no boat could be allotted a place which had not previously paid its licence. We ought to have told the Conservators that they represented the bobbies who march up and down at Epsom shouting 'All off the course' and that beyond this they had nothing to do with the arrangements. I am of course aware of their statutory powers with regard to regattas but these were meant to strengthen their position for keeping the course and not to admit of interferences with the legitimate functions and arrangements of regatta committees. Of course we ourselves made one great mistake and that was during the height of the houseboat boom, making or rather agreeing to a Conservancy regulation that no person should underlet his houseboat or launch after a position had been allotted. The ostensible reason given was that undesirable people were thus kept out, but the practical result was that the whole of the speculative element disappeared and we lost £600 or £700 a year – money which might have provided a nest egg which would have been very useful to us in after years when labour became so costly. However, I will not pursue the subject of what might have been – it was a very sore one with me, to think that the houseboat fund which had been nursed from £27 to over £1,000 in a dozen years or so was ruined and all our efforts nullified and overruled by the interference of a fussy and thirsty little Thames Conservancy inspector who really knew nothing about Henley and its ways. '*De Mortuis etc*' and he has been dead many years now. Perhaps I ought to explain that in these days houseboat owners consisted of two distinct classes – the well-to-do owner who brought his boat to Henley and right royally entertained not only his friends but his friends' friends also; and the speculative owner who applied for a place knowing that it was worth his while to subscribe handsomely in order to get near the winning post as the position obtained counted nearly if not quite as much as the appearance and accommodation on the boat. The profits from a good Henley let would very often pay his running expenses for the whole season on the river. Reverting to particular houseboats I suppose everyone of the olden times will remember the *Golden Grasshopper* in the days of Raymond Radcliffe of the *St. Stephens Review*. His scheme of decoration – an all one colour scheme – was quite novel in houseboats and like most novelties I think it paid him well. It was a little later that he let the boat to Colonel North of nitrate fame. I am sure

most of the old habitués of Henley will remember that year. Colonel North was then in the zenith of his fame and prosperity. He was one of those men, who, like some modern ladies, must be in the limelight and accordingly he appeared as the occupier of the *Golden Grasshopper* at Henley, in those days about the smartest and best known houseboat on the river. On the last night of the Regatta the Pierrots gave an entertainment off his boat and after it was over the Colonel was called upon for a speech. After mounting the steps to the roof he proceeded to ask the assembled company (who were gathered around in at least 300 or 400 boats, punts and canoes) to supper. However, he qualified his invitation by saying he was not sure if there was supper enough for all but he assured them there was plenty to drink. As one man the assembled company roared 'We're quite sure of that, Colonel'. That the opinion of the company was not far wrong was still further evidenced when the gallant Colonel attempted a hornpipe on the roof but got through very few bars before measuring his length on the floor. There are some who will remember Brooke's houseboat a little earlier in the houseboat annals. He had a lovely band on board of about twenty performers who played and played beautifully every evening and everything was done in the most elaborate style. Of course the boat was known as *Monkey Brand* but it was a fleeting appearance, and Brooke never appeared again – the amount which the fortnight was reputed to have cost him was something stupendous. Other well remembered houseboats are *The Fair Maid of Perth* which of course belonged to Sir Thomas (now Lord) Dewar and *The Scotland* belonging to Lady

Scott, and who does not remember Babs Scott, afterwards Countess Russell, in those days a really beautiful girl. But the houseboat era would not be properly described if I did not go into some details of the evenings. Every crew man turned out quite oblivious of the 10 p.m.-to-bed rule and hundreds of others in boats, punts and canoes. Truth to tell it got a little rowdy except round houseboats where The Pierrots under Clifford Essex or The Japs were performing. Music hath charms to sooth even the rowdy undergrad and both the above parties sang exceedingly well. Somehow I seem to remember the biggest noise being made by 'Bally-holl' among Oxonians and hearing that 'Trinity Hall the best of all' repeated almost *ad nauseam* among the Cantabs. If my recollections extend to 1887 I must admit the college cry was not far wrong. I should say there were always two or three thousand people at the least on the river on a fine night. How times have changed – if you go on the river now on a Regatta night I don't believe you will meet a couple of hundred people and there is no music around.

Both the Essex Pierrots and The Japs made a lot of money. I was in Barclays Bank in Henley one Saturday after the Regatta when the Jap lady who acted as Treasurer paid in over £200 in hard cash as the week's takings and complained that owing to the wet evening receipts were much below anticipation.

It might be said that the motor cruisers along the Regatta course today are the successors to the houseboats of the late Victorian or Edwardian eras. But even the most opulent launches are but pale ghosts of those houseboats. Some were seventy feet long, with sleeping accommodation for a dozen people, with kitchen and servants' quarters in separate 'tenders'. And they lined the Bucks shore all the way from Poplar Point to Fawley Court boathouse.

By 1914 the cost of staging Henley had climbed to £3,046. When the Regatta was revived in 1919 both Tom Steward and John Cooper forecast an annual bill of about £8,000. They were closely correct for the 1919 figure was £8,244.

It must have been shortly after this, possibly in 1920, that John Cooper wrote:

I have often had it said to me 'I cannot imagine how Henley Regatta costs such a large sum to run'. It has been said, too, by people who might be described as knowledgeable people on rowing subjects and sometimes by the managers of other regattas. One and all of them fail to realise the enormous difference between Henley and any other regatta. At no other meeting is the course piled and boomed, a matter which with labour at its present price means a charge representing at least £100 a year. At all other regattas the crews arrive on the morning of the races. At Henley we have to provide for three weeks housing and care of boats, for dressing-rooms and baths and the many exigences of crews in training, roughly an annual liability of £500, and bear in mind that these two items have no credit side to the account. At present prices to carry on we shall have to obtain from some source or other perhaps £8,000 a year. It will be hard work to do it for many difficulties are in the way. First of all we do not own a square inch of land abutting on the Regatta course neither have we other than a short tenancy of any of it. The meaning of this is that except the boathouse above the bridge we have no permanent buildings nor erections whatever. Everything required to carry the Regatta through has to be put up and taken down every year. Besides this we are, of course, in an unfortunate position. Imagine, let us say, the Epsom authorities running their meeting, and the whole of the vantage ground on one side of the course, belonging to someone else who takes the profits and pays no share of the expenses. And imagine, further, their having only a yearly tenancy of the vantage ground on the opposite side of the course and consequently being unable to erect permanent buildings thereon and having accordingly to erect annually such temporary stands as the meeting from year to year required. If you *can* imagine it then you get at something like the position of the Henley executive today, namely getting less than half the takings and having to make an inordinate outlay on the necessary work to obtain the smaller half of such takings, the lion's share of which goes to those who do not find any part of, or practically no part of, the expenses of the meeting. Of course Henley is run for sport not for dividends or gate money, but still it ought to be self supporting and how to make it so is the problem confronting the Committee today. The average pre-war income of something under £4,000 is no longer adequate, the total expenditure is, as I said before, likely to come to £8,000. The card is one item I think visitors will not resent our raising from 6d to 1/- as long as it is plainly stated that such addition is to bring grist to the Regatta mill. In 1919 we had an elaborate frontispiece on the card which cost a lot of money. A more economical front page yet in good taste with

a different colour for each day would probably sell as well and produce a larger percentage of profit for the fund. Then, of course, much depends on the profits of the Stewards' Enclosure. This has been considerably enlarged and planted and will in future years be a much prettier place than in the year of its initial trial. If we succeed in, say, three years in doubling the number of members it will go far towards providing the additional revenue required. An enclosure of this sort is its own advertisement – when everything is well done and no complaints are heard. One does not want to make profits out of lunches and teas. If they are well done the profits soon come in in the shape of subscriptions from new members recommended by their friends who have already joined the Club and have found out its advantages. Then there is the flag system. I have contended and still contend that the methods employed by us in the past are wrong. Not that it has not added to the fund – it has, and an average of £400 a year is not to be sneezed at, but it is to the method of collection that I take objection. I would ask anyone acquainted with income tax and the method of collection thereof 'which do you think you are going to get the most out of and in the easiest way, a tax on income and dividends after receipt, or a tax levied at source?' Why of course the latter and if the boat tax could be levied on the boatletters with their consent at 2/6 per day for each boat let, and collected by them in addition to the charge for the boat, I am perfectly satisfied our returns would be much larger and the method of collection much cheaper and less irksome to all concerned.

Now as to houseboat and launch

positions. There are a large number of houseboat and launch owners who will pay a good price for the position they want if they can take it on the course and see what they are paying for; but the old system of buying a pig in a poke they will not have and never will.

Then I must refer to the 'meadow tax' – once get it firmly into the heads of the many that this is their only contribution to the funds which provide the sport they come to see, and that the same funds go entirely to support the Regatta and not to the profit of any person or persons, and they will respond, I am sure. But example is everything, every Steward, every old and present rowing man ought to buy and wear a four-day button making the man, woman or child without it like a schoolboy on the 29 May who cannot show his oak.

Lastly, some form of propaganda, cleverly got up, setting out our position, our objects, our necessities and our hopes, would I believe largely improve our finances and make it impossible to feel that there is any chance of the decline of Henley Regatta through lack of funds.

Though it is not relevant to finance I must include here an anecdote of John Cooper's – since this is where he included it in his own memoirs. The story I believe has never been told before, and casts a fascinating sidelight on the character of this respected local solicitor, who, on this occasion at least, became the scheming architect of history beyond the confines of the Thames Valley.

Turning from the actual point of £ s. d. (i.e. 'Finance', for the benefit of younger readers today), Cooper wrote:

I hope our Committee will never blush to find themselves famous as we have perhaps done too much in the past. The fame of Henley in the States, in Canada, in Australia and nearly all the world over is much greater than we as a Committee ever allowed ourselves to think. A good crew in the USA is described as up to 'Henley form' and the premier Regatta is styled 'the American Henley'. Similarly is there not Henley on the Yarra and Henley on the Zambesi? Our modesty in this respect nearly led us to a great mistake in 1908 when the Olympic Regatta was held in England. This was, of course, quite rightly, under the auspices of the Amateur Rowing Association and it was originally arranged by them to hold it at Putney. This subject came up at one of our meetings in the autumn of 1907 and I asked the Committee to recommend the advisability of holding it at Henley, on the ground that all colonial and foreign oarsmen who came to row in England would naturally expect to row at Henley and nowhere else. My arguments however fell very flat on our Committee who did not wish to interfere with the arrangements of the ARA. However, feeling very strongly on the point, but still not quite certain as to how far one may legitimately do evil that good may come, I borrowed some Vincents Club paper in Oxford and wrote to *The Field* under the pseudonym of 'an American Oxonian' protesting against the Regatta being held at Putney, a place which *I, as an American, had never heard of before matriculating at BNC,* and using the same arguments as I had previously done at the meeting at Henley, winding up in a somewhat grandioso manner that if one went to Greece the Olympic Games would be absurd if not at Athens and

that in like manner no foreigner would come
to row in England if the Olympic Regatta
took place elsewhere than at Henley.
Imagine my surprise when at our very next
meeting 'an American Oxonian's' letter in
The Field was read out in full and voted a
remarkably good letter, and my suggestion
which the Committee had unceremoniously
rejected became the headstone in the corner.
I must confess to having felt rather mean
but the point was gained and I tried to
persuade myself that, as far as the Olympic
Regatta went, I was only one of the public
and consequently entitled to express my
opinion in any way I thought fit – perhaps
rather thin ice to tread upon. Unfortunately,
however, what might have been the finest
Regatta ever held was spoilt by the subsequent decision to hold the Olympics a
fortnight after Henley instead of con-
temporaneously as at first proposed, with
the result that both fell a little flat and the
Olympic in particular was a very dull affair.
I have quoted this incident at length because
it bears so strongly on the point I raised,
namely the unassertive modesty which our
Committee have always shown, sometimes
almost at the risk of the best interest of the
Regatta. Since those days however the
Committee has been very much strengthened by the infusion of young blood, quite
as enthusiastic as the older members, but
with the advantage of more modern ideas
which are indeed so necessary for the successful conduct of a great festival like
Henley Regatta.

When John Cooper penned his memoirs he had
retired as Secretary of the Regatta. He referred
in passing to the innovation of the Stewards'

Enclosure, but of course could not have fore-
seen that this was to prove to be one of the
most important developments in the Regatta's
history.

During the eighty years since the first
Regatta, the problem of accommodating spectators had been dealt with in many different
ways but without any ongoing policy. The
founding fathers, townspeople all, had been
concerned with bringing business to the town.
Henley Bridge itself, and the roadway from the
Red Lion to New Street were the preferred
spectator areas. The towing path, open to the
public, ran along the opposite bank, and at
various times various people erected stands in
the meadows. But the Committee had no interest in luring the public away from the town.

When rowing men took over the running of
the Regatta one of their first acts was to move
the finish of the course from the Red Lion
to Poplar Point, with the immediate object of
improving the course, but with the effect of
transferring the 'spectator area' from the town
waterfront to the Lion and Blandy Meadows
below Poplar Point.

From this time on, enclosures, grandstands
and refreshment tents sprang up along the
bank. But directly or indirectly this was oppor-
tunistic private enterprise and the Regatta saw
little direct financial benefit. And be it remembered that the years between 1890 and 1914
covered probably the greatest 'boom' in Henley's history up to that time.

Undoubtedly the boom was fuelled by the
growing popularity of the railway which put
Henley within easy reach of London. The
largest number of visitors carried to Henley in
one day was 17,727 in 1906. That, incidentally,

1. Lord Camoys's yacht at Henley in 1887, during the royal visit described in chapter 2. Seated in the bows of the launch, in a white hat, with her back to the camera, is Julia Stonor (later Marquise d'Hautpoul) Then, left to right, Princess Maud of Wales (later Queen Maud of Norway), Princess Louise of Wales (later Duchess of Fide) and facing the camera, holding her programme against the light, Princess Victoria of Wales (later Queen Alexandra). The Queen's Watermen are seated on the ledge facing the bank, while the portly figure of the Prince of Wales (later King Edward VII) can be seen to the fore of the funnel. Prince George (later King George V) in his characteristic light suit stands to the right of the funnel.

2. The Royal Barge conveying Their Majesties King George V and Queen Mary from Henley station to the Stewards' Enclosure, 1912.

3. Spectators 'tossing oars' as Their Majesties King George V and Queen Mary return to the Enclosure after lunching at Greenlands as guests of the Hon. W. F. D. Smith (Lord Hambleden) in 1912.

4. H.R.H. The Prince of Wales, wearing a straw boater, is seen in the bows of the umpire's launch *Magician* during a Royal visit to Henley in 1921. Also in the bows is the umpire R. S. Bradshaw (holding a megaphone); sitting next to him is C. D. Burnell. Behind the Prince of Wales is Lady Desborough, and talking to Lady Desborough is J. H. Gibbon (wearing a boater). Standing up in the launch is C. T. Steward (wearing a cap) and Lord Desborough facing towards the stern. Sitting on a gunwale and facing the stern, wearing an Oxford cap, is probably Guy Nickalls. Standing with a programme in his hand and wearing binoculars on a strap is L. G. Wormald. Standing in the stern, holding a notebook and with his hand cupped to his mouth, is probably Theodore Cook (timekeeper). Seated on the counter is A. F. R. Wiggins.

5. H.R.H. Princess Elizabeth presents the Grand Challenge Cup to J. Bradley, stroke of the Leander crew, at the first post-war Regatta. Following Bradley are P. N. Brodie, R. M. A. Bourne and R. D. Burnell. To the right of Princess Elizabeth is Princess Margaret. Behind the trophies, on the left is the Regatta Chairman, Harcourt Gold; A. S. Garton is on the right. Behind the Princesses is C. D. Burnell; to the right of P. N. Brodie is E. R. Burgess; and behind R. M. A. Bourne is J. H. Gibbon.

6. Members of the Harvard crew of 1914 being presented to Her Majesty Queen Elizabeth the Queen Mother in 1964. Obscured by the Queen Mother is Leverett Saltonstall (the crew captain and bowman); partly obscured is Charles C. Lund, then left to right, Louis Curtis, David P. Morgan, John W. Middendorf, Henry S. Middendorf and Henry H. Meyer. Out of the picture were James Talcott and Henry L. F. Kreger.

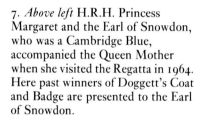

7. *Above left* H.R.H. Princess Margaret and the Earl of Snowdon, who was a Cambridge Blue, accompanied the Queen Mother when she visited the Regatta in 1964. Here past winners of Doggett's Coat and Badge are presented to the Earl of Snowdon.

8. *Above* H.R.H. Princess Alexandra, the Hon. Mrs Angus Ogilvy, during a visit to Henley in 1976.

9. H.R.H. Princess Anne, Mrs Mark Phillips, arriving by barge escorted by the Chairman, John Garton, in 1977.

10. Stewards on parade to welcome Princess Anne, 1977. *Left to right*: P. R. C. Coni, K. M. Payne, Lord Cottesloe, A. Burrough, J. G. P. Crowden, D. M. Jennens, J. R. Owen, W. A. D. Windham, C. G. V. Davidge, A. B. Hodgson, R. S. Goddard (Secretary).

11. Her Serene Highness Princess Grace of Monaco presents the Diamond Sculls to C. L. Baillieu of Leander Club in 1981.

12. H.R.H. Prince Andrew on the umpire's launch, accompanied by the Chairman, P. R. C. Coni, in 1985.

13. H.R.H. The Princess Royal braves the elements on board the umpire's launch in 1988. T. O'Neill, coach of the winning Leander and University of London crew, is on the right; Chairman and umpire P. R. C. Coni has his back to the camera.

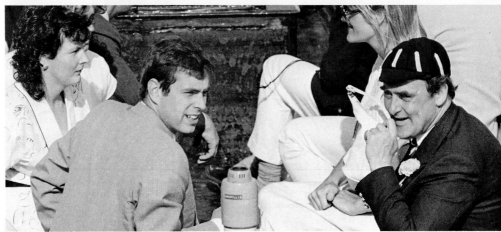

14. Probably the final of the Grand in 1842 when the umpire's crew joined in the race.

15. On the lawn of Bird Place. Second from the right is J. Cooper, son of P. B. Cooper, the first Treasurer. The boy at his knee is J. F. Cooper, Secretary of the Regatta from 1883 to 1919.

16. Watching the racing from carriages on Henley Bridge, c 1885 or earlier.

17. Henley Bridge with fairy lights, c 1903.

18. The first year of the booms, 1899.

19. A cannon on Blandy Meadow signals that a race has started, c 1903.

20. *Opposite* Arriving at Henley station, 1907.

21. Prize-giving, 1907.

22. Arcadia, 1914. A
month later the world
was plunged into war.

23. The first aeroplane
over Henley, 1914.

24. A peaceful picnic,
1923.

was six more than for all four days of the 1908 Olympic Regatta.

We have Cooper's evidence that the income from houseboats peaked at £1,000 a year but there is little evidence of prosperity in the minute books. In 1914, for example, £133 10s. came from 'letting enclosures to boat proprietors', £55 from 'enclosure for clubs', £101 1s. 6d. from 'permission to erect tents', £271 19s. from 'subscriptions and donations from owners of houseboats and launches', and £100 10s. 4d. 'from members of Phyllis Court Club'.

A pathetic record, one might say, from the world's premier Regatta, which, at that time, must have been one of the biggest events in any sport.

There had always been an Enclosure and Grandstand for the Stewards and Committee and their guests. The innovation in 1919 was the founding of a club, with a selected membership – candidates being elected then, as now, by the Committee of Management – paying an annual subscription for the privilege of access to the Stewards' Enclosure. Perhaps typically the minute book tells us very little about the setting up of the Stewards' Enclosure Club. It seems to have just happened; and I just happen to know – because my father, who was elected a Steward in 1919, told me so – that the idea emanated from Harcourt Gold. It was a conscious attempt to emulate the Royal Enclosure at Ascot, on the principle that people will pay to attend a sporting function, irrespective of whether they are personally involved in the sport in question, providing the facilities offered are sufficiently attractive.

And that is precisely what happened with the Stewards' Enclosure. The facilities, simple at first, became very good. Anyone who was anyone in the rowing world sought membership, and quite soon it became fashionable as well as convenient to be a 'Member of the Stewards'. Henley Royal Regatta became a feature of the London social season, as well as a great sporting occasion.

Of course there was opposition to the proposal, led by the habitual rebels, Sir John Edwards-Moss and W. B. Woodgate, who complained in the press that rowing men were to be squeezed out of Henley by the social butterflies. But what actually happened was that the Stewards' Enclosure, by attracting more spectators and ensuring an income which was not dependent on the vagaries of the English summer, secured the future for just those rowing men who were supposed to be squeezed out.

In the absence of such colourful eccentrics as 'Johnny' Edwards-Moss and 'Guts' Woodgate, some gentlemen of the press still endeavour to stir the social mud from time to time, suggesting that it is inappropriate for the *jeunesse dorée* to sip their champagne and Pimms without even bothering to take note of the sweating brows and gasping lungs on the river nearby. I can only say that I have seldom met an oarsman who saw it that way. Oarsmen are well aware that they enjoy the world's best regatta facilities by courtesy of the money paid by the spectators.

The Stewards' Enclosure started with a membership of 300 in 1919. By 1939 the number had risen to 704. In 1946 membership stood at 667. Ten years later it reached 1,500 and continued to rise until, after the 1980

Regatta, the Stewards announced a ceiling of 5,000 members, with priority to candidates who had rowed in the Regatta. In recent years there has been a steadily growing waiting list and one must suppose that this situation will continue, since there is really no scope for increasing the capacity of the Stewards' Enclosure.

Membership is only one facet of attendance. Each member has a quota of badges for his annual subscription, and can apply for additional badges for guests, though this privilege is now also 'on quota'. The Regatta Office of course know how many badges are issued, but there is no way of telling precisely how many are actually used.

But once again we have strayed from the chronological passage of events. Perhaps surprisingly in view of the depression years, costs seem to have increased relatively little between 1919 and 1939. The 1938 figure was still only £8,786. In 1939 the costs jumped to £15,358, but that was due to the special circumstances of the Centenary celebrations. During the 1940s and 1950s costs rose steadily but not dramatically. In 1952, Harcourt Gold's last year as Chairman, expenditure stood at £19,878.

But by this time the winds of inflation were beginning to blow cold. Chairman Harold Rickett saw the cost of staging the Regatta nudging the £50,000 mark. John Garton, taking over in 1966, saw it increase threefold in twelve years. At the December meeting of the Stewards in 1969 Garton expressed 'deep concern about the trend of the finances for the future'. The loss of many school entries had proved much worse financially than anticipated, the most recent increase in the sub-scription rate had led to many resignations, and the Regatta faced 'massive increases in the cost of tentage and installations'. Concluding his message of warning Garton announced a campaign of cost-cutting. Many will say that the manner in which he achieved economies without damaging the traditional background of the Regatta was one of his major contributions to Henley.

One step, in fact, had already been taken towards stabilizing the finances. In 1966 the fairground contract was terminated, most of the ground thus released being taken for car parking, whilst part was taken into a new public enclosure.

I can find no record of when a fair, recognizable as such, first appeared at Henley. The accounts for 1905 show an item of £86 17s. 6d. deriving from 'Hawkers, Motors and Bicycles'. But without doubt there must have been hawkers and itinerant entertainers long before that, as one would expect with any large gathering of people in search of amusement. But since the Regatta itself owned no land apart from a boathouse above Henley Bridge, any benefit probably accrued to others.

After 1920 the fair became a regular background to the enclosures. It was a major attraction to the young during the duller moments of the racing, to the oarsmen as they came out of training, and of course to the townspeople. The fair is still 'in town' during the Regatta week of course, but it has been banished to the Wargrave Road and is no longer a part of the Regatta. It was simple economics which tipped the scales; the space was needed, and could more profitably be utilized for parking cars.

Among many who bewailed the loss of the

fair, one did so in verse, and received her reply also in verse:

Henley Regatta without a fair is like a
    woman without hair,
All the colour, beauty dimmed, with sparkle,
    that did flow lit the sky with such a
    glow.
Children of the town itself cannot have their
    roundabouts,
Its always been their one delight to be taken
    to the fair at night.
After all they cannot see the races lest they
    climb a tree.
All the half-crowns that you take will always
    be a great mistake.
                    Ena Canvey (Mrs.)

Dear Madam, your communication didn't
    fill me with elation.
That you were sad I do not doubt. But I
    feel I must point out
That Henley Regatta without a fair meant a
    Regatta without a care.
Now for half-a-crown instead many an inno-
    cent child could tread
Down to the new enclosure, where, seated
    in a comfortable chair
He and his parents could enjoy watching the
    prowess of man and boy,
And, eating and drinking, pass the day in a
    more enjoyable way
Than pushing past the candy floss and on
    the swings taking a toss.
And it's so much safer after dark to have no
    fair, but just a park
For cars, and space for us to see the fireworks
    loved by you and me.
And it's a great deal quieter by Leander,
    Yours faithfully, A. L. Alexander.
                    Diana Southwell.

Well, one might say that the Poet Laureate was in no great danger of losing his job. But I doubt that many innocent children found sitting in a comfortable chair in the new public enclosure more enjoyable than searching for candy floss and chancing a tumble on the roundabouts!

In 1972 Garton reported that a surplus of £1,320 in 1971 had turned into a deficit of £2,756. Worse, he feared that the new VAT and other inescapable increases would raise expenditure by a further £60,000 (30%) in the ensuing year. Notwithstanding this dire situation the Stewards rejected the possibility of looking for sponsorship, to their eternal credit. But there was an important decision this year, to move the finals from Saturday to Sunday. This was not popular, but it increased income and paved the way for the Special Race for Schools, which in turn brought many school supporters back to the Regatta.

The cost of staging the Regatta exceeded £100,000 for the first time in 1975, an increase of 58% in two years. But the economies and drive for new income were beginning to bear fruit. There was a surplus of £524 in 1974, which crept up to £1,547 in 1975.

At the same time the seeds of another important development had been sown. Strenuous efforts were being made to interest business concerns in renting hospitality tents on the Fawley Meadows below Phyllis Court. About ten companies were captured in 1976, worth some £2,800 to the Regatta's coffers. Within three years this source of income had topped the £10,000 mark, and today 10% of the Regatta's earnings derive from hospitality tents.

It is hard to say whether corporate entertaining itself sparked off a new spectator interest, by bringing to Henley people who otherwise might never have sampled the Regatta's attractions, or whether this was caused by the rapid expansion of the sport of rowing itself. Certainly entries at Henley, which averaged 144 between 1946–50, were up to 243 between 1976–80; and more competitors must mean more spectators. Whatever the reasons, there is no doubt that the demand for access to the Stewards' Enclosure increased in a remarkable fashion after 1975, and has continued to do so every year since. In 1987 Henley earned £1m for the first time, and showed a profit in excess of £350,000.

With such a success story in the past decade, the financial future of Henley Royal Regatta may now look secure. And for the immediate future it surely is. But there is one factor which cannot be overlooked. The strong position today stems on the one hand from the tight financial controls imposed in John Garton's reign as Chairman, and on the other hand from the expansion and exploitation of the facilities by his successor as Chairman, Peter Coni. But

there is little scope left for further economies, since, for want of a better term, the 'gracious ambience' of Henley is an essential part of its attraction. Were it not for the immaculate lawns and flower beds, the Pimms and champagne bar, and the military band playing the Knightsbridge Suite and Iolanthe, the magic might fade and cash registers cease to ring. And if there is little scope for extending Garton's economies, it would be even more difficult to go further with Coni's exploitation of the facilities – for there is no more space available for parking cars, extending enclosures, or purveying food and drink.

This means that if the cost of staging the Regatta continues to increase, as it is bound to do, this can be met only by increasing charges. And at some point that must become counterproductive – unless, that is, Henley can find a new key to unlock a golden future. It is not obvious where this key may be found. But Henley has proved to be a great survivor in the last hundred and fifty years, and no doubt it will be done.

5 Henley as Landowners

In the early days Henley Regatta had no need of land. Spectators watched from the Bridge or from the roadway. Grandstands were erected, if not by the Town Council at least under the supervision of the Council's employees. Crews embarked wherever they could along the waterfront, or from the lawns of Bird Place, the then Cooper residence. But as the years passed problems arose with varnish blistering in hot weather; and competitors began to demand changing accommodation.

So it came about that the Stewards leased a plot of land between Mr Cooper's lawn and the bridge, and there erected a boathouse, to which in due course they added a plunge bath. In 1903 W. H. Brakspear, then as now the local brewer, offered this plot for sale and the Regatta acquired its first freehold property, which incidentally is now incorporated in the Headquarters complex.

There must have been other leasings, but only on a year-to-year basis. A Committee minute in June 1900 noted 'that sites in the Fawley Court Meadows should be granted as follows: Isthmian Club 190 ft., Thames Rowing Club 100 ft., Bath Club 150 ft., Sports Club 200 ft., R. E. Lunch Club 50 ft., Mr L. Hannen 50 ft.'.

Here we have not only a renting by the Regatta, but also a letting out, which was clearly the forerunner of the modern day amenity tents. Club enclosures were a feature of Henley for some years around the turn of the century but we know little or nothing about them because of the haphazard way in which the Stewards' and Committee minutes were kept.

At about the same time Phyllis Court, belonging to the Mackenzies of Fawley but empty of a tenant, was rented by the Stewards during the Regatta week. This practice seems to have commenced in 1901 or 1902, and probably ended in 1905, when there is a Committee minute that 'the public should be admitted to the Grandstand and Enclosure (on the Berks side of the river) at a charge of 2/6, *Phyllis Court being closed.*'

Hitherto the Stewards had shown no enthusiasm to become landowners in any significant degree. But in September 1924 Roderick Mackenzie noted his intention of selling a parcel of land in Lion Meadow, adjoining the garden of Leander Club. The Regatta had been renting the whole of Lion Meadow on a yearly basis, no doubt believing themselves secure in the knowledge that Mackenzie was one of the senior Stewards. But they certainly could not contemplate allowing this land to pass into other ownership, with the possibility, even, of houses being built.

In March 1925 Fred Pitman reported to the Stewards:

> Early in September last it became known
> that Mr. Mackenzie was negotiating for the
> sale of the portion of the Lion Meadow

immediately adjoining Leander Club. It was felt that if a sale of any considerable part of the Meadow were completed it must encroach on the space which has for many years been occupied by the boat tents, and that the very existence of the Regatta under modern conditions would be endangered. The Chairman of the Committee commenced a correspondence with Mr Mackenzie, and early in September had a meeting with him ...

Mr. Mackenzie intimated that he was not prepared to sell the main portion of the Lion Meadow on which the enclosures are situated, but that he did propose to sell the whole of the portion adjoining Leander Club, and which is occupied by the boat tents ... The negotiations ... were continued throughout December and January, but the Committee regret to state that so far they have not been able to come to terms ... the Committee has made an offer to purchase the whole of the portion of Lion Meadow which Mr. Mackenzie has for sale at a price which they are advised is far in excess of its market value on the condition that they should be granted a 21-year lease of the remainder of the two meadows ... Mr. Mackenzie, while prepared to sell the portion of the meadow above referred to, has so far refused to grant anything better than an annual tenancy over the remainder of the meadows.

The Committee have been compelled to inform Mr. Mackenzie that the high figure which was offered by them for the purchase of a portion of the meadow was based on the assumption that a lease for a reasonable period would be granted of the other portions of the meadow, and that in their opinion no Committee or body of Stewards would be justified in making a purchase unless such a lease is granted ... the meadows are essential to the Regatta as at present organized, and unless it is possible to retain control of them for a term of years without unreasonable restrictions it will be necessary to consider either a drastic alteration of the existing course or the removal of the Regatta to another reach of the Thames.

FRED. I. PITMAN
Chairman of the
Committee of Management

It was not a happy situation, but one can only wonder whither the Committee proposed to transfer Henley Regatta if Mackenzie did not back down. Fortunately, after further negotiations, back down he did, so that the minutes of June 1926 were able to report the purchase of three acres adjoining Leander for £2,250, and a twenty-one-year lease of $9\frac{1}{4}$ acres, 'the remainder of Lion Meadow and the southern half of Blandy Meadow, at £20 p.a. per acre, reducing to £5 if no Regatta should be held'.

In 1938 the Regatta purchased 'The Nook' – now the competitors' car park – and in the following year added the land which had been rented in 1926. The Stewards' minutes recorded 'that now all the land between the river and Remenham Lane from Leander Club down to the upper end of the meadow in front of Remenham Lodge (now Court) is the property of the Stewards'.

This year (1939) marked the Centenary of the Regatta's foundation, and it is interesting to reflect that although Henley was, and indeed had for long been, the world's premier annual

Regatta, at this point in time there was still no permanent headquarters. The Regatta had always been run from the offices or homes of its Chairmen, or Secretaries, or, between the two wars, of Tom Steward.

After the 1939–45 war, changes were afoot, and one possible development was of incalculable importance. For in the autumn of 1945 it was learned that Phyllis Court Club was likely to come on to the market for the first time since 1906. It would be hard to exaggerate, but even harder to quantify, the effect which possession of Phyllis Court would have had on the Royal Regatta. Certainly it would have extended far beyond the acquisition of additional enclosure space. For one thing it is a fair assumption that if the Stewards had owned Phyllis Court they would have had to tackle the problem of providing a bridge or tunnel link between the Oxfordshire and Berkshire shores. By the yardstick of 1945 requirements, Phyllis Court would have provided all the spectator facilities that could possibly have been envisaged. But equally importantly it would have made it possible to provide car parks along the Marlow road to serve the increasing crowds in the Stewards' and public enclosures, easing the traffic congestion on the approaches from London and Wargrave.

Only the vaguest and most fleeting references to this important matter appear in the minute books. Messrs G. O. Nickalls and Jack Beresford Jr, as 'younger Stewards', were invited to report on the possibilities, which they did with enthusiasm. It was suggested that some realignment of the course would be necessary, to improve the view from Phyllis Court. These matters were referred to in a lengthy and rather rambling letter to the Stewards, which, to judge by the address, came from Harcourt Gold:

PHYLLIS COURT
The above property has come into the market, including furniture and fittings inside and outside the house, and the vendors are prepared to give preference to the Stewards of Henley Regatta, if they should decide in favour of acquiring it.

In a short discussion between a few members of the Committee on the 15th November it was thought advisable to have the views of the younger generation and, accordingly, Messrs. Nickalls and Beresford were requested to go into the matter with the secretary of the Regatta, who would supply them with all available information. Their report, which covers a wide range of investigation, has already been circulated and, as will be seen, it is in favour of the scheme. They back their opinion by expressing a willingness to serve on a committee to manage the club side of the project.

From the Stewards' point of view the advantages are as follows:
1. To establish a headquarters of rowing.
2. The provision of permanent Regatta offices with accommodation for records. The purchase of a house for this purpose has become essential.
3. It is set in a unique position for all Regatta services, other than the officials and those requiring the enthusiasts' view of the racing.

From the members' point of view:
1. It is an excellent house and grounds for week-end visiting and entertaining.

2. Well adapted to requirements of a social club.
3. It is many years since it came into the market and the opportunity may not recur.

The letter then considers the possibility that some re-alignment of the Regatta course might be necessary in order to give a better view from Phyllis Court, and also contemplates the redistribution of spectator facilities on the two sides of the river, and finally moves to finances.

Finance.   This brings us to a point where the going is far from easy and comes under the heads:

The Purchase Price.   Provided the price was reasonable the raising of the money would not present insuperable difficulties. The interest charges which the Nickalls–Beresford report has taken into account would be a heavy item.

The Annual Expenditure.   As far as the club is concerned the income would depend entirely on its popularity and its ability to attract members, i.e. the rowing fraternity principally – at an adequate subscription.

Finally.   It may be thought that as the Regatta would benefit for only a very limited period in each year a way might be found whereby the club might be run as a separate entity and some reciprocal arrangement made with the Regatta. This arrangement would resolve itself into dual control, which sooner or later would probably prove an unsatisfactory arrangement to the Stewards.

It seems then to resolve itself into two headings:

1. Has the Nickalls–Beresford report convinced the Committee of the advantages which would accrue to rowing generally, and Henley Regatta in particular, with a reasonable prospect of financial profit.
2. Do their views represent the majority of their rowing contemporaries and a yet still younger post-war generation, for it is these that the Committee will wish to have in mind.

The Nickalls–Beresford Report does not appear in either minutes or files; nor does the plan of the proposed course realignment. There is a Committee minute on 24 February 1946 to the effect that: 'After inspecting the property ... it was decided to open negotiation for the purchase of Phyllis Court at a figure not exceeding £14,000.'

After that there is tantalizing silence. The popular story in Henley's corridors of power is that 'Uncle Tom' (C. T. Steward) found the Phyllis Court drains to be less than satisfactory. The tale may well be true. What is certainly true is that the members of Phyllis Court Club held a Special General Meeting in London, on 29 May 1945, to vote on a proposal to sell the club, when a contrary motion was raised from the floor and carried. So Henley could not have had Phyllis Court, even if they had been more forceful in their quest.

Although Phyllis Court slipped out of the net, Henley did get their first permanent headquarters in 1945, when they purchased the lease of Baltic Cottage to provide accommodation for the Secretary, and for the Regatta Office.

Despite their less than enthusiastic reaction to the Phyllis Court episode, it may nevertheless have focussed the vision of land ownership in the minds of the Committee, who now began a campaign of land procurement.

In 1948 the Regatta purchased Selwyn's Field, originally the local cricket club, but more recently the Henley Tennis Club ground. The immediate purpose was to provide a site for luncheon tents, thus releasing land on the enclosure side of Remenham Lane for the additional car parking required for the Olympic Regatta. Three years later the adjoining field was purchased for the same purpose.

Roderick Mackenzie of Fawley Court died in 1952, and the Regatta asked his daughter, Margaret Mackenzie, for a 'first refusal' if she should ever wish to sell Temple Island. History does not relate whether any understanding was reached. But at the same time the Mackenzie Executors sold more than 1,000 acres on the Berks side of the river to a speculator who offered the land for resale in lots which would have meant Henley Regatta acquiring some 417 acres, at a cost of £50,000, in order to secure the river frontage between Phyllis Court and Fawley Boathouse.

By now the Committee had recognized how vital it was to secure as much as possible of the land on both sides of the river, for the future protection of the Regatta if not for its immediate requirements. So the Regatta agents went to the auction, buying what they could, selling what was not required, and using the proceeds to make further purchases. In this manner they acquired all of the riverside Fawley Meadows between the Boathouse and Phyllis Court.

More land on the Bucks shore, between Fawley and Temple Island, and known as the Park Farm Meadows, was purchased in 1955.

Thus the process of securing the future of the Henley Royal Regatta against undesirable development seemed to be making good progress. But in 1957 there were some setbacks. First Remenham Farm came on to the market. The Committee indicated that they would not bid against the sitting tenant but would like a first refusal if he was not a bidder. The property was withdrawn, and subsequently sold without Henley having an opportunity to bid.

In July 1957 Remenham Lodge, known today as Remenham Court but as the White House to older generations of Henley oarsmen, was offered for sale for £15,000. This time one must say that the Committee of Management made a blunder of some magnitude. They decided that the White House would make a suitable headquarters, which was a glimpse of the obvious, but jibbed at the price, partly, it seems, because one of the fields involved was subject to grazing rights which could, they feared, interfere with its use during the Regatta. The chance was lost; Remenham Lodge, with the field in front – but without the field subject to grazing rights – was sold to a Dr Davies, since when it has changed hands several times at orbitting prices. It was not so much the loss of the house as the loss of the field in front of it which was a tragedy, as today it is the site of amenity tents which earn large sums of money for someone else.

A year later the Committee purchased the field known as Green's Field for £2,500, and bought out the grazing rights for £500. It is used as an overflow car park. With the advantage of hindsight one may say that for £12,000 Remenham Lodge would have been the best bargain Henley ever bought, with or without grazing rights. But in fairness one must also

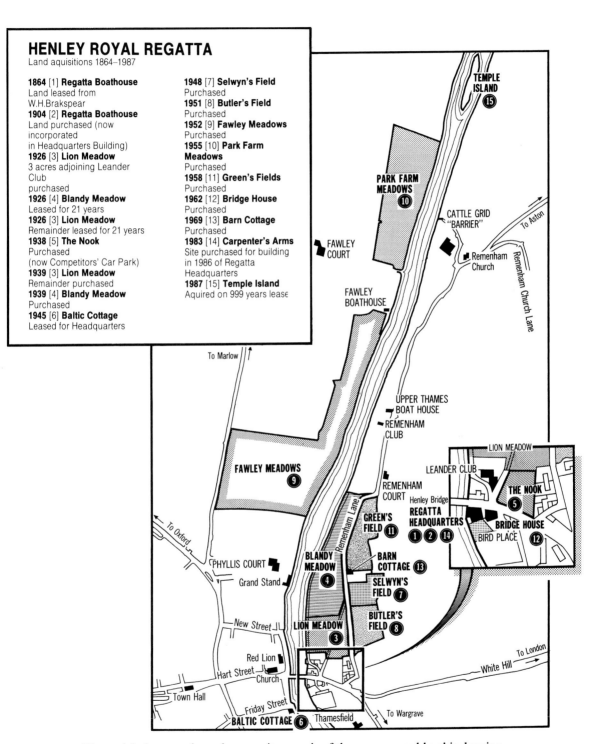

HENLEY ROYAL REGATTA
Land aquisitions 1864–1987

1864 [1] **Regatta Boathouse**
Land leased from
W.H.Brakspear
1904 [2] **Regatta Boathouse**
Land purchased (now
incorporated
in Headquarters Building)
1926 [3] **Lion Meadow**
3 acres adjoining Leander
Club
purchased
1926 [4] **Blandy Meadow**
Leased for 21 years
1926 [3] **Lion Meadow**
Remainder leased for 21 years
1938 [5] **The Nook**
Purchased
(now Competitors' Car Park)
1939 [3] **Lion Meadow**
Remainder purchased
1939 [4] **Blandy Meadow**
Purchased
1945 [6] **Baltic Cottage**
Leased for Headquarters

1948 [7] **Selwyn's Field**
Purchased
1951 [8] **Butler's Field**
Purchased
1952 [9] **Fawley Meadows**
Purchased
1955 [10] **Park Farm Meadows**
Purchased
1958 [11] **Green's Fields**
Purchased
1962 [12] **Bridge House**
Purchased
1969 [13] **Barn Cottage**
Purchased
1983 [14] **Carpenter's Arms**
Site purchased for building
in 1986 of Regatta
Headquarters
1987 [15] **Temple Island**
Aquired on 999 years lease

The aerial photograph on the opposite page is of the area covered by this drawing.

recognize that £15,000 was a substantial sum in 1958, nor was there any indication of the huge rise in house prices which was to follow, nor of the potential value of riverside land for corporate entertaining.

The failure to acquire Remenham Lodge was the more surprising because the lease of Baltic Cottage was due to expire in 1964. In 1962 Bridge House was purchased, but with a sitting tenant in the ground floor. The Secretary took up residence but the office remained at Baltic Cottage. In fact it remained there on a day-to-day basis for some time after the expiry of the lease. Shortly before the 1966 Regatta the office moved to the premises of the Henley Squash and Badminton Club. In September the office moved again to Leander Club, until finally, in April 1967, possession was gained of the ground floor of Bridge House which then became the official headquarters, being renamed Regatta House.

In 1969 the remaining land in the immediate vicinity of Barn Cottage was purchased and leased back to the occupant, the lease being determinable on the sale of Barn Cottage. In the previous year the Stewards had empowered Trustees to purchase such land as might be necessary to provide a four-lane racing course. Three schemes were prepared from an aerial survey during 1969. The 'Berks Scheme' would have been the simplest, requiring the excavation of about $3\frac{1}{2}$ acres of land along the line of the towpath; this scheme was frustrated because the owner of Remenham Farm refused to sell. The 'Bucks Scheme' required the excavation of a long but quite narrow strip of the Bucks bank; this was frustrated because Miss Mackenzie was not prepared to sell the Fawley Boat-

house site 'for aesthetic reasons'. It should be added that the Boathouse was already a ruin and subsequently collapsed altogether. The third alternative, the 'Centre Scheme', would have required no land acquisition but the removal of almost the whole of Poplar Point, including a large area of the Stewards' Enclosure.

Not surprisingly these schemes were all dropped. By this time, as already mentioned, the Regatta's finances were coming under increasing pressure from inflation. In 1972 Regatta House was sold, and headquarters moved into accommodation across the road in Leander Club, to the mutual benefit of both institutions.

In 1983 an opportunity arose to acquire the site of the derelict Carpenters Arms Inn, on the end of Henley Bridge and adjoining the original Regatta boathouse, which was still in use as a store. Fortunately the economic climate was improving by this time, and the Stewards made sure the chance of providing a purpose-built headquarters was not missed. In 1983 the Carpenters Arms site was purchased; plans were drawn up and the necessary building application instituted without delay. In 1986 the new Regatta Headquarters were opened by Her Majesty Queen Elizabeth II.

And so, looking at the map on the preceding page, it might seem that as Henley approached its 150th Anniversary, all the land which could be obtained to ensure the Regatta's future well-being had been obtained. But yet there was one thing missing, which might be described as the 'jewel in the crown'. The jewel of course was Temple Island, the 'folly' thought to have been built in 1771 by the famous architect James Wyatt, surveyor of Westminster Abbey, for

John Freeman of Fawley Court, which had become for many the epitome of the Henley reach.

For a time before the building of their clubhouse near Henley Bridge, Leander Club had an enclosure on Temple Island. Members and guests used to drive by coach to Remenham Church and thence via the towing path to be ferried over to the Island. There seems to have been no use of the Island for Regatta purposes.

But the real importance of Temple Island was not that it might be put to good use by the Regatta, but rather that it might one day be put to bad use by somebody else. Whilst it remained the property of the Mackenzie family there was probably no risk of this. But the sudden advent of corporate entertaining, and the huge rents paid for sites on which amenity tents could be erected, put a different complexion on the potential value of the Island. From 1983 onwards the Regatta began to make overtures for the purchase of the Island, and in the spring of 1986 it came on to the market. This could hardly have happened at a worse moment, coinciding as it did with the heavy cost of building the new headquarters. Also it was very much a seller's market, with everyone well aware that the Regatta deemed it vital to secure the Island. Fortunately by this time Henley's finances were in a buoyant state, matched by the Stewards' determination that Temple Island, the backcloth to nearly a century and a half of Regattas, had to be secured for posterity at any price. Negotiations were opened, and successfully concluded in December 1987, with a 999-year lease. For once courage and determination were abundantly rewarded, for at the December meeting of the Stewards, Peter Coni was able to announce not only the acquisition of Temple Island but also a magnificent gift of £515,000 from Alan Burrough and his wife Rosie to cover the cost. In all their long history no meeting of the Stewards can have received more welcome news.

In their 150th Anniversary year the Stewards hold all the land which might be described as essential to the running of the Regatta. But they would certainly like to gain control of the Berkshire bank below the enclosures. When Cooper bewailed the fact that someone else was taking the lion's share of the profits, while making no contribution to the cost of running the Regatta, he was probably overstating his case. Seventy years on his complaint would be much more apposite. The amenity tent complexes near Temple Island, and at Remenham, and the viewing and car parking area at Remenham Farm, not only profit from the Regatta without contributing to it, but greatly increase the intractable traffic problem.

6 The Course

The length of the Henley Regatta course, long described as 'about one mile and 550 yards', is an instance of how geographical chance can profoundly influence the development of the sport. When Messrs Nash and Towsey set about organizing their Regatta, in 1839, they naturally though ill-advisedly placed the finishing line at the bridge, and the start line at Temple Island, at the far end of their stretch of open water. The distance at the time was supposed to be 'about a mile and a half'.

It is unlikely that the start was opposite the Temple, as some have claimed, for that would have partially hidden the crews from the spectators on the towing path on the Berkshire bank, including the umpire who was on horseback and had to align and start the races. Probably the start was opposite the drainage ditch on the Oxfordshire bank, just above the head of the Island. According to H. T. Steward that became the established start for the 'Old Course', and one of the earliest Henley photographs (see Plate 25) confirms this. If this reasoning is correct then the first Henley races were over a distance of about one mile and 600 yards.

The dangers inherent in finishing races at the bridge itself must have become immediately apparent, and in 1840 the finish was moved downstream, some have said by ten, and some by as much as sixty yards. What matters is that the finish of the Old Course settled down on the steps of the Red Lion lawn. This turned out to be one mile and 570 yards from the start. But as the crews were aligned by their sterns at the start, and judged by their bows at the finish, shorter boats had to row further than longer boats. The assumed length of an eight was about sixty feet, or twenty yards, and thus the Henley course came to be described as 'about one mile and 550 yards', which was the distance to be covered by a sixty-foot eight.

As Henley was the first, and before long the most famous, Regatta, this distance gained acceptance as the classic distance for regatta racing. When boat racing began to flourish in the United States, Canada and Australia, oarsmen there adopted the Henley distance, and in some cases described their courses as 'Henley courses'. The Emperor Napoleon having imposed the metre unit on Europe, the Continental countries adopted the nearest convenient distance of 2,000 metres, which is about 123 yards short of the classic Henley distance.

Looking at the map, or at pictures of the Henley reach today, it may appear incredible that anyone should have laid out a racing course. with a major left-hand bend in the last quarter-mile. But the founders of Henley Regatta were not so much concerned with the niceties of boat racing as with providing a fine spectacle for their spectators, not to mention a convenient grandstand for Stewards and Committee, built over the roadway with direct access to the comforts of the Red Lion Hotel.

It was soon realized that the Old Course offered a huge advantage to the crew on the Berkshire Station, not only because of the bend at Poplar Point, but also because there was shelter from the stream in the bays below the Point.

Paradoxically the unfairness of the Old Course was mitigated by the unfairness of the old rules, which gave to a crew which succeeded in crossing in front of an opponent, the right to claim their 'water'. Since the crew on the Bucks side of the river enjoyed some advantage in the opening stages of the race it was not uncommon for a Bucks crew to cross in front of a Berks crew, and so to obtain the inside berth before Poplar Point. But for this rule Berks would no doubt have won an even higher proportion of the races.

As it was, in the last twenty years (1866–85) on the Old Course, 57.7% of all races were won by the Berks crew, with the Bucks and Centre crews sharing 42.3%. When only two crews raced, the Centre Station was not used.

Attempts were made to reduce the Berks advantage by roping poles across the bays below Poplar Point, and in 1884 a sub-committee considered the possibility of cutting off Poplar Point. They concluded that this would be too costly, and unlikely to achieve a worthwhile improvement. Instead they proposed that the finish should be moved downstream to Poplar Point, and the start to the bottom of Temple Island.

This proposal was certainly not universally popular. It deprived the townspeople of their view of the finish from the roadway outside the Little White Hart Hotel, the Stewards of their grandstand in front of the Red Lion, and the gentry of the possibility of watching from their carriages parked on Henley Bridge. But now rowing men were taking charge of the Regatta. Backed by replies to a questionnaire to club captains, the Committee reported in favour of moving the start, and also recommended that only two crews should race abreast. That entailed a three-day Regatta. But both recommendations were accepted and put into effect for the 1886 Regatta.

The New Course, as it came to be known, started just below the tail of Temple Island, on the Bucks side, with the finish opposite the upstream end of Phyllis Court, almost as it is today. There were two slight bends, one opposite Remenham Rectory, and the other 150 yards below Fawley Boathouse. The start line was staggered so that both stations were equal in length. And for the first time the course, 150 feet wide, was piled though not boomed. To replace the Stewards' Grandstand and Committee Room the Exeter College barge was towed down from Oxford and moored at the finish.

Alas, though the New Course looked fairer, it proved to be quite the reverse, but with the advantages now transferring to Bucks. This was because the first half of the course now hugged the Buckinghamshire shore, along which, below Fawley, there was a strong growth of bushes, offering shelter from the prevailing wind. This was the era during which the term 'Bushes Wind' came into being. At the same time the New Course deprived the Berkshire crew of compensatory advantage at the finish. During the ensuing twenty years the statistical advantage swung emphatically to Bucks, with 59% wins to 41% for Berks.

About this time Dr Warre made an interesting comment about the course, overheard and recorded for posterity by the ubiquitous Secretary, Cooper:

> Given a fine calm day there is nothing in the stations except this – any duffer can steer the Bucks Station, keeping a course say twelve feet away and perfectly parallel to the piles. But it takes a really good cox to steer the Berks course as he leaves the head of the Island until the half way mark.

To reduce the effect of the Bushes Wind the course was pushed further out towards the centre of the river, and narrowed to 135 feet in 1887, 120 feet in 1888, and then progressively until by 1914 it was down to 100 feet at the start tapering to 80 feet at the finish. In the meantime partial booming was introduced in 1899, to keep spectators off the course.

After the 1914–18 war a survey was carried out to see if the notorious 'Bushes Wind effect' could be overcome by moving the start to the Berkshire side of Temple Island. The Berkshire channel was then very much a winding backwater, shallow in places, and it was clearly not possible to achieve the full Henley distance. Nevertheless the Stewards decided as an experiment to try out a straight course on the Berkshire side of the river, although this meant starting above the Island and accepting a shorter course.

In 1923 this Experimental Course produced 53.2% wins for Bucks and 46.8% for Berks. This was much better than the 59%–41% advantage which Bucks had shown before, but unusually calm weather meant that the Bushes Wind effect had not been in evidence in 1923.

Nevertheless, according to Tom Steward, the feeling generally was that there must be advantages in moving the course to the Berkshire side of the river. The decision was made; Lord Hambleden agreed to give up land on the Berkshire bank, Mr W. D. Mackenzie likewise agreed to a trimming of the Temple Island bank; 10,000 cubic yards of material were excavated, 800 feet of new campshedding erected, and the new Straight Course, 80 feet wide and back to the original one mile and 570 yards length, was ready for the 1924 Regatta.

Results during the first ten years of the Straight Course seemed to confirm the 1923 pattern. Thereafter the gap narrowed, and since 1939 there has been no significant statistical difference between the total number of wins for Berks and Bucks. Understandably the Henley management have tended to quote these statistics as proof of the fairness of the course. But an objective study of the results hardly substantiates this claim. For example, the twenty-four Regattas between 1939 and 1968, which showed only $1\frac{1}{2}$ percentage points difference between the winning stations, also reveal

Percentages of races won from each Station

			Bucks	Berks
Old Course	(ii) 1866–1885	(i) 42.3	57.7
New Course	(ii) 1886–1905		59	41
Experimental Course	(ii) 1923		53.2	46.8
Straight Course	(ii) 1924–1955		53.3	46.7
	(iii) 1939–1968		49.11	50.61
	(iii) 1975–1984		50.52	49.31

(i) Bucks and Centre: when only two crews raced, the Centre Station was not used.
(ii) Races in Grand, Ladies' Plate and Thames Cup.
(iii) All races (small percentage discrepancy due to dead-heats being included in total 100%).

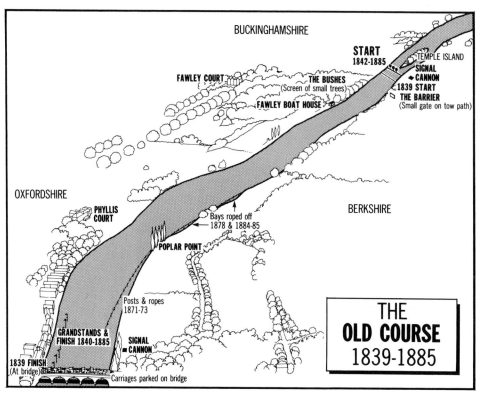

BUCKINGHAMSHIRE

START
1842-1885

TEMPLE ISLAND

SIGNAL
CANNON

1839 START

THE BARRIER
(Small gate on tow path)

FAWLEY COURT

THE BUSHES
(Screen of small trees)

FAWLEY BOAT HOUSE

OXFORDSHIRE

BERKSHIRE

PHYLLIS
COURT

Bays roped off
1878 & 1884-85

POPLAR POINT

Posts & ropes
1871-73

**THE
OLD COURSE
1839-1885**

GRANDSTANDS &
FINISH 1840-1885

SIGNAL
CANNON

1839 FINISH
(At bridge)

Carriages parked on bridge

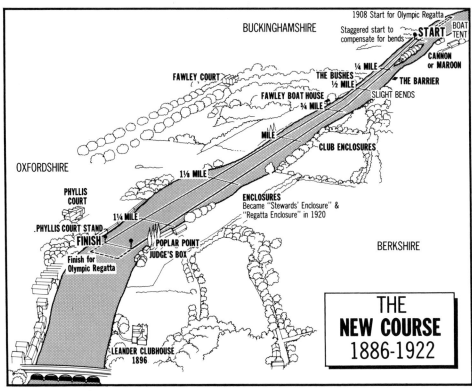

1908 Start for Olympic Regatta

BUCKINGHAMSHIRE

Staggered start to
compensate for bends

START

BOAT
TENT

¼ MILE

CANNON
or MAROON

FAWLEY COURT

THE BUSHES
½ MILE

THE BARRIER

FAWLEY BOAT HOUSE
¾ MILE

SLIGHT BENDS

MILE

CLUB ENCLOSURES

OXFORDSHIRE

1½ MILE

PHYLLIS
COURT

1¼ MILE

ENCLOSURES
Became "Stewards' Enclosure" &
"Regatta Enclosure" in 1920

PHYLLIS COURT STAND

FINISH

POPLAR POINT

JUDGE'S BOX

BERKSHIRE

Finish for
Olympic Regatta

**THE
NEW COURSE
1886-1922**

LEANDER CLUBHOUSE
1896

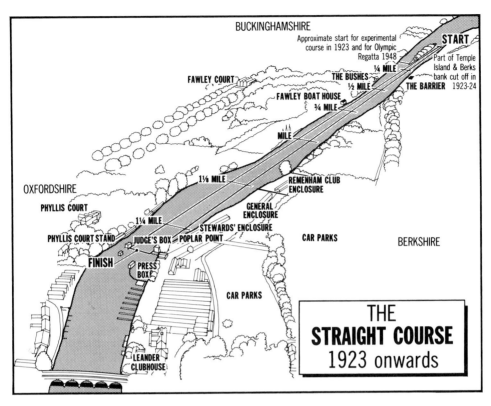

BUCKINGHAMSHIRE

Approximate start for experimental
course in 1923 and for Olympic
Regatta 1948

START

¼ MILE

Part of Temple
Island & Berks
bank cut off in
1923-24

THE BUSHES

½ MILE

THE BARRIER

FAWLEY COURT

FAWLEY BOAT HOUSE

¾ MILE

MILE

OXFORDSHIRE

1½ MILE

REMENHAM CLUB
ENCLOSURE

PHYLLIS COURT

GENERAL
ENCLOSURE

1¼ MILE

STEWARDS' ENCLOSURE

PHYLLIS COURT STAND

JUDGE'S BOX — POPLAR POINT

CAR PARKS

BERKSHIRE

FINISH

PRESS
BOX

CAR PARKS

LEANDER
CLUBHOUSE

THE
STRAIGHT COURSE
1923 onwards

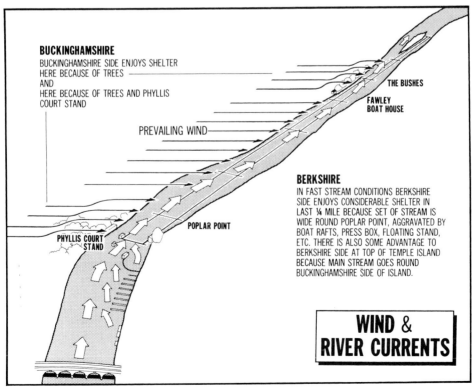

BUCKINGHAMSHIRE

BUCKINGHAMSHIRE SIDE ENJOYS SHELTER
HERE BECAUSE OF TREES
AND
HERE BECAUSE OF TREES AND PHYLLIS
COURT STAND

THE BUSHES

FAWLEY
BOAT HOUSE

PREVAILING WIND

BERKSHIRE

IN FAST STREAM CONDITIONS BERKSHIRE
SIDE ENJOYS CONSIDERABLE SHELTER IN
LAST ¼ MILE BECAUSE SET OF STREAM IS
WIDE ROUND POPLAR POINT, AGGRAVATED BY
BOAT RAFTS, PRESS BOX, FLOATING STAND,
ETC. THERE IS ALSO SOME ADVANTAGE TO
BERKSHIRE SIDE AT TOP OF TEMPLE ISLAND
BECAUSE MAIN STREAM GOES ROUND
BUCKINGHAMSHIRE SIDE OF ISLAND.

POPLAR POINT

PHYLLIS COURT
STAND

WIND &
RIVER CURRENTS

that there were five years in which Berks showed an advantage of 10% or more, whilst in four other years Bucks enjoyed a similar ascendancy. The truth is that conditions – and therefore the possible advantage to one station or the other – vary not only from year to year but also from day to day, and sometimes, at least so far as the wind is concerned, from hour to hour.

Given that the Bucks crew enjoys some shelter from the prevailing wind, and that the Berks crew can avoid the full force of the stream when the river is running strongly, it would be astonishing if conditions were always 'fair'.

But this fact also needs to be considered objectively. On the courses on which international championships are held, the outside lanes are further apart than the full width of the river at Henley, so that conditions on lanes 1 and 6 may vary dramatically. At Henley the course is only eighty feet wide, the crews start forty feet apart, and with good steering can row within thirty feet of each other. Coaches are quick to blame the conditions when their crews are beaten, but often they are victims of their own bad steering, or, according to how you look at it, of those same coaches' failure to brief their crews properly.

Another factor which is often overlooked is the wide difference in the quality of the competing crews. In a World Championship final there may be six crews within a length of each other, sometimes less: in those circumstances racing conditions are critical. They can sometimes be critical in one particular race at Henley, too. But when one is looking at the overall statistics on a particular day, or in a particular event, the picture is quite different. Often there is a difference of many lengths between the competing crews. We can see this if we look at one year, 1959 for example, which might easily be quoted as grossly unfair because 78 (60%) out of a total of 129 races were won off the Bucks Station. But eighty-four races that year were won by margins of two lengths or more. The losers in those races would have lost whatever conditions they encountered. Of the twenty-seven 'close' races in 1959 (verdicts of one length or less), in which the outcome might have been influenced by the wind, thirteen were won from the Berks Station, and fourteen from the more sheltered Bucks Station.

The conclusion is clear. When there is a strong south-westerly wind it is better to be on the Bucks Station, and when the stream is strong it is better to be on Berks. But the number of races which are actually lost because of the draw is quite small, and insignificant compared with the races lost through bad steering and failure to understand, or react to, the tactical requirements of the race.

To return to the history of the Henley course, when the 1908 Olympic Regatta was held at Henley the start was moved downstream to provide a distance of a mile and a half. For the 1948 Olympics, with the need to provide three racing lanes, the start was moved upstream to the top of Temple Island.

A new factor entered Henley's calculation after 1948. By this time British crews were beginning to compete regularly in the European Championships, so the Amateur Rowing Association awoke to the fact that if Britain aspired to hosting such events it was necessary to provide a multi-lane 2,000-metre course.

A committee was set up by the Amateur Rowing Association to find, or stimulate the construction of, such a course, and various possible sites came under discussion, among them Pangbourne, Eton, Theale, and particularly Sonning, which progressed to the point of feasibility plans being drawn. All those locations had one point in common: they were close to Henley. The committee believed, and pointed out to Henley, that the appearance of a purpose-built multi-lane course in the Thames Valley would pose a threat to the Royal Regatta, and suggested that they ought to consider the possibility of providing such facilities themselves. The most that could have been hoped for would have been four lanes, but even that might have discouraged the construction of a rival course nearby.

Harold Rickett, whom we have already identified as the 'conservator', showed no enthusiasm for such a drastic proposition. But his successor, John Garton, faced with daunting financial problems, ordered an aerial survey in 1969 to establish the feasibility of providing four lanes. With opposition from riparian landowners a four-lane course was impossible. Furthermore, with the advent of the new National Watersports Centre at Nottingham, enthusiasm for 'updating' the Henley course was ebbing. From around the world the message was clear, 'nothing should be done to detract from the unique character of the two-lane racing at Henley.' So for better or for worse the Henley course remains unchanged – in all but one small detail. Since 1967 the distance is no longer described as 'about one mile and 550 yards'. In that year the start line was re-located exactly one mile and 550 yards from the finish, and arrangements made for all boats, irrespective of their class and length, to be aligned by the bows, on that start line. The small boats today find the course a few yards shorter than it used to be.

7 The Events

The conditions under which Henley events are contested are described in Appendix 3, but some general comments may be of interest here.

In the early years the Stewards and Committee were searching for events which would attract competitors and spectators, sometimes with a degree of desperation to judge by the frequency with which the qualifications for the local events were adjusted. At times they even looked beyond the confines of rowing in their search for entertainment. In 1862, according to *Bell's Life*: 'The Regatta was threatened with the indignity of a canoe race, but the list not filling, this misfortune was averted.' Five years later that indignity actually occurred, with a 'canoe chase over land and water'. Herbert Steward commented that 'this was so justly condemned that the experiment was not repeated'.

But these were passing fantasies. The inauguration of the Thames Cup in 1868 completed the basic programme which was to remain unaltered for seventy years. The Grand, Stewards', Goblets and Diamonds were the open events for eights, fours, pairs and sculls; the Ladies' Plate and Visitors' were for college and school eights and fours; and the Thames and Wyfold Cups were for lower ranking eights and fours. A bias in favour of 'student' rowing was already apparent, for colleges and schools could enter for any of these events whereas clubs could not enter for the Ladies' Plate or Visitors' Cup.

The Double Sculls was added to mark the Centenary Regatta in 1939, and in recognition of the fact that this was the only event in which Great Britain had won a gold medal in the Berlin Olympics, three years earlier. And in 1946 the Princess Elizabeth Cup was introduced as an encouragement to schools which were not strong enough to have realistic prospects in the Ladies' Plate.

No new categories of boats had been considered since coxed fours were abandoned in favour of coxless fours in 1868. But a new factor was now at work, for the amalgamation of the National Amateur Rowing Association with the Amateur Rowing Association, after the Second World War, meant that there were now many provincial and even coastal clubs eligible to race at Henley. And for these clubs coxed fours were an important event.

The view of the Stewards was that coxswains were not necessary in fours, so coxed fours should be regarded as second-class and therefore inappropriate to Henley. But at the same time British oarsmen were beginning to look towards the Continent. The first British entry for the European Championships came in 1947, and the Amateur Rowing Association affiliated to the Fédération Internationale des Sociétés d'Aviron. Coxed Fours were an important event internationally, and could scarcely be termed 'second-class'. But an open event for coxed fours at Henley was likely to find no home crews capable of defending the trophy, whilst a closed event would encourage a large entry of poor quality.

The conclusion of the Henley Committee was that they would consider adding a coxed fours event when there was evidence that domestic entries would be competitive. The contrary argument, of course, was that leading British clubs would not invest in a new class of boat, or waste their best oarsmen in an event which was not included in the programme of Britain's premier regatta.

This was a classic 'chicken and egg' argument which persisted for fifteen years, until finally resolved with the introduction of the Prince Philip Cup for coxed fours in 1963. The Britannia Cup, for second-flight coxed fours, followed six years later.

In 1974 the International Rowing Federation introduced a new category of racing for Quadruple Sculls. This revived the same argument, but by now the Committee were more open to change and the Queen Mother Challenge Cup for Quadruple Sculls was introduced in 1981.

Another decade passed and yet again the same argument cropped up, this time more controversially because it involved women at a time when sex discrimination was becoming an increasingly popular – or according to your view point unpopular – cause. Women's events had long been included in the European and World Championships, and from 1976 onwards were also included in the Olympic programme.

Internationally women's rowing was, and to an extent remains, dominated by the Soviet-bloc countries. One may say that this is due to male prejudice, but it is also due to lack of adequate finance in those countries in which government does not assume prime responsibility for financing sport for political and socio-logical reasons.

However that may be, women's events were introduced experimentally at Henley in 1981 and 1982 on a limited invitation basis. The experiment was deemed to be successful, but when the Committee came to consider making the events permanent, and open to entries as opposed to invited crews, they concluded that the congestion of the programme, and of the boating facilities, would make it impractical to accommodate women's events without dropping or curtailing some existing event. This argument lost some of its credibility in 1986 when the Regatta was extended to five days, and the opportunity afforded by the extra day was utilized not to accommodate women's events but to increase the number of entries accepted in the Thames Cup and Diamond Sculls.

Without doubt a case can be made for changes in the Henley programme, but there are probably as many views on what these should be as there are pundits and pressure lobbies to expound them. Certainly women want a place, and will campaign vigorously until they are admitted. Lightweight rowing, too, has grown in importance and is presently knocking at the door of Olympic recognition. A glance at the programme shows that individual lightweights account for a sizeable proportion of the total number of oarsmen competing; but there is no lightweight event; nor is there an event for the Under-23 class which thrives internationally. The same is true of Junior (Under-18) rowing. Schools are well catered for, but frequently have individuals who are above this age-limit.

In theory the top crews are well catered for in Henley's open events. But here there is a problem of another sort. Many of today's top crews are composite or 'national squad' crews preparing for the World Championships. Their participation is important to Henley because they set the seal of excellence on the Regatta. But at the same time their presence inhibits the better club and university crews – or if you like, 'private enterprise' crews – from entering for these events. There is, after all, no great incentive for such crews to enter for an event in which they are likely to find only three or four competitors, two of which may be of world class.

The subsidiary events pose yet another problem, one which the Committee have recently tried to ameliorate, but have certainly not yet resolved. One can look at this problem in terms of the eight-oar events, but it applies also to the fours. Apart from the Grand Challenge Cup, there are today something of the order of eighty eights seeking to row at Henley each year, and there are only two events to accommodate them. The problem can be illustrated visually on the following pages in performance profiles for the two events.

These profiles are based on 'distance behind the winner'. It should be emphasized that this method does produce distortion, in that crews which are winning races easily are unlikely to be rowing as fast as they can whilst, conversely, crews which find themselves outclassed in the early stages of the race sometimes stop trying. Also the outcome of a race may hang in the balance until one cracks and the other cruises home to an easy victory, which verdict technically denotes a margin of the order of five

lengths. It would therefore be wrong to compare one particular crew with another, and to deduce that the profile shows the distance by which one would have beaten the other. What the profiles can do is demonstrate the overall performance pattern in the two events, and changes brought about by alterations in the qualification rules.

The first performance profile which I produced was in 1970, when I was making a case to the Stewards for the need to consider various changes, and sought to demonstrate that the standards in the Ladies' Plate and Thames Cup were too similar, and the margin between the fastest and slowest crews in each event, too wide. The 1970 profile illustrated this point very well, the profile of the Ladies' Plate, apart from the smaller entry, being almost a mirror image of the Thames Cup profile. My argument fell on deaf ears of course, and at risk of breaching the confidence of a Stewards' Meeting (after almost two decades) I will reveal that I found only one supporter, the late Hubert Hartley, who awoke from a deep sleep just in time to raise his hand in favour of my motion which he had not heard.

The 1984 profile reveals a sharp increase in the number of entries, whilst the Thames Cup standard had clearly outstripped the Ladies' Plate. Nevertheless within each event the spread of performance was not much changed.

In the 1985 profile the change is dramatic, reflecting the altered qualification rules, which at long last opened the Ladies' Plate to other than student crews, aiming to concentrate the best club and student crews in the senior event.

PERFORMANCE PROFILE
1970

LADIES' PLATE

Winning Time: 7min. 1sec.

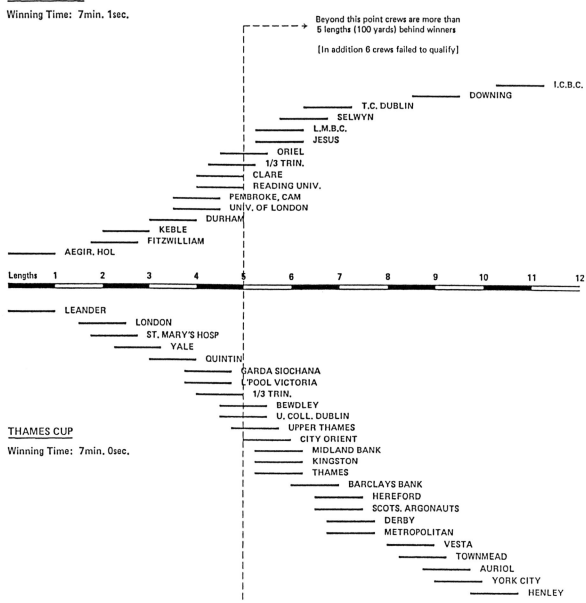

Beyond this point crews are more than
5 lengths (100 yards) behind winners

[In addition 6 crews failed to qualify]

I.C.B.C.

DOWNING

T.C. DUBLIN

SELWYN

L.M.B.C.

JESUS

ORIEL

1/3 TRIN.

CLARE

READING UNIV.

PEMBROKE, CAM

UNIV. OF LONDON

DURHAM

KEBLE

FITZWILLIAM

AEGIR, HOL

Lengths 1   2   3   4   5   6   7   8   9   10   11   12

LEANDER

LONDON

ST. MARY'S HOSP

YALE

QUINTIN

GARDA SIOCHANA

L'POOL VICTORIA

1/3 TRIN.

BEWDLEY

U. COLL. DUBLIN

UPPER THAMES

CITY ORIENT

MIDLAND BANK

KINGSTON

THAMES

BARCLAYS BANK

HEREFORD

SCOTS. ARGONAUTS

DERBY

METROPOLITAN

VESTA

TOWNMEAD

AURIOL

YORK CITY

HENLEY

THAMES CUP

Winning Time: 7min. 0sec.

PERFORMANCE PROFILE
1984

LADIES' PLATE

Winning Time: 6min. 42sec.

CHRIST'S, CAM.
MANCHESTER UNIV
TRINITY HALL
CHERWELL 'A'
ST. CATHARINE'S, CAM
CHERWELL 'B'
CLARE
SELWYN
KING'S, LONDON
U.C. & H.
U.C. DUBLIN
1/3 TRIN
ORIEL
DURHAM UNIV.
L.M.B.C.
RUTGERS UNIV.
DOWNING
NEWCASTLE UNIV.
NOTTINGHAM UNIV.
PEMBROKE, CAM
EMMANUEL
T.C. DUBLIN
I.C.B.C.
UNIV. OF LONDON
HARVARD UNIV.
YALE UNIV.
UNIV. OF BRISTOL
ISIS B.C.
TEMPLE UNIVERSITY
PRINCETON UNIV.
UNIV. OF WASHINGTON
BROWN UNIV.

Beyond this point crews are more than
5 lengths (100 yards) behind winners

[In addition 7 crews failed to qualify]

Lengths 1   2   3   4   5   6   7   8   9   10   11   12   13   14   15

CANTABRIGIANS
THAMES
VESTA
LEANDER 'A'
NAUTILUS LWT
PETERBORO' B.C. CAN
ORMSUND, NOR
ARGONAUTS, CAN
LEANDER 'B'
HARVARD UNIV.
ST. CATHARINE'S B.C. CAN
THAMES TRADESMEN 'A'
STOURPORT
LEA 'A'
LONDON 'A'
LEA 'B'
READING UNIV.
MOLESEY
TWICKENHAM
QUINTIN 'A'
TEES
LONDON 'B'
ABERDEEN UNIV.
QUINTIN 'B'
CITY OF CAMBRIDGE
BARCLAYS BANK
WORCESTER B.C.
AGECROFT
THAMES TRADESMEN 'B'
DERRY R.C.
KENT SCHOOL
CLYDE (N.R.O.)

Beyond this point crews are more than
5 lengths (100 yards) behind winners

[In addition 11 crews failed to qualify]

THAMES CUP

Winning Time: 6min 30sec.

PERFORMANCE PROFILE

1985

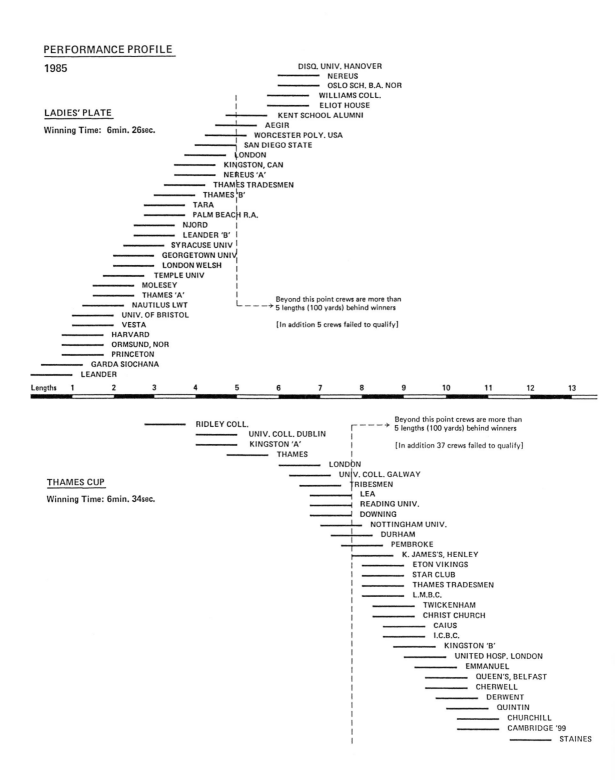

LADIES' PLATE

Winning Time: 6min. 26sec.

DISQ. UNIV. HANOVER
NEREUS
OSLO SCH. B.A. NOR
WILLIAMS COLL.
ELIOT HOUSE
KENT SCHOOL ALUMNI
AEGIR
WORCESTER POLY. USA
SAN DIEGO STATE
LONDON
KINGSTON, CAN
NEREUS 'A'
THAMES TRADESMEN
THAMES 'B'
TARA
PALM BEACH R.A.
NJORD
LEANDER 'B'
SYRACUSE UNIV
GEORGETOWN UNIV
LONDON WELSH
TEMPLE UNIV
MOLESEY
THAMES 'A'
NAUTILUS LWT
UNIV. OF BRISTOL
VESTA
HARVARD
ORMSUND, NOR
PRINCETON
GARDA SIOCHANA
LEANDER

Beyond this point crews are more than
5 lengths (100 yards) behind winners

[In addition 5 crews failed to qualify]

Lengths   1   2   3   4   5   6   7   8   9   10   11   12   13

RIDLEY COLL.
UNIV. COLL. DUBLIN
KINGSTON 'A'
THAMES
LONDON
UNIV. COLL. GALWAY
TRIBESMEN
LEA
READING UNIV.
DOWNING
NOTTINGHAM UNIV.
DURHAM
PEMBROKE
K. JAMES'S, HENLEY
ETON VIKINGS
STAR CLUB
THAMES TRADESMEN
L.M.B.C.
TWICKENHAM
CHRIST CHURCH
CAIUS
I.C.B.C.
KINGSTON 'B'
UNITED HOSP. LONDON
EMMANUEL
QUEEN'S, BELFAST
CHERWELL
DERWENT
QUINTIN
CHURCHILL
CAMBRIDGE '99
STAINES

Beyond this point crews are more than
5 lengths (100 yards) behind winners

[In addition 37 crews failed to qualify]

THAMES CUP

Winning Time: 6min. 34sec.

PERFORMANCE PROFILE

1987

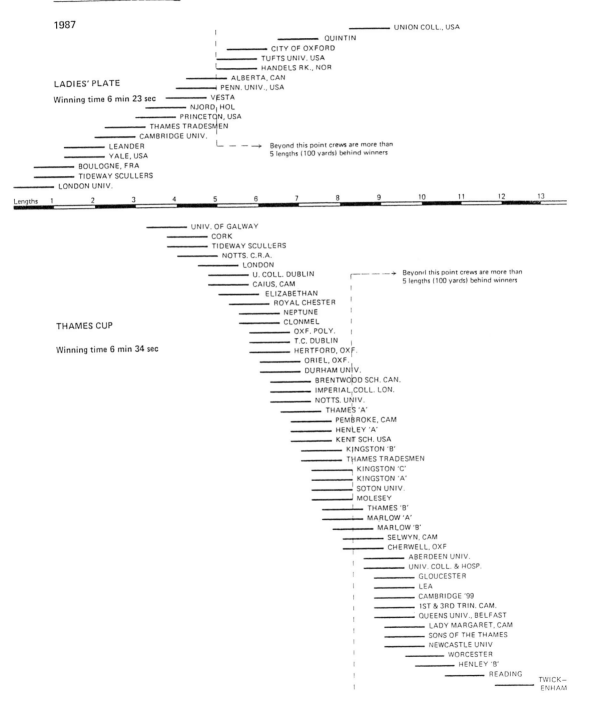

UNION COLL., USA

QUINTIN

CITY OF OXFORD

TUFTS UNIV. USA

HANDELS RK., NOR

ALBERTA, CAN

PENN. UNIV., USA

LADIES' PLATE

Winning time 6 min 23 sec

VESTA

NJORD, HOL

PRINCETON, USA

THAMES TRADESMEN

CAMBRIDGE UNIV.

Beyond this point crews are more than
5 lengths (100 yards) behind winners

LEANDER

YALE, USA

BOULOGNE, FRA

TIDEWAY SCULLERS

LONDON UNIV.

Lengths 1   2   3   4   5   6   7   8   9   10   11   12   13

UNIV. OF GALWAY

CORK

TIDEWAY SCULLERS

NOTTS. C.R.A.

LONDON

U. COLL. DUBLIN

CAIUS, CAM

ELIZABETHAN

ROYAL CHESTER

NEPTUNE

CLONMEL

OXF. POLY.

T.C. DUBLIN

THAMES CUP

HERTFORD, OXF.

ORIEL, OXF.

Winning time 6 min 34 sec

DURHAM UNIV.

Beyond this point crews are more than
5 lengths (100 yards) behind winners

BRENTWOOD SCH. CAN.

IMPERIAL COLL. LON.

NOTTS. UNIV.

THAMES 'A'

PEMBROKE, CAM

HENLEY 'A'

KENT SCH. USA

KINGSTON 'B'

THAMES TRADESMEN

KINGSTON 'C'

KINGSTON 'A'

SOTON UNIV.

MOLESEY

THAMES 'B'

MARLOW 'A'

MARLOW 'B'

SELWYN, CAM

CHERWELL, OXF

ABERDEEN UNIV.

UNIV. COLL. & HOSP.

GLOUCESTER

LEA

CAMBRIDGE '99

1ST & 3RD TRIN. CAM.

QUEENS UNIV., BELFAST

LADY MARGARET, CAM

SONS OF THE THAMES

NEWCASTLE UNIV

WORCESTER

HENLEY 'B'

READING

TWICK–
ENHAM

In addition 31 crews failed to qualify.

The profile here confirms the success of this policy. At the same time the consequent lowering of the Thames Cup standard predictably fuelled an unprecedented increase in the number of entries for what was now the 'soft option' event. No less than seventy crews entered, of which one withdrew and thirty-seven failed to qualify.

Finally the 1987 profile is of considerable interest. It clearly shows the Ladies' Plate standard drawing ahead of the Thames Cup. Probably for this reason the 1987 entry fell to seventeen. But this seems to have been a passing hiccup for in 1988 the field rose again to twenty-six, indicating a very healthy 'new look' Ladies' Plate. On the other hand the quota admitted to the Thames Cup was increased from thirty-two to forty-eight in 1987 and this immediately and predictably led to a huge entry of seventy-nine crews, thirty-one of which had to be eliminated before the Regatta.

Looking at the overall picture it is evident that the Ladies' Plate has been successfully re-established as the Regatta's second senior eight-oar event. But the situation still gives cause for concern. For there are now around 100 crews, the great majority of which are seeking to compete in one event; and the difference between the fastest and slowest of those crews is certainly in excess of ten lengths or 200 yards. There must be a case, surely, for subdividing them into smaller events?

Finally, one category not yet considered is sculling, which presents a different problem. Whereas in the rowing events there is a choice of standard in each discipline, the three sculling events are open to the world. An oarsman in international class competes in the Grand, or in the appropriate four-oar or pair-oar event; an oarsman below that class competes in the Ladies' Plate or Thames Cup, or the Visitors', Wyfold or Britannia Cups. But a sculler must compete in the Queen Mother Cup, the Double Sculls, or the Diamonds – or not at all. His standard may compare well with the standard of most of those who are rowing at Henley; but he must be matched against scullers of world class. That cannot be good news for anybody, and inevitably results in processional races and humiliating defeats. Without doubt there is a case for an event, or events, for second-flight scullers.

All this sounds like an appeal for more races at Henley. But in fact I generally concur with the sentiments of the anonymous poet quoted by Harold Rickett that 'It seems better to go a bit steady and not to start off at a run'. At the same time one must remember the Red Queen's advice to Alice, 'it takes all the running you can do, to keep in the same place.' With ever more young people, men, women, lightweights, juniors, seniors and the 'in-betweens', seeking to enter the sport every year, that advice might be appropriate to Henley.

Henley is a magnet, and there will always be a demand for more and different events. But every golfer and tennis player in the country cannot expect to play in the Open, or at Wimbledon. There may be a case for providing more races, or races in different categories, but there is not a case for admitting competitors of lower standard. Nor is time the only limiting factor to the number of races that can be held. The boat tents are already full to overflowing, and late arrivals can only be accommodated when boats belonging to crews knocked out in the qualifying races have been removed. And crews must train as well as race. Congestion on the river is already at saturation point.

But the fact that it is impracticable to have more races, and undesirable to have more competitors, does not mean that there could not be more events. At present, for example, the Ladies' Plate is limited to thirty-two crews and the Thames Cup to forty-eight crews, a total of eighty crews. It takes seventy-eight races to produce the two winners. If there were four events instead of these two, the Ladies' Plate (sixteen crews), Thames Cup (thirty-two crews), Lightweights (sixteen crews), and Under-23's (sixteen crews), for example, it would require only seventy-six races to produce the four winners.

I hasten to add that this is not a recommendation, but simply a provocation to thought. The same process could be applied elsewhere, to the fours and single sculls perhaps, resulting in fewer but certainly more closely contested races, and a more flexible programme with less congestion on the early days, and more finals spread over Saturday and Sunday when there is time to spare. Somewhere along the way the women might breach the male bastion of the Royal Regatta.

25. *Above* The three-lane start on the Old Course, 1885 or earlier.

26. Club Nautique de Gand, Belgium: V. Molmans (bow), A. Heye, A. Van Roy, G. Visser, M. Orban, R. Orban, O. de Somville, R. Poma (str.), R. Van der Waerden (cox) beating Magdalen College, Oxford: Hon. R. P. Stanhope (bow), C. L. Garton, J. A. Gillan, J. L. Johnson, A. G. Kirby, L. R. A. Gatehouse, C. R. Cudmore, E. H. L. Southwell (str.), A. C. Clarke (cox) in a heat of the Grand Challenge Cup, 1906. The bend below Fawley can just be seen in the distance.

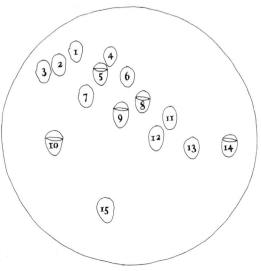

27. Winning Leander crews framed in the 1908 Olympic Regatta winning-post: 1. G. L. Thomson, 2. H. C. Bucknall, 3. J. R. K. Fenning, 4. B. C. Johnstone, 5. C. A. Willis (coach), 6. A. C. Gladstone, 7. F. S. Kelly, 8. H. G. Gold (coach), 9. C. D. Burnell, 10. G. S. Maclagan, 11. R. H. Sanderson, 12. R. B. Etherington-Smith, 13. P. R. Filleul, 14. H. R. Barker, 15. Guy Nickalls. (Identification of nos. 2, 3 and 13 is tentative.)

28. *Above* Third Trinity BC, Cambridge: C. R. M. Eley (st.), J. A. Macnabb, R. E. Morrison, T. R. B. Sanders (str.) winning the Stewards' Challenge Cup in 1924. They went on to take the gold in the Olympic Regatta that year.

29. The record breakers, 1934. Leander Club: J. H. C. Powell (bow), J. M. Couchman, J. H. Lascelles, A. V. Sutcliffe, P. Hogg, K. M. Payne, D. J. Wilson, W. G. R. M. Laurie (str.), J. M. Duckworth (cox) beating Princeton University, USA: R. Hallett (bow), A. Gawthrop, R. Zundel, H. Dicke, H. Rutherfurd, A. Howell, W. Pflaumer, A. Armstrong (str.), R. S. Firestone (cox) in the final of the Grand Challenge Cup.

30. Dead Heat. J.
Beresford Jr and L. F.
Southwood (Thames
RC) and G. Scherli and
E. Broschi (Trieste,
Italy) in the final of the
Centenary Double
Sculls, 1939.

31. Lt. Col. C. D.
Burnell judging one of
the informal schools
races held in 1942.

32. *Above* The final of the first post-war Grand Challenge Cup, 1946. Leander Club: R. M. T. Raikes (bow), A. J. R. Purssell, P. Bradley, H. W. Mason, R. D. Burnell, R. M. A. Bourne, P. N. Brodie, N. J. Bradley (str.), G. D. Clapperton (cox) beating RC Zurich, Switzerland: H. Zoller (bow), W. Stapfer, J. Knoepfel, E. Knecht, P. Stebler, R. Reichling, E. Schriever, W. Stapfer (str.), F. Brentani (cox). Their Royal Highnesses Princess Elizabeth and Princess Margaret followed the race in the umpire's launch.

33. Olympic Double Sculls, 1948. B. H. T. Bushnell (Maidenhead RC) and R. D. Burnell (Leander Club) winning from A. E. Larsen and E. V. Parsner (Denmark) and J. A. Rodriguez and W. Jones (Uruguay).

34. *Above* The Grand Challenge Cup in 1949 was the last occasion on which a crew rowing with fixed-pin rowlocks won the Grand. Leander Club: J. G. C. Blacker (bow), R. M. T. Raikes, J. R. L. Carstairs, J. R. W. Gleave, W. A. D. Windham, R. D. Burnell, P. A. de Giles, P. Bradley (str.), Alan Palgrave-Brown (cox) are here shown beating Thames RC: P. S. Pusey (bow), A. J. G. Wood, P. R. Simmett, B. R. Worsnop, J. L. Sangster, T. H. Christie, A. S. F. Butcher, P. C. Kirkpatrick (str.), J. G. Dearlove (cox).

35. Diamond Sculls, 1954. P. Vlasic (Yugoslavia) in danger of fouling A. Colomb (Switzerland) in winning the Diamond Sculls. Vlasic won by 6 feet.

36. The Russian boats
for Henley are unloaded
during the 1955 dock
strike.

37. G. Zhilin and I. Emchuk (USSR) beating H. Vollmer
and T. Keller (Switzerland) in the final of the 1955 Double
Sculls. Keller later became President of the International
Rowing Federation.

38. Man overboard. Methodist College, Belfast lost a man overboard and also this heat in the Princess Elizabeth Cup by a canvas in 1955. Methodist College: H. F. McMahon (bow), J. K. McCartney, A. Hamilton, W. J. Palmer, J. W. Carson, W. V. McQuoid (presumably underwater in this picture!), E. B. McGarry, P. R. M. Stratford (str.), D. G. T. Maxwell (cox). Their opponents, The King's School, Chester, were represented by A. G. Evans (bow), J. C. Groome, J. A. Simmons, R. H. S. Mills, R. W. Owen, R. S. Dickinson, J. A. Melling, C. P. Oliver (str.), J. R. Houghton (cox).

39. S. A. Mackenzie (Sydney RC, Australia) leading V. Ivanov (USSR) in the final of the 1957 Diamond Sculls. Ivanov closed to 4 feet at the finish.

PART TWO

The Racing

8 The Old Course: 1839–1885

1839 Henley Regatta may have been founded for the benefit of the local inhabitants rather than for the oarsmen. But to the wider world beyond the Thames Valley it was the prospect of boat racing on a scale hitherto unknown which caught the interest. The newly appointed Stewards and Committee could scarcely have hoped for better publicity, both before and after their first Regatta.

On 8 June 1839 the *Berkshire Chronicle* reported that 'from the interest which the Regatta excites to a considerable distance, it is calculated there will be from 15,000 to 20,000 persons present. "Mine Hosts", with smiling faces, anticipate, of course, a "regular squeezer". Stands will be erected in various places commanding a complete view of the course...' Whether the squeezer referred to a full house, or to inflated prices, is left to the reader's imagination.

The Aquatic Register correspondent of *Bell's Life and Chronicle*, as befitted the country's leading sporting publication, even concerned himself with crew preparations. Reporting that Trinity Boat Club in their craft *Black Prince*, the only entry from Cambridge, were currently training at Oxford, he opined 'that Oxford appears to us to be a singular training ground for the Cantabs to select, as we think they are likely to partake more freely of the hospitable conviviality of the sister university than is quite consistent with the task they have before them'. Events were to prove that either the Trinity

men were made of sterner stuff than *Bell's* man had anticipated, or the Oxonians were less Machiavellian.

The great day started early, for the *Reading Mercury* recorded that 'At five o'clock a merry peal aroused the inhabitants and the busy din of preparation was heard in finishing the various erections by the waterside ... these buildings flanked the river from the Red Lion to New Street; and there were two others, one near Phyllis Court, and one near the bridge, on the Remenham side, the latter of which, we fear, was a losing speculation!'

Another local paper, the *Bucks Herald*, we may deduce, rushed their report to press in time for their second edition, for we have the actual manuscript, and it will be noted that their reporter changed tense in the penultimate paragraph, unable to wait to see whether the display of fireworks had survived the earlier rains.

Second Edition
June 1839 Herald Office, Saturday Morning
HENLEY REGATTA

During the past week great preparations had been made in the Town of Henley, for the reception of the company expected to be present at the Regatta; but, unfortunately, after a fine week, on Thursday night a storm arose and for some time the rain poured in torrents, amidst the most terrific thunder and lightning. The chimney of Mr. Cooper's Assembly Rooms in Bell Street, was struck by the electric fluid and fell, many of the windows were also broken, and the wall crushed in two places, several persons were knocked down by the fluid in various parts of the Town, but happily none that we heard of sustained any serious injury...

At 11 o'clock the Stewards and Captains of the different boats attended at the Town Hall and tossed for the choice of places; the situation nearest the Bank on the right hand side of the Bridge being considered the most advantageous. Of the two boats for the first heat, the Brasenose and the Etonian, the former gained the choice; for the second heat, the Wadham had the preference of the Cambridge; and for the Town Cup, the *Albion* took the inner bank, the *Dreadnought* the outer, and the *Wave* in the centre...

About 11 o'clock the Leander Club arrived from London, drenched with rain. They rowed the distance each heat with the racing boats, in good style.

About 3 o'clock the weather cleared in a slight degree, and the spectators to the amount of 9,000 or 10,000 assembled on the Bridge, and on either bank of the River, also in stands which had been erected for the purpose, or on barges in the water decorated with flags. The bells of the Parish Church were ringing the best portion of the day, and cannon fired at intervals, and two bands of music on the water playing popular airs alternately.

Previous to each race, a signal gun was fired at the Bridge, to clear the course, another when the course was clear, a third at the Island, when the boats started, and a fourth at the Bridge, to announce that the race was ended.

The writer went on to record that the Etonians beat Brasenose with some ease, and 'the Cambridge' beat Wadham by a length and a half after a stern battle. In the Town Cup the *Dreadnought* led at first, but was passed by the *Albion*, and then by the *Wave* who won 'in gallant style'. He then concluded:

> The third and last heat for the Grand Challenge Cup between the Winners of the first and second heats, the Etonians and the Cambridge, took place at seven o'clock. The Cambridge having won the choice of situations, took, of course, the inner side ... the excitement was very great, and the cheering from both parties tremendous. The Cambridge obtained the start and kept the lead all the way, winning by only half a length ... The distance was performed in seven minutes and forty-five seconds.
>
> At ten o'clock in the evening there was to be a grand display of fire-works on the river.
>
> (During the interest of the second heat some miscreants (who are luckily known) entered the building where the *Albion* boat was kept and chalked the bottom completely over; fortunately it was discovered in time to remedy the defect.)

Bell's Life also had their say, but at more leisure:

> The first annual regatta at the delightful town of Henley-upon-Thames took place on Friday last. This aquatic festival had for some time past been looked forward to with an unusual degree of interest, and had caused considerable excitement in various parts of the country especially among the cutter crews at Oxford, Cambridge and London. The members of the London

Leander Club proceeded up the river on Thursday in their cutter, and arrived at Henley early on Friday morning. An eight manned by Cambridge men was also taken from Searle's (Lambeth), and a new and beautifully light four, built by Springett, containing Mr. Layton and two other members of the London Scullers Club, and Phelps the waterman, went from Putney.... many of the inhabitants also busied themselves in erecting stands for the visitors ... the gentlemen of the Corporation attending to see that the stands and booths were properly and firmly erected. The Stewards' stand was in front of Mr. Cooper's house on the Thames side, and that gentleman set apart a room for their exclusive use – altogether there were seats for about 10,000 persons, and the innkeepers looked forward to a rich harvest ...

The reference to Mr Cooper's house, which was Bird Place, is interesting. It is known that crews embarked from the lawn and kept their boats here in the early years. But if the Stewards really had their stand in the garden they certainly cannot have used it for watching the racing which finished at Henley Bridge.

There was of course the inevitable reference to the 'electric fluid', but *Bell's* man perhaps more privileged than the local *Herald* reporter, managed to find some compensations from the abominable weather, commenting that 'previous to the Regatta and also between the various heats, a number of gentlemen were invited to partake of excellent cold collations at the residences of Messrs. Brakspear, Nash, Hickman, Stubbs and other gentlemen of the Committee'.

These divertissements however did not deflect the seasoned scribe from taking note of the sartorial efforts of the competitors:

The Etonian Club were dressed in white guernseys with pale blue facings, rosette sky blue. Brasenose had blue striped guernseys, blue cap with gold tassel, rosette yellow, purple and crimson. Wadham wore white guernseys with narrow blue stripes, dark blue cap with light blue velvet band, and light blue scarf, and Trinity were attired in blue striped guernseys, rosette French blue.

The waiting may have been long, but once racing got under way there was no dawdling. The first heat of the Grand Challenge Cup, inaugurating the new Regatta, started at four o'clock, followed immediately by the second heat. A pair-oar match for watermen from Henley Bridge round Temple Island and back followed at five o'clock, the Town Cup for local fours at six o'clock and the final of the Grand, won by Trinity College, Cambridge, as described in the *Herald* report, at seven o'clock. Which makes it the more remarkable that the gentlemen of Leander were reported to have 'rowed the distance, each heat, with the racing boats in good style'. Unlike his colleague from the *Herald*, *Bell's* man was able to stay on for the prize-giving, to watch a 'splendid display' of fireworks.

1840 Perhaps the competitors did not relish being shadowed by the gentlemen of Leander 'each heat in good style', for in 1840 it was ruled 'that no boat under any pretence whatever (the umpire excepted) shall accompany the racing boats during the matches'. Some concern was caused before the Regatta when it was rumoured that the dons had forbidden the Oxford colleges to compete. But it transpired that the objection was only to crews appearing under the names of their colleges; so Wadham turned up as 'The Admiral', University College as 'The John Cross', and Brasenose as 'The Childe of Hale' – the names of their respective boats.

Leander entered for and won the Grand Challenge Cup with some ease, which was not surprising in view of their demonstration of stamina in the previous year. But they cannot have been wholly confident, for *Bell's Life* records that they had objected to the Cambridge Subscription Rooms (London) being permitted to compete, on what grounds we do not know. Their objection was overruled by Lord Camoys and the Cambridge Rooms entered but withdrew.

1841   Leander entered again in 1841 and so became the first crew to defend the Grand Challenge Cup as 'holders'. For under the original rules the Grand was indeed a Challenge Cup which the holders were required to defend only in the final against the winner of the Challenge heats. The Cambridge Subscription Rooms earned this right by beating Trinity and St John's Colleges, Oxford. Leander, on the unfavoured Bucks Station, fouled the Subscription Rooms whilst attempting to cross ahead of them and were disqualified.

A second open event was added in 1841, the Steward's Challenge Cup which was to become the blue riband for four-oars, rowed at that time with coxswains of course.

1842

Berkshire Chronicle   18 June 1842

Amongst the list of entries, it will be remembered that the two eights whose wager last Saturday so distinguished those engaged,* were both entered for the Grand Challenge Cup at this place (Henley); and it was of course generally supposed and equally much desired that a second struggle should take place between them ... The present holders of the Cup, the Cambridge Subscription Rooms ... declared that should the Oxonians win the race with their opponents of Saturday last, the Cambridge Subscription Rooms crew would be justified in selecting any member of the Cambridge University boat, and substituting them for others who might not feel disposed to contend.

Oxford did not relish the idea that if they beat Cambridge for the second time in three days they might then find some of the same men drafted into the Subscription Rooms crew in the final, and protested to the Stewards that it would be unfair to permit any man to race in two different crews in the same event. The Stewards evidently saw the force of Oxford's pleading for they changed the rules in the following autumn. But for the time being they declared that there was nothing in the Rules to prevent such a substitution. Oxford consequently withdrew in protest.

---

*The Oxford and Cambridge Boat Race, which took place this year at Westminster, on 11 June. No University Boat Race was ever a 'wager match', but journalists of that time found it difficult to believe that anyone would race other than for money. Oxford won this race by 13 seconds.

Cambridge won their heat against King's College, London, and the semi-final against the Oxford Aquatic Club. In the final they lost to the Subscription Rooms by only a few feet, which suggests that the latter might well have strengthened their crew by calling on some members of the university crew, had the opportunity arisen.

To add to the excitement this year the watermen's crew, which was carrying the umpire in this race – and therefore following behind the two Cambridge crews – decided to 'have a go' themselves. At Poplar Point they spurted round the outside of the bend 'so that on approaching the Stewards' stand all three boats were stem and stem', reported *Bell's Life*, '... The shouting was deafening – the shrieks of the exhausted runners – the clearer words of encouragement from the fixed spectators – the guns – the bells – the hoarse voices of the three coxswains exciting on with a last gasp their various crews.'

An heroic scene – particularly if, as was probably the case, the umpire was himself holding the rudder lines in the stern, and so, with his last hoarse gasp, encouraging his crew of watermen in their highly unorthodox exploit!

1843 As already remarked, a new rule was drafted before the 1843 Regatta stating 'That no member of a club shall be allowed to be substituted for another who has already rowed in a heat ... nor to row with more than one crew for the same cup.' This rule, intended to prevent disputes, paradoxically led immediately to one of the historic dramas in Henley's history.

Oxford University started with a comfortable win over the Oxford Etonians, but all was not well. Fletcher Menzies, the Oxford stroke and captain, had been unwell for several days. The *Oxford Chronicle* thought it doubtful whether he would row again – 'but his heart was in the right place, and, though he had lived for twenty-four hours only on water gruel, when the time was called he was at his post ...' Once again Oxford won, this time against Trinity College, Cambridge, qualifying them for the following day's final against the Cambridge Subscription Rooms. Then as they prepared to row down to the start, Menzies fainted. The Cambridge men were not agreeable to a substitute, nor indeed would a substitute have been permitted under the new rule. Oxford were granted one hour's postponement, whilst, to quote a verse written by Tom Hughes, brother of the Dark Blues' replacement stroke:

Within a darkened chamber,
Wrapped in his tartan plaid,
Fevered in mind and body,
Our Captain brave is laid.
To keep him from the river
They've ranged stout waiters four,
And they've barred the windows firmly,
And firmly locked the door.

Meantime, no doubt closing their minds to the distressing image of their gallant captain struggling vainly against four stout waiters to make his escape via the firmly barred windows of his sickroom in the Red Lion Hotel, the Oxonians determined to race with seven men. That proposition was far from welcome in the Cambridge camp, but Lord Camoys, as acting Steward of the Regatta, decided that there was no rule to the contrary.

And so there occurred the famous Seven-

Oar Race which was to become legend on the day. It was all surprisingly easy. Hugging the Buckinghamshire (or Oxfordshire as it was then often described) shore, no doubt on a day when the prevailing wind was blowing from the south-west, Oxford soon began to forge ahead and were able to cross in front of the Cambridge Subscription Rooms below Poplar Point, winning by about a length. The aftermath was quite spectacular, for Oxford supporters went mad with delight and, headed by a small man in spectacles who had never handled an oar in his life, stormed the toll gate on the end of Henley Bridge and heaved it into the river. Happily the Justices took a benign view of their behaviour.

Apart from the furore of the Seven-Oar Race the 1843 Regatta was a rather dull affair. There were only ten entries and six races, and the Committee must have begun to realize that it was one thing to found a regatta but quite another to wean it into a viable annual fixture. The main problem, as remarked elsewhere, was one of logistics. The only way to reach Henley was by coach, on horseback, or by river. And to aggravate the problem the Londoners inaugurated their own rival regatta in 1843. *Bell's Life* commented, 'We have earnestly considered the effect which the new [Thames] Regatta may have on its parent, viz. that of Henley, and *vice versa*, under a strong feeling of hope that all collision will be avoided, which has this year been prevented by the concession of the Henley management to alter their chosen days.'

1844   But the chosen days were important, for clashing with the Thames Regatta was not the sole consideration. Henley also depended on an influx of visitors from Oxford, and on 4 June 1844 *Jackson's Oxford Journal* reported:

> The approach of this annual aquatic festival had this year lost much of its interest in being no longer the close adjunct of the Oxford Commemorations,* an arrangement which, if it did not mar the pleasure, at least materially diminished the profits of the inhabitants of this picturesque little town ... No bugle sounds proclaimed the coming teams; for the Oxford 'going down' was an event of the previous week, and the excitement of the first day was virtually gone down with it ...

The Times man took a more relaxed view, commenting that 'after the excitement and bustle of the Thames Regatta the quiet meeting at Henley was a very happy relief'; also that 'the speedy transit from the Metropolis by the Great Western Railway, and a short drive, brought a great many people to Henley ...'

But 1844 heralded another significant landmark in the introduction of the Diamond Sculls, which at one stroke doubled the number of races in the Regatta.

'Open to all England' – and later of course to the world – the Diamond Sculls was destined to become Henley's most prestigious event after the Grand Challenge Cup, and some might say even more prestigious than that. For whilst the Grand has attracted some of the world's finest eights over the years, the relative ease of transporting one man and a sculling boat has meant that most of the world's single sculling stars have been able to make their bid

---

* Festivities at the end of the summer term before the students 'went down' for the long vacation.

for the Diamonds at Henley. Since 1908 the only Olympic gold medallists not to have tried for the Diamonds are J. B. Kelly whose Henley entry was rejected in 1920 (see page 25), G. Schafer (1936), J. Malischev (1972), who did however compete unsuccessfully in the Double Sculls at Henley in 1973, and P. Karpinnen (1976–84).

1845 There were more innovations to come. The watchful correspondent of *Bell's Life* saw changes in the air, and secured himself a minor scoop:

> 27th April, 1845.   Henley-on-Thames
>
> We learn that some important additions at this Regatta are contemplated by the Committee, and that the necessary propositions will be submitted for the consideration of the Stewards on Tuesday next. Oarsmen, *in pairs*, and also crews of oarsmen in eight-oared boats, who have not yet had a fair opportunity of testing their powers, at this aquatic festival, will do well to be on the alert...

Bell's man was right. Encouraged by the success of the Diamond Sculls the Stewards introduced two more new events in 1845. The first was the New Challenge Cup, open to eights 'from Colleges and amateur clubs other than University crews and Subscription Rooms and clubs similarly constituted'. The difference between a 'subscription room' and a 'club' lay in the fact that a 'subscription room' might have no fixed geographical headquarters, and, at any particular moment in time, no individually named membership. The 'Etonian

Club, Oxford (or Cambridge, or London)' would be a good example – a notional club, or in modern parlance perhaps a 'flag of convenience', available to any group of Eton oarsmen wherever they might be.

In 1845 the trophy was not ready and presentation medals were given.

The second new event was for pair oars, as *Bell's* had foretold. Like the Diamonds the race was for presentation prizes, silver wherries, which were described as 'perfect gems of their kind'. The event was named 'The Silver Wherries' until 1850 when the prize, and the title, was altered to 'The Silver Goblets'. In 1895 Tom Nickalls, to celebrate the successes of his sons Vivian and Guy Nickalls in winning the event for two years in succession, gave a silver cup as a challenge trophy and the event became 'The Silver Goblets and Nickalls' Challenge Cup'.

The Ladies' Plate could not be described as an immediate success, for it attracted only three entries in 1845 and did not exceed this number for another sixteen years. The Wherries attracted five pairs in the first year, and six in the following year, but once the novelty had worn off it seemed that the demand for such an event had been over-estimated. It was to be twenty years before the entries of the first two years were exceeded.

Nevertheless there was optimism in 1845. 'At an early hour,' *Jackson's Oxford Chronicle* reported, 'the town presented a very bustling and animated appearance; the Great Western Railway poured in company by every down and up train throughout the morning, and the arrivals of visitors from the immediate district by every description of conveyance that could be put into requisition were momentary. The attendance was, at the time the races commenced, the greatest we ever remember to have seen at this regatta … The grandstand and the Phyllis Court grounds, on the banks of the Thames, were thronged with the gentry of the neighbourhood, who were admitted by Stewards' tickets.'

It would seem that the promise of the founding fathers that the Regatta would bring benefits to the town, was being fulfilled, but can we also discern the first sign of the acquisitive nature, in terms of securing to themselves and their friends the most favoured viewing positions, of which the Henley Stewards have sometimes been accused? If so, one should also note that annual expenditure at that time was running at £200, with receipts from entry fees averaging only £55. Most of the balance was contributed by the Stewards.

However that may be, the spectators in 1845 were well rewarded. They saw history made in the Diamonds when J. W. Conant appeared in an outrigged sculling boat.* 'In a few strokes,' reported *Bell's Life*, 'Mr. Conant led by over one length … Mr. Bumsted [winner in 1844] fairly turned round on his thwart to see what had become of Mr. Conant.' But surprisingly Conant's new device did not bring him victory in the final, which was won by F. S. Wallace over H. Chapman on a foul.

For the first time at Henley, Oxford and Cambridge met in a straight fight in the Grand, though Oxford showed four and Cambridge two changes from their Boat Race crews. Oxford's number seven was the same Mr Conant, of St John's College, who had reached the final of the Diamonds in his outrigged sculling boat; he also contested the final of the Stewards' Cup, so perhaps he was feeling a little tired. At any rate Cambridge won the Grand by 'more than two lengths'.

Mr Conant might lay some claim to have been Henley's first rowing personality, as this was the first time that a competitor had entered for three events. His third final, in the Stewards' Cup, was the closest to date. 'A grand race,' wrote Herbert Steward, 'At the half distance St George's were leading by an eighth of a length, but the crews were oar and oar before the Point. Half way between the Point and the goal St. George's were leading again by an eighth of a length, and at the finish it seemed impossible to say which had won. A Mr Forrest, who seems to have been appointed judge, but about whose appointment there seems also to have been some informality, declared the race to have been a dead-heat. Mr Bishop, the umpire, however, said he was certain the Oxford crew had won.' But George Treherne told a somewhat different story.† 'At Henley at this time no judge was stationed at the finishing post. Arthur Shadwell, a famous Oxford coxswain and coach, seeing the race for the Stewards' Cup to be a very close thing, ran in front of the boats, and, by covering both posts with his eye, was able to discern that Oxford passed the goal first.' After this, says Treherne, a judge was stationed at the finish by

---

* The invention of the outrigger, generally credited to Henry Clasper in 1844, was the most important single innovation in the development of racing boats (*Swing Together* by Richard Burnell, Oxford University Press).

† *Records of the University Boat Race, 1829–1883* by Geo. G. T. Treherne.

the Committee. Steward, the official historian, however, says that judges were not officially appointed until 1847. Of what St George's Club said, on being deprived of a dead-heat by a self-appointed Oxonian judge, there is no record.

1846 The District Cup for local fours received no entries at all in 1846, but a new event, the Silver Wherry for local scullers, boosted the entry to a record thirty-one. The Thames Club – no relation to the modern Thames Rowing Club – broke the university monopoly in the Grand. On the favoured Berkshire Station they beat First Trinity by more than three lengths. But in the Ladies' Plate, on the Centre Station, they lost to the same Trinity crew, drawn on Berks, by a quarter of a length.

In the challenge heat for the Stewards' Cup the umpire declared a dead heat between Guy's Club, London and the Dreadnought Club, Henley. The local crew insisted they had won and refused a re-row, so were disqualified. But Guy's were easily defeated by Oxford in the final.

1847 *Jackson's Oxford Chronicle* was enthusiastic about the prospects for 1847, commenting, 'The annual meeting at Henley ... next to the Thames Regatta, certainly ranks as the most important and attractive in the kingdom.'

The *Chronicle* reported that the 1847 Regatta programme 'exceeded that of any other year' which leads one to suspect that their reporter had consulted the entry list rather than the starting programme, for withdrawals had reduced the entries to twenty-seven, four less than in the preceding year. Nor can the *Chron-*

icle's man have endeared himself with the Stewards by commenting that 'The annual meeting at Henley' ranked next after the Thames Regatta. But it must be conceded that the latter had already achieved Royal patronage, which Henley had not.

But if the racing was unremarkable, at least 1847 was a busy year. Mr Donkin presented a new challenge cup, named after his home, Wyfold Court. There being no event without a trophy already, the Wyfold Challenge Cup was allotted as a prize for the winner of the trial heats for the Grand. No doubt the Stewards hoped that this would attract more entries for their premier event. But in fact the first year was the only occasion on which the Wyfold Cup was presented to a 'challenger' – Oxford University who beat Cambridge in the only challenge heat and went on to beat the Thames Club in the final. For the next seven years there were insufficient entries to require a challenge round. In 1855 the Wyfold Cup became a trophy in its own right for fours.

The Thames Club entered for both the Grand and the Ladies' Plate but were ruled ineligible for the Ladies' despite the fact that they had entered and lost in the previous year.

St George's Club failed to make their entry for the Stewards' in time, leaving Christ Church to row over. The local Dreadnought Club were the only entry for the Town Cup, and there were no entries at all for the District Fours. This meant that there would have been no four-oared race at all, so the Stewards put on a special event at the last moment, and advertised 'A Scratch Match in Four-oared Boats for Henley Regatta Medals'. They then decided to make over the District Challenge

Cup to the new event, renaming it the Visitors' Challenge Cup. Christ Church were the first winners from St George's Club.

1848   The entries fell to twenty-three in 1848 and, short of hard news for his preview on 9 July, Mr O'Grady of *Bell's Life*, who had become a subscriber to the Regatta three years earlier and no doubt felt in duty bound to keep his end up, embarked on a eulogy which, if it adds little to our knowledge of Henley Regatta, is surely worthy of preservation as an example of contemporary journalistic prose:

How many of those, it has been frequently asked, who dilate with so much apparent warmth, and even ecstasy, on the 'beauties of the Rhine' ... have threaded the windings of our own beautiful Thames, aye, even from the almost worn out bridge at Westminster into Oxfordshire. Very few, we fear; but we only wish they would do so, for unless they are prejudiced indeed, they will, we opine, confirm that there is not a more noble river in the world. Take for instance the beautiful Reach of Henley, with its fine architectural bridge, Thames and Isis adorning on either side the central arch – the domains approaching to it – the ancient church – the island in the distance – the 'wood-covered heights' ... and, on so splendid a day as Thursday, the sun sending forth its almost too refulgent rays through an Italian sky – who, we would ask, that was present on that occasion – the annual aquatic festival – that did not feel, as we felt, it to be one of the most charming scenes in nature, enhanced perhaps by the gay paraphernalia of a regatta, and the multitude of persons congregated to witness the exciting sports by

some of the manliest of Britain's manly sons ... But enough of this ...

Enough indeed! With such a public relations officer who needed a regatta?

The sparse entry in 1848 signalled a sharp decline in Henley's fortunes, which may have been in part due to growing opposition from the heads of Oxford colleges to their undergraduates competing at Henley. Perhaps the same problem convinced the Stewards of the need to foster college rowing, so important to their entry list. At any rate in this year they altered the qualification rule for the Ladies' Plate, and placed the new Visitors' Cup under the same qualification, barring university clubs and subscription rooms, and non-university clubs unless their membership was restricted to one profession, or to one particular town or place 'distant at least seven miles from Westminster Bridge'. Clearly the signal was that the Ladies' and Visitors' were to be events which Oxford and Cambridge college crews could aspire to win. And on this occasion Christ Church duly won the Ladies' Plate from Worcester College, the Stewards' and Visitors' Cups on row-overs, and the Silver Wherries on a foul.

1849

Bell's Life   17 June 1849
It is now eleven years since this annual regatta was established, and it has ever been looked forward to with more than ordinary anxiety by amateurs and the admirers of rowing generally, as one of the most interesting and important *aquatic fêtes* of the season; and how could it be otherwise under the patronage of Lord Camoys, the stew-

ardship of J. W. Gardiner Esq., the High Sheriff, the worthy Mayor of Henley, the Marquis of Downshire, the Earl of Orkney, Viscount Palmer, the Earl of Falmouth, the Earl of Kilmorey, and a host of other stewards, together with the excellent working committee ... and so indefatigable and talented an honorary secretary and founder of the regatta, Mr. James Nash.

Thus the faithful Mr O'Grady switched the spotlight from the problems besieging the Regatta to the fine folk who patronized and organized it, and perhaps assured himself of another free luncheon. Unfortunately he had to add that only one entry had been received for the Grand Challenge Cup, and that the Committee had been constrained to accept late entries up to 7 June.

If memorable for no other reason, 1848 must surely have seen one of the latest starting hours in the history of the Henley Regatta. The Oxonians were not permitted to leave their dreaming spires until four o'clock in the afternoon, and then had to cover twenty-two miles by horse and carriage. The Regatta waited for them; to have done otherwise would have meant no races. Perhaps it was as well that there were no challenge heats for the Grand and Ladies' Plate, which were started not much before 8 p.m. on the Monday and Tuesday respectively.

To escape the wrath of their heads of colleges, Oriel entered as 'An OBC', and Wadham as 'The St John of Malta'. There were two fine races between Wadham and Second Trinity, Cambridge.* In the Grand the crews raced stroke for stroke, with Trinity, on the Berks Station, just ahead at the finish, but, quoting Herbert Steward, 'a slight foul took place which the umpire decided in favour of Wadham'. In the Ladies' Plate, with the Stations reversed, there was again a close race as far as Poplar Point, where Wadham, with the inside Station, went ahead to win by a third of a length.

Bell's Life thought it worth noting: 'no thunderstorms this year, a circumstance which for its novelty ought, we think, to be recorded in the annals ...'

The Regatta opened with a professional scullers' match, 'in no way connected with the regatta' Herbert Steward was at pains to note – though it did head the Regatta's race-card! The match was for £25 a side between 'The Oxford Pet', Mark Cook, and Thomas Coombes of London. Coombes was firm favourite, but, *Bell's Life* commented, 'the race is not always to the swift'. Coombes, using a boat with a flush deck from stem to stern with only 'a small hollow for the heels', led all the way, but, hugging the Berkshire bank too closely, hit a stake and capsized within yards of the finishing post.

As a postscript *Bell's* added, 'Henley is likely to be even more strongly supported than it hitherto has, from the fact which cannot be concealed, that the Thames Regatta will probably cease to be an arena for contests between amateurs.'

A few weeks after the 1849 Regatta, perhaps sensing the growing discouragement among the Regatta hierarchy, the local inhabitants penned a Public Address to the Stewards exhorting them to continue the good work (see page 41).

---

*Trinity, Cambridge, being much the largest college at either university, used to support three boat clubs. 'First' consisted of all students except the 'scholars', who rowed as 'Second Trinity', and the Etonians and Westminsters who rowed as 'Third Trinity'.

1850 Some encouragement was certainly needed, for Henley Regatta reached its nadir in 1850. It was advertised as usual for two days but, with only fifteen entries of which five were for the local restricted events, it occupied only one day. Oxford University rowed over in the Grand and the Stewards', and Lincoln College were unopposed in the Ladies' Plate. There were no club crews at all, nor any Cambridge starters. But despite the thin entry 1850 was important in Henley history for the introduction of the first comprehensive Laws of Boat Racing. Also in this year the Stewards agreed to give Presentation Cups for the pair-oars and sculls, in place of the Silver Wherries and Diamond Scarf Pin. The Silver Wherries thus became the Silver Goblets. The Diamond Sculls retained their original title.

As *Bell's* had forecast, there was some comfort at hand, for now they were reporting:

> ... lower downstream we have to lament the loss of the Thames Regatta ... and ... we have to record the progress towards convalescence of its parent, for that we presume is the relationship in which the Henley-on-Thames Grand Regatta may fairly be considered to stand.

1851–1854 One might naturally suppose that the patronage of Prince Albert in 1851, making Henley a 'Royal Regatta' – the only one, since the Royal Thames Regatta was now defunct – was the accolade bestowed on a successful sporting event. But despite the fulsome reports written by Mr O'Grady of *Bell's Life*, and other journalists, the truth is that Henley was still fighting for survival in the year of the

Great Exhibition. It was to be another decade before the entries would increase significantly.

In 1851 there were but two entries for the Grand, Oxford beating Cambridge by some six lengths after the Light Blues' no. 3 broke his rowlock about 300 yards after the start. In the Ladies' Plate Christ Church entered as the 'Westminster and Eton Club', under assumed names, but this time an over-zealous journalist published the true names, which landed the 'House' men in serious trouble with their Dean. Whether the same occurred to the Brasenose crew, which won comfortably under the banner 'Childe of Hale', is not known. Brasenose also won the Stewards' Cup by default, their only opponents, Balliol, being prevented from leaving college in time. Messrs Clarke (Wadham) and Vaughan (Oriel) struck back at the authorities by entering for the Goblets as 'Hawkins and Symonds', the names of the heads of their colleges. One can see that the problems of getting entries for the Royal Regatta were not inconsiderable.

There were no challengers at all for the Grand in 1852, so Oxford, at the request of Lord Camoys, entered two crews, it being agreed that whichever won should be called the 'Oxford University Boat Club' (thus remaining 'holders') whilst the losers would be recorded as the 'Oxford Aquatic Club'. The tally of entries fell to twenty in 1853, but the racing was better. Cambridge had challenged Oxford to a summer Boat Race this year but Oxford suggested that they should meet at Henley, 'which having already shown symptoms of decay it was desirable by all means to endeavour to support'. A splendid race resulted, with Oxford, on the Berks Station, edging past Cambridge at Poplar Point, to win by only eighteen inches. Oxford had thus won Henley's premier trophy four years in succession, a record never surpassed and equalled only by Leander Club (1891–4, and 1898–1901).

First Trinity and Wadham were the only eight-oar entries in 1854, the Cambridge men winning both the Grand and Ladies' in spite of catching a crab, 'a sea fish, not common in these parts' was *Bell's* comment.

If the racing lacked inspiration in 1854 it seems that somebody had nevertheless turned it to some account, for a week after the Regatta *Bell's* correspondent wrote:

> We have received a communication concerning some bets in connection with the late Henley Regatta, and requesting our interference and decision; now we are always unwilling to have to do with such affairs, but the writer will see the utter impossibility of our giving an opinion in this instance without hearing both sides of the question. We strongly recommend a settlement by private arbitration, as should both parties ultimately agree to refer the matter to us, circumstances might possibly be brought to light, which we should feel bound in duty to make public, and the less of this sort that transpires the better for the interests of London rowing...

A simple case of a repudiated debt, a disputed decision, or something more sinister? We will never know.

1855–1857 Though the entry lists were still ailing there were important landmarks in the next three years. In 1855 there appeared on the scene A. A. Casamajor, who must be recognized

as the first Henley 'star'. At his first venture he won both the Diamonds, easily, and the Goblets, of which *Bell's Life* wrote:

> A capital race for half a mile, when the great strength of Mr. Casamajor began to tell, and he appeared to be lugging both his boat and his partner along; indeed, he must have had a skeg [rudder] on his sternpost, or Mr. Nottidge never could have kept the steerage against such continuous hard rowing. In the end they won as they liked.

Casamajor went on to win the Stewards', Wyfold Cup, Goblets and Diamond Sculls in 1856. In 1857 he took the Grand, Stewards' and Diamonds. In 1858 he held these three titles, added the Goblets, and was referred to as 'a blight on the entries' – because no one would waste their time sculling against him. In the ensuing three years he won respectively the Grand, Goblets and Diamonds, sadly dying suddenly a few weeks after his last Henley victory.

Also in 1855 Royal Chester Rowing Club brought off the first successful invasion from the provinces, winning both the Stewards' and the Wyfold Cup, which became a four-oar event for the first time this year. That was nothing compared to their performance in 1856, when they brought to Henley a keelless eight built by Matt Taylor of Newcastle. They could not balance their new-fangled craft and were soon the laughing-stock of the towpath – until they romped away with both the Grand Challenge Cup and the Ladies' Plate. For good measure four men from their eight were also runners-up in the Visitors' and Wyfold Cups, and withdrew from the final of the Stewards' Cup.

Perhaps such a potent demonstration by a club from the River Dee was unpalatable to the gentlemen of the Thames, for in 1856 the Stewards changed the rules to limit entries for the Ladies' Plate and Visitors' to Oxford and Cambridge colleges and Eton and Westminster School, and barred double entries in the Stewards' and Wyfold Cups.

Another important event in 1856 was the foundation of London Rowing Club, though not in time to compete that year under their own colours. In 1857 they won the Grand and Diamonds. London never failed to enter a crew for the Grand Challenge Cup from 1857 until 1968, a unique record in Henley annals. But the significance of the foundation of LRC is that it was the first modern rowing club on the Thames – though I suspect Chester may claim to have ante-dated the pattern on the Dee. Prior to 1856 rowing clubs were of the 'subscription rooms' type, with membership by invitation, and often limited by rule to a small number of members who were required to attend on specified days or face substantial fines for absence. Leander Club, for example, was at first limited to sixteen, and in 1856 was still limited to twenty-five. The new principles upon which London Rowing Club was to run were announced by its promoters. It was to enrol

> a large number of members at a small annual subscription ... perfect freedom to its members from all fines ... a well-assured immunity from any calls beyond their annual subscriptions, and an extensive fleet of boats, so that racing crews may be formed

when necessary without interfering with the usual pleasure-rowing of the members.

It is scarcely possible to exaggerate the importance of the founding of London Rowing Club, which soon became the pattern for healthy and prosperous rowing clubs countrywide, which in their turn not only provided a counterweight to the universities, but a wide range of entries which enabled Henley, and other regattas, to flourish.

1858 Despite *Bell's* optimism, it was still more a case of intensive care than of convalescence in 1858, when the entry list further slumped to fifteen, mainly because the presence of Casamajor and H. H. Playford scared all but one other crew out of the Goblets, whilst Casamajor found no challengers at all in the sculls. The Grand final was some compensation, and a typical example of the difficulty of winning on the Old Course from the Bucks Station. London Rowing Club, with Casamajor at no. 7 and Playford at stroke, were just clear of Cambridge University at Poplar Point. They tried to cross in front of Cambridge to take the Berkshire water but were driven out by a fine spurt which took the Light Blues through to win by nearly half a length.

1859 One might say that an era ended in 1859. London Rowing Club beat Oxford University in a heat and Cambridge in the final of the Grand Challenge Cup, and this was to be the last appearance of a representative university crew at Henley for a hundred years – surely an astonishing reflection today. In the seventeen Regattas since Henley's foundation there had been only five occasions on which one, or other, or both the University crews had not contested the Grand. Oxford had won seven times and had been runners-up four times, and Cambridge, facing more difficult logistical problems of course, had reached the final six times with three wins.

Whilst all were representative university crews, and some actually the same crews which had rowed in the University Boat Race, in many cases these crews were only assembled for Henley after the conclusion of the College Bumping Races, and were consequently short of practice. The twin defeats in 1859 seems to have persuaded them that it was more profitable to leave the honour of their universities in the hands of their colleges. In the short term at least they seem to have been right, for in the ensuing five years seven college crews reached the final, and three were winners, whilst between 1866 and 1871 the Oxford Etonian Club won five times.

1860–1863 Apart from 'a foul wind and a heavy stream' there was little of interest to report in 1860, save that First Trinity won the Grand, Ladies' Plate, Stewards' and Visitors' Cups. With no intent to detract from Trinity's achievement, but to put these results, which seem astonishing today, into perspective, one should add that Trinity beat London, the only other contender in the Grand, and that four men from each of these crews were also the only contenders for the Stewards'. The self-same Trinity eight rowed over unopposed in the Ladies' Plate, and the same Trinity four were unopposed in the Visitors' Cup.

First Trinity repeated their quadruple

success against stiffer opposition in 1861, which was the first year in which Eton and Radley raced in the Regatta; but it was not their first race on Henley waters, for they had met in a private match in 1858 – not in the autumn of 1860 as reported by the usually reliable H. T. Steward. On that occasion Eton were the winners by three-quarters of a length. Strictly by the rule book Radley should not have been eligible to compete in the Ladies' Plate, as the qualifications stipulated only Eton and Westminster as eligible schools. Radley suffered misfortune at the start, when their rudder fouled the bung line.* Eton led to Fawley, when First Trinity went ahead to win.

The main feature of 1862 was the performance of W. B. Woodgate, who had made his Henley debut in the previous year. On this occasion he won three races on the opening day of the Regatta, and on the following day covered the course five times, losing only the re-row of a dead-heat with E. D. Brickwood in the final of the Diamond Sculls.

Apart from remarkable Oxford successes – University and Brasenose Colleges between them winning the Grand, Ladies' Plate, Stewards', Visitors' and Goblets – 1863 was most notable for another Committee decision which illustrates the scant respect accorded to the Rules in the days when the Henley Regatta still counted no oarsmen among its governors. London Rowing Club, as holders of the Wyfold Cup, protested that both Kingston and Third

---

* At that time crews started with their coxswains holding a wooden 'bung' attached to a rope which was dropped when the umpire started the race. As a result of Radley's mishap stakeboats were introduced in 1862, with men to hold the stern or rudder of the competing boats.

Trinity were boating men who had previously competed for the Stewards' Cup. Their protests were rejected 'on what principle it is difficult to imagine', wrote H. T. Steward, 'as the qualification rule for the Wyfold expressly disqualified anyone who had contended, or was entered to contend, for the Stewards' Cup'. Steward, presumably, was too strict in his own interpretation of what was right and proper to grasp the principles on which the Town Committee operated. They needed races to swell their programme, and Kingston and Third Trinity were the only challengers for the Wyfold Cup that year.

1864–1866 The entries, which had been creeping up for several years, slumped in 1864, so that there were only ten races and three row-overs. Eton, destined to become the most prolific winners of the Ladies' Plate, scored their first victory. In 1865 they entered both the Grand and the Ladies' but without success, being disqualified in the second event for fouling Third Trinity no less than four times.

In 1866 dissatisfaction with the Committee's somewhat cavalier approach to the Rules came to a head. At the draw in the Town Hall protests were lodged against several competitors on various grounds. All were overruled, but in the autumn certain changes were made, viz:

i) No one to be eligible to row for a club unless he had been a member for at least three months. This, it is said, was provoked by Kingston who had made a habit of last-minute recruiting.
ii) A limit on the number of names and substitutes (twice the number in the crew).

iii) No assumed names permitted.
iv) No one to enter twice for the same event. This with particular reference to W. B. Woodgate, who had sought to enter twice for the Goblets, once under his own name, and once under the name 'Wat Bradford'.

The Thames Conservancy first assumed authority over the river in 1866, but the most remarkable feature of that year's Regatta was recorded by *The Field*:

Out of twenty-eight medals given to oarsmen for winning the eight- and four-oar events, twenty-seven were won by Etonians. These twenty-seven medals were won by nineteen men, of whom seventeen had been pupils of Mr. Edmond Warre, of Eton.

1867 In an attempt to stimulate spectator interest the Committee again tried the expedient of a canoe race in 1867. This time it was a 'chase' over land and water, open to the Canoe Club and all Henley competitors:

If Henley had been an ailing concern [wrote *Bell's Life*] and required propping up by having recourse to any of those inferior strategies by which we continually see minor affairs of this kind (seeking to survive) . . . it would have been more dignified . . . that it should have gathered its imperial robe around it and died with dignity. But what is to be said when . . . the Stewards have consented to invite the desecration of their peerless regatta by establishing a prize for canoemen? It is as if donkey races were added to the attractions of Epsom.

In such circumstances it is scarcely surprising to hear from John Cooper that this was also the only occasion that a man won a medal at Henley and played in the Varsity cricket match in the same year. This was W. H. Lipscombe who steered University College to victory in the Stewards' Cup.

1868　A cox was in the news in the following year too. For this was the historic occasion on which W. B. Woodgate announced that Brasenose intended to race in the Stewards' Cup without a coxswain, the boat to be steered by himself via wires attached to his feet. He was duly advised that since the Stewards' Cup was an event for coxed fours Brasenose would not be permitted to start without a cox. But 'Guts' Woodgate was not the man to be deterred by that sort of legalism, and promptly announced that Brasenose would comply with this requirement – but that their cox would dive overboard as soon as the umpire started the race.

The chosen sacrifice was Fred Weatherly, later King's Counsel and destined to give the world some of the best-loved Victorian ballads, notably 'Danny Boy' and 'Roses of Picardy'. Writing some sixty years later,* by which time he had forgotten which event he never actually took part in – he thought it was the Ladies' Plate – he recalled his ordeal after receiving his summons by telegram from Woodgate:

> I was at my window looking across the Bristol Channel at the Welsh Mountains, just finishing the first of my songs that was ever set to music, '*A message o'er the sea*'.

* Piano and Gown, Fred E. Weatherly (G. P. Putnam & Sons, 1926).

> Arriving at the Red Lion I was told what I had to do. I was to squat on the dummy seat of our boat at the start, and at the word 'Go', go overboard, quietly, so as not to rock the boat. I could not swim a stroke, and by way of encouragement I was told that the river was fifteen feet deep...

Weatherly took advice 'from a fatherly waterman' who further explained that the river near Temple Island was full of dangerous weeds. He then practised 'jumping overboard from a chair at the Red Lion'. In view of his subsequent career as a lyricist one can hardly describe Fred Weatherly as an 'unsung hero' of the Regatta. But it seems hard that he was not even recorded as a competitor. Brasenose of course were disqualified.

This was the first year of the Thames Cup, which was won by Pembroke College, Oxford. *Bell's Life* thought Eton 'the best crew seen for the Ladies' Plate for many years' and 'to get to the final heat for the Grand Challenge Cup after beating such crews as Kingston and University College was as great an honour almost as securing the prize itself'.

Bell's also thought that 'the beautiful sight which the Queen of Regattas offers should not be dimmed by the smoke of nearly a dozen steamers ... [which] darted about among the boat loads of aristocratic people, regardless of the perils to which they exposed them'.

1869–1871　Following the Fred Weatherly affair the Stewards offered a Presentation Cup for Coxswainless Fours in 1869. There were only two entries, the Oxford Radleian Club winning from the Surbiton club, Oscillators.

There was major revision of the Rules this year.

Henley received their first 'overseas entry' in 1870, from Trinity College, Dublin. It was not a 'foreign' entry, of course, and TCD have enjoyed a special relationship with Henley ever since, continuing to be accepted as a 'home entry' for the Ladies' Plate and Visitors' Cup even after the foundation of the Irish Republic. TCD have never done things by halves, and at their first attempt went for the Grand, Ladies', Visitors' and the Wyfold Cup. According to *Hall's History of Irish Rowing*, 'several of the Trinity oarsmen were still suffering from sea-sickness after the notoriously rough Irish Sea crossing. They had to borrow boats ... had never before sat in a fine racing eight ... and had a peculiar high feather no doubt due to training on rougher water ...' Notwithstanding these handicaps they reached the final of the Ladies' Plate, succumbing to Eton who completed a record sequence of five successive wins this year, and won the Visitors' Cup from University College, Oxford. They withdrew from the Wyfold Cup.

In 1871 Pembroke, Oxford, ended Eton's sequence of five wins in the Ladies' Plate, a sequence, incidentally, which only they themselves were ever to beat, twenty years later. At the same time the Oxford Etonian Club won their last Grand from the up-and-coming London Rowing Club. In the Visitors' Cup First Trinity gave Cambridge their first victory, apart from John B. Close in the previous year's Diamond Sculls, for six years.

1872

1872 was a busy year at Henley, with major Rule changes which ended a crew's right to take – and then keep – their opponents' water. And in accordance with the wishes of the oarsmen the Stewards also abolished the Rule whereby the holders of the previous year's challenge trophies did not have to race in the challenge heats.

London Rowing Club, who were now well established in their first great period of success, brought sliding seats to Henley for the first time this year, winning both the Grand and the Stewards' with some ease. 'The advantage,' according to Herbert Steward, 'being then so apparent, nearly all the other crews adopted them at the last minute.'

John Cooper remarked that, 'Unlike most other clubs London did not concentrate on the eights, but set as much store on winning the Stewards' as the Grand,' an opinion borne out by the tables of winners. The Close brothers, John and James, A. de L. Long, F. S. Gulston, Le Blanc Smith and F. L. Playford, in various combinations formed these hugely successful fours, at the same time often turning out against each other in the Goblets. The first two foreign entries were made in 1872, the Atlanta Rowing Club entering for, but subsequently withdrawing from, the Presentation Cup for Coxswainless Fours, whilst E. Smith from the same club appeared in the Diamond Sculls but with no success.

1873

The Irish took two trophies home in 1873, Trinity Dublin winning the Visitors' and Kingstown Harbour defeating first Thames, and then London, to win the Wyfold Cup which was no mean achievement at the first time of asking. Perhaps because of this discomfiture of the home crews *Bell's* man remarked that 'Worse rowing, worse form and worse watermanship, taking the crews all round, were never witnessed at Henley'.

The amenities on the other hand were certainly improved. Two large tents were erected below the bridge for additional boat storage, and a dressing-room and plunge bath added to the existing boathouse above the bridge – though the 'plunge' was into the chilly waters of Old Father Thames. Carriages on Henley Bridge were limited to a single rank to ease traffic congestion, and a parking place for carriages provided in the Lion Meadow. Near Poplar Point a 'speculative gentleman' (John Cooper's description) put up a stand for spectators which threatened to cut off the view of the course from the Red Lion Hotel where many of the crews stayed. After dinner on the night before the Regatta the young gentlemen of University and Brasenose Colleges, encouraged needless to say by Woodgate, set out on a demolition job, cheered on by the locals and watched by half a dozen policemen who made no attempt to intervene until the task had been completed, when they ruled that the planks should not be tossed into the river for fear of causing a hazard to navigation. One senses that the entrepreneur was not popular.

The Presentation Cups offered for Coxed Fours in 1868 and 1872 having met with a poor response, the Stewards concluded that clubs would not provide themselves with a new class of boat unless there was a permanent event for them in the Henley programme. So they made the Stewards' Challenge Cup into a coxless event in 1873, following suit with the Visitors' and Wyfold Cups in the following year. With the benefit of hindsight one may conclude that

it would have been wiser to have kept at least one event for coxed fours, for it took a long struggle, with the same argument in reverse, that clubs would not purchase a type of boat for which there was no Henley event, when it came to reintroducing coxed fours ninety years later.

1874–1876 Cooper thought that the London Rowing Club fours of 1874 and 1875 were the best of all, and certainly they won the Stewards' Cup easily, from Thames Rowing Club in 1874 and from Leander in the following year. F. S. Gulston stroked and steered both crews. In partnership with Albert de Lord Long, 'Gully' Gulston also won three out of five finals of the Goblets at this time. One of their rare defeats came in 1875. 'Gully loved to give his opponents some backwash,' Cooper explains. 'In the final they were opposed to a pair of selling platers (W. Chillingworth and C. Herbert) . . . the L R C pair who had the Centre Station at once took the lead and as usual Gully took his opponents' water and gave them the benefit of his wash all the way from Remenham to the Point . . . but he [then] began to take life very easily. About two hundred yards from home the two pairs were less than half a length away and Chillingworth and Herbert, suddenly spurting, just touched the stem of the L R C boat with the inevitable result.'

So Gully Gulston lost a race which he should have won. Today washing an opponent is forbidden. But that stems from the fully buoyed lanes of straight international courses. In the University Boat Race and Wingfield Sculls, both contested on the tortuous Putney to Mortlake course, it is still legitimate and practised.

Whether the faithful Mr O'Grady was still writing for *Bell's Life* is not known, but in 1874 their Aquatic Correspondent displayed unprecedented venom:

> If we could slay or drown the Committee,
> if we could weed out the Stewards, replace
> the many anile incapables with a few prac-
> tical men who really knew one end of an oar
> from the other; chop off Poplar Point and
> choke all the itinerant Christy Minstrels,
> what a vision of an ideal regatta bursts on
> our view.

1877   Cheltenham College joined the ranks of 'Henley Schools' in 1877, entering for the Ladies' Plate with a request to be drawn against Radley. That the Stewards declined to do, but declared that if the two schools did not meet in the Ladies' they would allow a private match between them. In the event both lost their heats of the Ladies', and in a special match for medals presented by the Regatta, Radley were the winners by several lengths. Cheltenham entered for the Ladies' Plate again in 1878, and won the Public Schools Challenge Cup, which was instituted in 1879. In 1881 they dis-appeared from Henley as suddenly as they had come, not reappearing until 1951.

1878–1879   Henley Regatta realistically attained international status for the first time in 1878, with entries from two scullers, G. W. Lee of New Jersey and G. Lee of Boston, and two fours, the Shoe-wae-cae-mette B.C., Monroe, entered for the Stewards', and Columbia College for the Stewards' and Visi-tors'. The Bostonian sculler made no impression, but G. W. Lee lost his Diamonds

heat on the post to T. C. Edwards-Moss, the ultimate winner.

The American fours met in the Stewards', with Dublin University, who fouled Columbia. But Monroe were easy winners. In the final Monroe, using swivel rowlocks which were said to be audible from one end of the course to the other, started at 50 and led at once. But London, rating 8 strokes a minute less, gradu-ally pulled them back. At the White House, London edged into the lead and the Americans stopped, one of the crew 'not feeling well' as H. T. Steward put it. In the Visitors' Cup Columbia became the first foreign winners of a Henley trophy.

Unhappily the first foreign invasion of Henley had a sour aftermath, with accusations that both G. W. Lee and the 'Shoes' were not truly amateurs. This led to considerable acri-mony, and a tightening up of the Henley rules in the following year.

1879 produced more acrimony from *Bell's* correspondent, too, and perhaps a clue as to why he had become disenchanted with the Henley management:

> The umpire's launch as usual was early
> occupied by more than a dozen favoured
> individuals, most of whom seemed to take
> very little interest in the racing, but the
> polite request made to the Committee in our
> 'Aquatic Notes' last year to allow a couple
> of members of the Fourth Estate to go on
> board, so as to obtain a correct account of
> the racing, was entirely disregarded.

This year also saw Twickenham Rowing Club win the Thames Cup at their first attempt, heralding a remarkable six-year run of success, for they won the Thames Cup again in 1881 and 1884, and were three times losing finalists in the Grand Challenge Cup, from 1883 to 1885. Cooper said that 'unlike Kingston [they] were a Local Club who at any rate at first made their own oarsmen'. They had the advantage of J. H. D. Goldie as coach, and when they went for the Grand they also had four Hertford College men, G. Q. Roberts, E. Buck, J. Lowndes and D. E. Brown to help them.

1880–1881

Germania Ruderclub, Frankfurt, became the first European entry, and the first foreign entry for the Grand Challenge Cup, in 1880, but went out after a good race with London Rowing Club in a heat.

Great administrative changes were introduced before the 1881 Regatta and quickly put to the test. Cornell University sent in a late entry for the Stewards' and Visitors' Cups, which the new Committee, rightly by the book, rejected. Cornell arrived all the same and petitioned the Stewards to overrule the Committee, in which they were supported by a number of English clubs, and by the press. In the end, by the President's casting vote, they were accepted for the Stewards' but not for the Visitors'. This did not placate Cornell who particularly desired to race against Hertford in the Visitors'. They did meet in a private match after the Regatta. Unfortunately the Americans ran into the bank twice before Fawley which put an end to their aspirations. In the Stewards' Cup they fouled London early in the race. The umpire bent the Rules, taking all three crews back to the start, but Cornell finished last behind Thames and London. Later Cornell raced in Vienna where, according to H. T.

Steward, 'the stroke oarsman pretended to faint when they were well ahead, and he was accused by the rest of the crew of having sold the race ... there could be no doubt that such had been the case'.

Bedford School also indulged in some rule-bending in the Public Schools Cup in 1880. They fitted wide thwarts which they greased, and were thus able to 'slide' in what was supposed to be a 'fixed seat' event. *Bell's Life* of course had its say:

> There were three fouls but as no disinterested persons were on the launch (devoted to 'deadheads' and ladies), we must decline to deceive our readers by giving imaginary descriptions.

1882–1885

Exeter College won the Grand for the only time in their history in 1882. Entries were increasing by the year, and success was widely distributed. More races brought more technical problems and the realization that at last the Royal Regatta was firmly established as a successful and major sporting event. Indeed at this time Henley was surely the major sporting event in the country, and fast growing in international renown.

The days when Henley could be run by a committee of local dignitaries, on a blatantly unfair course, were numbered. In March 1884 a sub-committee considered the practicability of cutting off Poplar Point, but instead proposed moving the finish downstream. Their recommendations were rejected by the full Committee, but in 1885 the old Committee was abolished, and a new Committee of Management set up on which rowing and local

Stewards were to be equally represented. A new code of Rules was adopted, and in the autumn the 'New Course' was approved.

The Public Schools Cup was discontinued, but a proposal to scrap the Thames Cup, to reduce the number of races, was rejected.

If 'modern Henley' had not yet quite arrived, 'old Henley' was definitely on the way out.

9 New Course to Success: 1886–1914

1886–1888 Without doubt 1886 marked a watershed in the history of Henley Regatta, not so much because it saw the introduction of the New Course, which was expected to be fairer but turned out not to be, but because at last rowing men were taking charge of the Regatta. Maybe they did not always take the right decisions, but at least their concern was to promote rowing rather than the pecuniary interests of the local community. Some may say that they went too far in this.

Also 1886 may fairly be said to mark the commencement of the 'Golden Age' at Henley. The Regatta, no longer struggling for stability, found a new self-assurance in the expansionist climate of the late Victorian epoch. The Empire was in its heyday and Society was basking in the wealth created by the Industrial Revolution. Those 'Dark Satanic Mills' cast no shadow over Henley Royal Regatta.

Racing honours were well distributed in the first year of the New Course, but 1887 proved to be an *annus mirabilis* for Cambridge rowing. Trinity Hall won the Grand, Ladies' Plate, and Thames, Stewards' and Visitors' Cups, an achievement which has never been equalled. Pembroke, Cambridge, won the Wyfold Cup, C. T. Barclay and S. D. Muttlebury of Third Trinity took the Goblets and J. C. Gardner of Emmanuel completed the clean sweep by defeating Guy Nickalls in the final of the Diamond Sculls. Surprisingly the Hall held only the Stewards' in 1888, and could manage no entry at all in the following year.

1889–1890 This was the era of many legendary names in Henley history, Guy Nickalls and his brother Vivian, Muttlebury, W. A. L. Fletcher, G. C. Bourne, and C. W. Kent among them.

In partnership with Gardner, Muttlebury won the Goblets by two feet from Guy Nickalls and Lord Ampthill in 1889, the pairs racing almost level over the whole course. In 1890 Kent, weighing 10 st 10 lb., stroked Brasenose to victory over Leander in a heat of the Stewards' Cup, H. T. Steward's description of the race being so remarkable an understatement that it surely deserves repetition:

> Brasenose seemed ahead half way up the Island, but at the top of it Leander was ahead, and led by a quarter of a length at the quarter-mile mark. Brasenose however led at Remenham [Farm], but the crews were level again at Fawley. Brasenose led slightly at the three-quarter mile post, but the boats were alongside at the mile post. Off Phyllis Court Leander seemed to be getting the best of it, but Brasenose passed the post first by two feet.

Brasenose went on to win the final from Thames Rowing Club. Kent, recruited by his 1890 victims, stroked Leander to victory in the next four Grand Challenge Cups.

1891 Freak weather conditions affected the racing in 1891. 'Tuesday: A gale of wind from the South West and torrents of rain,' *The Field* reported. 'Wednesday, a thunderstorm … more like a tropical storm which for a time killed the wind.'

Kent, stroking Leander for the first time, found his crew, on the Berkshire Station, passed by Thames Rowing Club in the second half-mile, but in the end managed to force a dead-heat. Re-rowing on the following day, when the tropical storm 'killed the wind', Leander won easily, demonstrating the Bucks advantage in a south-westerly wind which was to become a feature of the New Course. On the last day, when *The Field* reported, 'A really fine summer's day, with no atmospheric drawbacks', Leander won the final by a length from London Rowing Club, in 6 minutes 51 seconds, a record which was to stand for forty-three years. This, incidentally, was the first of an unrivalled run of twelve Grand wins in fifteen years for Leander Club.

At the draw this year someone pointed out that one of the boats was six feet longer than the rest, which resulted in all boats being measured, and the longer boat in each race being pulled back so that the bows would be level at the start.

Ampthill and Guy Nickalls had the closest possible verdict in the Goblets. On the disadvantaged Berkshire Station they were two lengths behind F. Wilkinson and W. A. L. Fletcher at Remenham Rectory, a length behind at the White House, and still half a length behind at the Isthmian Enclosure, but 'made a rush' at the finish and won by one foot.

Incidentally this description by H. T. Steward establishes the position of the long-since defunct Isthmian Club enclosure, which must have been at the downstream end of the present general enclosure.

1892–1894 Royal Chester returned to the winner's list in 1892, with a quarter-length victory over Thames Rowing Club in the Stewards' Cup, but there were few other close races. In 1893 Henley signed an agreement with the Sociétés Françaises des Sports Athlétiques and the French were permitted to make entries up to 1 June instead of 31 March. This became the pattern for future Agreements with foreign governing bodies. Unfortunately a French crew was involved in controversy at their first appearance through no fault of their own. Approaching the Barrier in a heat of the Stewards' Cup, S N Basse Seine were pushed off the course by Thames Rowing Club and collided with a pleasure boat. Basse Seine claimed a foul but were ordered to withdraw it by Baron de Coubertin of Olympic fame. The Committee summoned Thames next day to explain their conduct and accepted their assurances that it had been a mistake. An hysterical outburst then accused Thames of disgraceful behaviour (presumably for making a steering error), the Committee for a 'disgusting' decision, and the umpire for referring the matter to the Committee in the first case. If there was one thing the Victorians were better at than raging at alleged unfairness to their own crews, it was raging at alleged unfairness to foreigners!

In 1893 the entries rose to a record fifty-three and there was a proposal in 1894 to extend the Regatta to four days. This the Stewards declined to do, but reserved the right to require some preliminary heats to be rowed on the day before the Regatta if the number of entries so demanded. The Nickalls brothers, Guy and Vivian, remarkably won the Goblets in partnership and contested the final of the Diamond Sculls against each other. Harcourt Gold, one of the great strokes of all time, stroked Eton to the second of three consecutive wins in the Ladies' Plate. His aggregate margin of victory for the three finals being an astonishing sixteen or seventeen lengths. The 1894 win, in which Gold was joined by my father making his first appearance as a 13 st. 2lb. schoolboy, was 'five or six lengths' over Trinity, Oxford. For the first time this year the swans were removed from the reach before the Regatta.*

1895   Racing was closer, and controversy fiercer in 1895. In a heat of the Grand, Leander were left on their stakeboat, hands raised to indicate that they were not ready when the umpire called 'Go'. Cornell University went on alone. It is said that the umpire believed Leander had simply made a bad start. But it was Cornell rather than the umpire who attracted the wrath of the crowd. One must say that it was unusual, at that period, to take advantage of opponents' mishaps. Later in the same Regatta St John's College, Oxford stopped when Eton caught a crab on the third

* Thames swans are owned by the Queen or, by Royal Grant, by the Dyers' and Vintners' Companies. Dyers' swans are identified by one 'nick' or 'notch' on the beak, Vintners' swans by two nicks. Royal swans are unmarked, so the Queen gets all which are not marked at the annual 'Swan Upping'. In olden times the penalty for stealing a swan was that the bird was suspended by its beak and the felon was required to cover it completely with wheat. Likewise stolen cats were suspended by their tails, which gave rise to the theory that swans were bred for their long necks, and cats for their long tails!

stroke. Next day Trinity Hall rowed Cornell to a standstill, sparking off the noisiest night of rejoicing that Mr Cooper could remember. The Hall went on to win the final from New College; but Leander, and in particular, Kent at stroke, had lost the chance of a unique sequence of five Grand wins in five years. The closest race of the year, however, was the first heat of the Stewards' Cup between London Rowing Club and the Argonaut Rowing Club of Toronto. The crews raced neck-and-neck to the mile, when London forged ahead to lead by three-quarters of a length at the Isthmian Enclosure. The Canadians counter-attacked and took the lead opposite the grandstand, but London, stroked by Guy Nickalls, with his brother Vivian at no. 3, snatched victory by two feet. 'One of the finest races from start to finish ever rowed' was Herbert Steward's verdict.

The Nickalls brothers won the Goblets again, and so became the first recipients of the new Nickalls' Challenge Cup, presented to the Regatta by their father, Tom Nickalls, this year to celebrate the fact that one or other, or both of his sons had won the Silver Goblets for the preceding five years.

Nereus Boat Club, Amsterdam, became the first foreign crew to win the Thames Cup, and I believe their no. 4, R. van der Veen, to have been the first 14-stone oarsman to race at Henley, though this claim is incapable of substantiation as the weights of scullers and pair-oar competitors were not recorded at that time. Van de Veen weighed 14 st. 9 lb.

1896–1898   The weather was hot and sultry in 1896, and the crowds on the river were said to be greater than ever before. Leander had a hard semi-final in the Grand, beating New College by half a length, but won easily against Thames in the final. The Nickalls brothers won the Goblets for the third time in succession. New College took their revenge on Leander in 1897, coming from behind at the mile post to win by two feet and equalling the course record of 6 minutes 51 seconds. It was a fast year, for records fell to Eton in the Ladies' Plate, Leander in the Stewards' Cup, and H. T. Blackstaffe in the Diamond Sculls. Blackstaffe however lost the final to E. H. Ten Eyck of Massachusetts. It transpired later that Ten Eyck's amateur status was in doubt, and despite the fact that he was the holder his entry was refused in 1898. There were no particular excitements in 1898 apart from several collisions with piles and pleasure boats, which led to a decision in the autumn to protect the course by fixing booms between the piles on the Bucks side of the river. A motion proposing that the Thames Cup should be relegated to fixed seats because the standard was so low was rejected.

1899–1900 The installation of booms in 1899 had a beneficial side effect in making it possible to row races at much shorter intervals. Nevertheless entries were so numerous that preliminary heats before the Regatta became necessary for the first time. Leander won the Grand with some ease, so that at the turn of the century they had failed only twice in ten years to take the premier trophy and one of those occasions had been the muddle with Cornell in 1885. Eton's record in the Ladies' Plate, at that time, was even more remarkable

than Leander's record in the Grand, for in 1899 they won for the seventh year in succession. This was to be followed by four losing finals and two more victories, so that by 1905 they had raced in thirteen consecutive Ladies' Plate finals.

The dawning of the 20th century does not seem to have attracted special notice at Henley, but there was one significant event which could not have been recognized as such at the time. For in 1900 the Club Nautique de Gand appeared in the Grand for the first time. Leander rowed past them at the bottom of the enclosures to win by three-quarters of a length, going on to beat Trinity, Cambridge, in the final. But in the ensuing decade the crews from Ghent were to shake British rowing to its foundations.

1901–1902 The Belgians were back in 1901 but the honour of becoming the first foreign crew to reach the final of the Grand fell to the University of Pennsylvania. They disposed of both London and Thames Rowing Clubs in the heats, but could not manage Leander in the final. Pennsylvania led to Remenham Rectory, but Leander came through to lead by a canvas at Fawley, going on to win by a length. Ghent fell to Leander by a trifle less in the semi-finals.

Ghent scratched from the Grand when their boat was damaged before leaving Belgium in 1902, but a fine Third Trinity crew beat the Argonauts from Toronto in the semi-final and Leander in the final – the only club to do so, incidentally, in eight years between 1898 and 1905. Trinity also beat Leander in the Stewards', whilst C. W. H. Taylor and W. Dudley-Ward made it a personal hat-trick, rowing in the winning Third Trinity eight and four, and also winning the Goblets.

The popularity of the Regatta may be gauged from the fact that the Great Western Railway was running twenty-six trains from Paddington to Henley on the Tuesday and Wednesday, and twenty-eight on Thursday, which was then finals day. Twelve were non-stoppers. There were also through trains from Windsor, Didcot and Oxford, and railway staff were drafted in from as far afield as Hereford, Chester and Liskeard in Cornwall.

1903–1904 A signal was introduced at Fawley in 1903, so for the first time spectators in the enclosures knew how races were progressing before the crews arrived. Third Trinity, seeking to defend the Grand, lost their no. 5, C. J. D. Goldie, on the morning of their first race. They contemplated starting with seven men, as Oxford had done in 1843, because their spare, C. H. Chalmers, was not in training. The Committee ruled that this was permissible, but after a trial spin with W. Dudley-Ward stroking from the no. 7 seat, and their regular stroke, R. H. Nelson, rowing at no. 5, they dropped the idea and put Chalmers in at no. 3.

Trinity beat London in their heat, and in the final were leading Leander by a quarter of a length at the White House. But Leander spurted along the enclosures to win by six feet. 'Third' had some compensation, for their four, which was not affected by Goldie's sickness, beat Leander and then the Royal Netherlands Rowing Club to win the Stewards' fairly easily. Partnered by C. W. H. Taylor, Goldie insisted on rowing in the Goblets. Skill and the use of the rudder against Taylor enabled the Trinity men to hold on for three-quarters of a mile, but L. Klaus and A. Ehrenberg, of Berlin, beat them by two lengths, and the next day easily beat D. C. R. Stuart and C. M. Steele, of Kingston, to become the first foreign winners of the Goblets. Several of the strongest Trinity men had moved on to Leander in 1904, and Leander were easy winners against New College. Nevertheless Third Trinity still took away three trophies, the Stewards' and Visitors' Cups, and the Goblets, which this year Goldie and Taylor won as they liked. The surprise of the Regatta came in the semi-final defeat of F. S. Kelly in the Diamond Sculls. After winning for the past two years Kelly was a hot favourite. But he was short of training and despite allegedly clearing Temple Island in forty-eight seconds, and leading by two lengths at Remenham, he was caught by the Canadian, L. F. Scholes. At the bottom of Phyllis Court Kelly stopped and had to be lifted from his boat. In the final, Scholes had another sensational battle against A. H. Cloutte of London Rowing Club, who also had to be helped ashore after chasing the Canadian all the way. Nor was that the end of the Scholes story. After the Regatta a newspaper report revealed that the cherished Diamond Sculls were on public display in the Toronto bar kept by his father. As Scholes senior's hotel was known to be a 'sporting establishment' this news does not seem to have worried anyone unduly, but Scholes' comment that the Diamonds 'at times get mixed up with the cigar boxes' caused no little stir in the British press, ever ready in those days to attack 'foreigners' even if they happened to be Dominions' sportsmen.

1905 After his failure in the previous year, F. S. Kelly's was the outstanding achievement in 1905. After winning his three heats in the Diamond Sculls Kelly allowed H. T. Blackstaffe to lead him to Fawley in the final. Kelly then quickened to take nearly four lengths in the next half-mile, winning by almost a quarter of a minute in the record time of 8 minutes 10 seconds. At that time this was five seconds faster than the record for the pairs, and it stood as the Diamonds' record until 1938. Kelly was also rowing in the Leander eight which won the Grand Challenge Cup, beating Jesus College, the Vesper Boat Club of Philadelphia, and Sport Nautique de Gand. The Belgians were checked when their stroke caught a crab on the fifth stroke in the final. They nevertheless managed 44 strokes in the first minute. Leander, at 42, reached the Remenham Barrier in a shade under two minutes, leading by half a length. Beyond Fawley Leander rowed away to win comfortably by three lengths according to H. T. Steward, two and a quarter according to Theodore Cook.

The Vesper crew were subsequently involved in an unhappy dispute about amateur status which is discussed elsewhere (see page 22).

1906–1907 The Great Western Railway conveyed 31,000 passengers to the Regatta in 1906, but the bottom dropped out of England's rowing world. After winning the Grand Challenge Cup twelve times in the preceding fifteen years, Leander Club had no eight at Henley. Who then was to stem the Belgian invasion? Faint hopes were raised when Trinity Hall won a titanic struggle against the Argonauts from Toronto in the semi-final. But Club Nautique de Gand had beaten Magdalen by a length and a half, and Third Trinity by two lengths. In the final, at 42 to the Hall's 41, Ghent went clear at the quarter-mile, and the Hall, perhaps feeling the effects against the Argonauts, could do nothing to hold them. Still at 38, Ghent rowed right away to win by three lengths, and so became the first foreign club to wrest the coveted blue riband of rowing from Britain's shores.

Worse was to follow in 1907 when Leander, with a crew based on the winning Cambridge Boat Race crew, set out to recover the Grand. Confrontation came in the second heat. The crews raced level up Temple Island, Ghent at 43 and Leander at 42. There was a strong 'Bushes' wind, favouring Leander on the Bucks Station. After half a mile Leander led by six feet. Beyond Fawley D. C. R. Stuart, stroking Leander on bowside, spurted to 37 in a desperate effort to shake off the Belgians, and at the three-quarter mile Leander led by half a length. Then the Belgian stroke, R. Poma, quickened to 38, taking the lead along the Phyllis Court wall to win by a third of a length. Christ Church made a gallant effort in the final, Theodore Cook pointing out that they had the disadvantage of the Berks Station, a fact which he omitted to mention in the case of Ghent the previous day. At Remenham the Belgians were at 38 and Christ Church still at 40, and at the half-mile Ghent pulled clear. Christ Church were still at 40 opposite the Grosvenor Club (above the mile), but there was nothing more they could do, the Belgians winning by a bare length. In the Stewards', Leander were almost caught by Ludwigshafener, Germany. In fact the Germans got their bows in front along the enclosures, but when Leander came back at them they stopped, completely rowed out. Leander stopped too, but then paddled on to the finish. It was, however, Magdalen's year in the fours. Four of their men, stroked by the veteran Guy Nickalls, easily beat Leander in the Stewards' final, and four other Magdalen men won both the Visitors' and Wyfold Cups. This was the only occasion when one club won all three four-oar events at Henley – an achievement only possible, of course, for a college, because of the Visitors' Cup student qualification. *The Times* correspondent commented: 'Henley finished as it opened – in blustering rain … it was Guy Nickalls's day, for in addition to stroking the Magdalen four which beat Leander in the Stewards' Cup, he coached his old College crew that won both the Visitors' and Wyfold Cups. There was quite a pretty domestic scene when Guy Nickalls came into the enclosures after winning his race, Mrs Nickalls, in her enthusiasm, running up to the hero and kissing him. Twenty-two years ago Guy Nickalls rowed in the Eton boat that won the Ladies' Plate at Henley, yesterday he stroked the Magdalen College four to victory against Leander in the Stewards' Cup – a record without compare in the history of rowing.'

After the racing was over in 1907 an unidentified lady complained that the Royal Regatta had corralled the Royal swans in a less than Royal pigsty. Sir Douglas Dawson, Comptroller of H M Household, wrote to the Stewards to administer a Royal rebuke which was initially ill received. But after some tetchy correspondence the matter was satisfactorily resolved and the Stewards, resourceful as ever,

elected Sir Douglas, who resided at the top of White Hill, to be a Steward himself.

1908   Because the Olympic Regatta was to take place over the Henley course in late July the Royal Regatta was closed to foreign entries in 1908. The furore which arose over the consequent exclusion of the Belgians, as holders of the Grand, is discussed elsewhere (see page 23).

The two crews nominated to represent Great Britain in the Olympic Eights, Cambridge University and Leander, were absent, making the Grand Challenge Cup look like an easy option. As a result there were no less than ten entries. Six of these crews also entered for the Ladies' Plate, including Eton College, who beat Pembroke and Caius Colleges with something to spare, and Thames Rowing Club after a hard race, to reach the final. Christ Church, who did not enter for the Ladies', were the other finalists after a close race against Jesus, Cambridge, and an easy win over New College. In the meantime, in the Ladies' Plate, Eton had beaten First Trinity safely, but succumbed in the semi-final to the same Jesus crew which had pressed Christ Church so hard. Members of that Eton crew used to claim that if their coach, R. S. de Haviland, had not entered them for the Ladies' Plate as an 'insurance policy' they could have been the only school crew ever to win the Grand Challenge Cup. That we will never know, but in the event with five races already behind them in three days, the boys could not match the 'House' who had raced only twice before, and after the mile post had the Grand final well in hand. The outstanding crew of the 1908 Royal Regatta, however, was undoubtedly the Magdalen College four which had won the Wyfold and Visitors' Cups in the previous year. In the Stewards' this time they fought off strong challenges by Thames and London Rowing Clubs, setting a new record in the process. In the Visitors' they easily beat Trinity, Oxford, and Jesus, Cambridge, rowing themselves right out in the final despite having the race in hand after Fawley, and clipping no less than seven seconds off the record.

1908 Olympics

The Henley course was lengthened to a mile and a half for the Olympic Regatta which took place at the end of July. Competing countries were permitted to enter two crews for each event, but none did so apart from the United Kingdom. There were only four events, for Single Sculls, Coxless Pairs, Coxless Fours and Eights, and only the Eights produced an international final. But that compensated in excitement for an otherwise rather unspectacular regatta. Anticipation was focussed on the Belgians, who had won the Grand Challenge Cup in 1906 and 1907. Cambridge University, having won the University Boat Race for three years in succession, were nominated as Britain's first-string eight. But the pundits were not impressed by their style of rowing, and so, as their second string, assembled a Leander eight comprising the best available oarsmen of several years past, and headed by the veteran Guy Nickalls, now forty-two years of age, and C. D. Burnell, now aged thirty-six. There was no doubt of their prowess and strength; their stamina remained to be proven.

Leander won their first heat against Hungary very easily, and their second, against Canada, safely by a length after a hard race. Cambridge drew the redoubtable Belgians, who led by three-quarters of a length at Fawley and held off a spirited attack to win by a length and a third. Excitement was intense when the final started, and a cheer arose when the signal showed that Leander, who had started at 42 to the Belgians' 43, led by half a length at the first signal. Despite a spurt by the Belgians Leander had almost a full length at Fawley, now rowing at 36 to the Belgians' 38. Leander just had the legs of the Belgians, and continued to inch ahead all the way to the finish, winning by two lengths. In the fours Magdalen and Leander easily won their heats against Canada and Holland, and Magdalen comfortably won the final against Leander. Leander provided both the British pairs, which duly reached the final with minimum exertion. J. R. K. Fenning and G. L. Thomson then won easily from G. E. Fairbairn and P. Verdon. It was a similar story in the Sculls, but the final in this case produced a good race in which H. T. Blackstaffe, of Vesta Rowing Club, held off a determined attack to win by just over a length from A. McCulloch of Leander.

1909–1910

There was a record entry for the Royal Regatta in 1909 and 'Les Braves Belges' returned with seven crew members who had won the Grand before. They did it again, though some thought that Magdalen might have stopped them if the Oxford men had not been drawn on the Berks Station with a strong 'Bushes' wind blowing. Forty-five races were won this year from the Bucks Station, to only eighteen from Berks. It was a popular win, however, for everyone agreed that the Belgians

JAMES NASH
1791–1856.
JOINT HON. SEC. HENLEY REGATTA 1839.

1. James Nash, the founder of the Regatta.
(From a portrait in Henley Town Hall.)

2. The finish of the Regatta and Henley Bridge
seen from Phyllis Court, c. 1853.

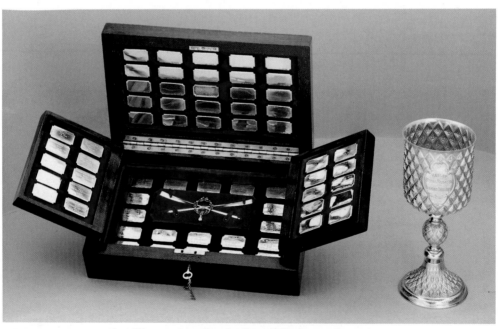

3 and 4. The trophies for the Grand Challenge Cup (*opposite*)
and the Diamond Sculls, and the Pineapple Cup (*above*).
The Regatta's other trophies appear in Appendix 3.

4

*'One of
the summer's
great
occasions.'*

5

6

7

8

9

10

11. Her Majesty the Queen arriving to open the Regatta's new Headquarters in 1986.
The building stands on the site of the Regatta's first boathouse and the Carpenter's Arms inn.

12. Looking downstream to Henley Bridge
with the new Headquarters on the right.

13. The Regatta's new Headquarters ablaze with light.

had taught British rowing a salutary lesson in the past five years. Supported by the Burgermaster of Ghent they danced in joy after their victory and John Cooper had difficulty in extracting himself from the demonstration, claiming he was 'too old to play Round the Mulberry Bush'.

The weather was rough again in 1910, but there was an unusually large number of close races. One was of historic interest. A strong south-westerly 'Bushes' wind in those days was reckoned to be decisive if crews were closely matched. On the day on which Magdalen faced Leander in the Grand semi-final Theodore Cook considered that the difference between the stations was 'at least two lengths'. That sounds unlikely, but there was nobody around at that time better qualified to judge. However that may be, Magdalen decided they had no chance if they remained on the Berkshire Station. Starting at 44 to Leander's 37 they were clear in 75 seconds. Their coxswain, A. W. F. Donkin, unhesitatingly steered across Leander's bows, making for the shelter of the famous 'Bushes', and two minutes after the start the crews were rowing in line-ahead. One touch would have brought disqualification but it is said that Donkin never looked round at Leander until beyond Fawley, when he took Magdalen back to the Berkshire side of the course. Exhausted by their early efforts Magdalen were nearly rowed out, but they made it to the finish with three-quarters of a length to spare. 'A. S. G. was sick,' wrote A. S. Garton, Magdalen's no. 6, in the margin of Cook's *Henley Races*. In the final Magdalen proved too strong for Jesus, Cambridge, who had beaten Thames R C by two feet. For the first time not one, but two, foreign crews reached the final of the Stewards' Cup. Mainzer Ruderverein from Germany were the heaviest crew yet to compete, with three men over 14 stone, but in the final they fell to Winnipeg R C, conceding nearly 4 stone a man.

1911 Magdalen won again from Jesus in the final of the Grand in 1911, but *The Times* correspondent thought that 'Eton's win in the Ladies' Plate ... was the most memorable achievement. Twice they touched the record, equalling it on Friday and beating it on the last day with 6 minutes 56 seconds against First Trinity. But the heroes were the veterans J. Beresford and A. Hamilton Cloutte, who won the Goblets. They were the oldest two men competing at the Regatta, their combined ages being 83 years ...'

Incidentally this was the year in which the finals were first held on the Saturday. It was also the year of HM King George V's Coronation, in celebration of which (quoting *The Times* again) there was a 'Maori procession in which about sixteen of the Te Arawa tribe paddled a war canoe over the full course ... making nearly sixty strokes a minute. On arriving in front of the enclosures the tribe chanted a Maori war song and indulged in several movements that much mystified us. The tribute was loudly cheered but the proceedings appeared to be a little out of place at Henley.'

1912–1913 Henley was honoured by its first visit from a reigning Sovereign in 1912. Leander, with a crew based on the recent Magdalen crews, were unexpectedly beaten by

Sydney Rowing Club, from Australia, in the final of the Grand. This result was reversed in the Olympic Regatta in Stockholm a fortnight later. W. D. Kinnear went out in the first round of the Diamond Sculls, and he too went on to win in Stockholm. After a gap of seven years Leander won the Grand again in 1913. In beating the Toronto Argonauts in a heat they equalled the record of 6 minutes 51 seconds, and if the timing was correct at Fawley, must have covered the second half of the course in 3 minutes 32 seconds. Mainzer Ruderverein beat Leander in a heat of the Stewards' by two feet, but lost the final to New College on a foul.

1914   Not only because it was to be the last Regatta at Henley for five years, 1914 was not a happy occasion for British rowing. In the four heats of the Grand Challenge Cup Winnipeg, Canada, beat Thames Rowing Club; Boston University, USA, beat London; Harvard Athletic Association beat Leander; and Mainz beat Jesus, Cambridge. Harvard went on to win and this was the crew which returned fifty years later for a celebratory outing at the scene of their triumph in 1964. The Stewards' Cup gave British supporters their only cause for comfort in 1914, when Leander rowed the Mainzer Ruderverein to a standstill at the bottom of Phyllis Court wall. John Cooper commented, with true-blue jingoism, 'so long as a German is top dog he can fight well and row well but once collared he showed in the race in 1914 as he was to show in 1918 that he is not endowed with the cut-and-come-again qualities of the Britisher.' The trouble about Henley Regatta in 1914 was that too many of the Britishers got 'collared' without the chance to 'cut and come again'.

10 Straight Course Between the Wars: 1919–1939

The rapidity of Henley's recovery from the 1914–18 war was remarkable. But whilst the two decades separating the two world wars may look today to have been 'business as usual' for the Royal Regatta, it was in fact a period of considerable change.

The two most obvious changes came quickly, with the foundation of the Stewards' Enclosure in 1919 and the switch to the Straight Course on the Berkshire side of Temple Island in 1924. Both are considered in Chapter 6. On the rowing front there were two less obvious, and more gradual, changes.

First, entries increased by around 60% between 1919 and 1939, with foreign entries almost doubling. Second, from 1924 onwards Oxford rowing at Henley virtually collapsed. To put this in perspective one has to remember that the support of the Oxford crews had been crucial to the Regatta's survival in the early years. Looking back only as far as the inauguration of the New Course, in 1896, Oxford had provided nearly as many finalists and winners as had the larger University of Cambridge. They continued to do so until 1924, providing nine finalists and six winners in the eight-oared events in the five-year period 1920–24. In the ensuing fifteen years only three crews from Oxford reached the finals of their events – and none was a winner.

Beyond pointing out that during these same fifteen years Oxford lost the University Boat Race thirteen times, and that Eton rowing, generally more important to Oxford than to Cambridge, was in decline at the same time, the reasons for this collapse are beyond the scope of this book. But the effect on the Ladies' Plate was profound.

1919 A letter appeared in *The Field* within a fortnight of the signing of the Armistice in November 1918, urging the revival of Henley. Leander took the initiative in calling a meeting of rowing men in January 1919. They concluded that it was too soon to revive the Royal Regatta, but requested the Stewards to stage a Peace Regatta. With difficulty this was achieved, and in the end a successful four-day Regatta took place for special events suited to the special circumstances. The King's Cup for eights, the Leander Cup and the Wargrave Manor Cup for fours were 'armed services' events, and the Hambleden Pairs and Kingswood Sculls were restricted to oarsmen and scullers from the 'allied countries'.

The Australian Army crew disposed of the Cambridge University Services crew in the semi-final of the King's Cup, and the Oxford Services crew in the final. It had been agreed that if the Oxford and Cambridge crews did not meet in the King's Cup they would row a private match. But with Oxford involved in the King's Cup final this proved to be impossible.

1920–1923 The revival of the Royal Regatta in 1920 saw the debut of two new Henley 'stars', Jack Beresford Jr and G. O. (Gully) Nickalls, son of Guy Nickalls. Nickalls was to become the most prolific winner of the Grand Challenge Cup of all time, and Beresford was to dominate British sculling for the ensuing twenty years.

Magdalen College, Oxford, with Nickalls at no. 7, easily won the Grand in 1920. In partnership with R. S. Lucas, Nickalls also won the Goblets, and four other members of the Magdalen crew won the Stewards' Cup.

This was the year in which the Committee refused to accept the entry of the American J. B. Kelly for the Diamond Sculls (see page 25). Beresford won without difficulty, and was subsequently runner-up to Kelly in the Olympic Single Sculls.

Magdalen won the Grand again in 1921 from Jesus, Cambridge. Oxford and Cambridge colleges have met in the final of the Grand Challenge Cup on seven occasions and three of these, in 1910, 1911 and 1921, were between these two colleges.

'As bad as it could be,' described the weather in 1922, but there was some compensation in a remarkable run of close finishes in the Thames Cup. On the Thursday Henley Rowing Club beat Kingston by two feet, only to succumb next day to Queens' College, Cambridge, by the same margin. London Rowing Club beat Jesus, Cambridge, by four feet. In the semifinal Worcester College beat Queens' by a third of a length after racing level all the way to the mile; and in the final they won from Clare by three feet.

G. O. Nickalls and Lucas won the Goblets again, recording the thirteenth and last Nickalls success in this event. One of Henley's finest fours won the Stewards' Cup under Eton Vikings colours, and the Visitors' under Third Trinity colours. They were to win the Stewards' Cup for Trinity for the next two years, culminating with an Olympic victory for Great Britain in 1924.

The shortened Experimental Course was used in 1923 (see page 69). Thames Rowing Club won the Grand for the first time since 1889, heralding a revival of London tideway rowing, inspired by the coaching of Steve Fairbairn.

It would be difficult for the oarsman of today to comprehend the passion which was generated by the controversy on rowing style which reached a peak during the 1920s and 1930s. 'Orthodoxy', as propounded in G. C. Bourne's *Textbook of Oarsmanship*, on the one hand, and 'Fairbairnism' on the other, became articles of faith to their supporters, and dire heresy to their opponents. One can only say that whilst the conflict between the two extremes may have been detrimental at the time, the interaction between them was beneficial to rowing in the long term.

1924 The full-length Straight Course was used for the first time in 1924, and in a blustery southwesterly wind which fully tested its fairness – and some might say quickly revealed its shortcomings. Forty-three races were won off the Bucks Station, and thirty-three off Berks.

Significantly, perhaps, Jesus College, making a double entry in the Grand and Ladies' Plate, lost the senior event to Leander by only six feet, rowing on the sheltered Bucks Station, and then, on the Berkshire Station, lost the Ladies' final to Shrewsbury by a length and a half. It was argued that Jesus had thrown away their chance by attempting both events, and also that Shrewsbury were an exceptionally fast school crew who might well have won the Grand this year. Their winning time, in a comparatively easy race, was only one second slower than that in which Leander won the Grand.

However that may be, the most remarkable race, without doubt, came in the final of the Goblets. Nickalls and Lucas, both Magdalen men though rowing under Leander colours, were confidently expected to thrash G. K. Hampshire and W. Philipps, also of Magdalen.

But, as C. T. Steward put it, 'It was not generally known that they (Nickalls and Lucas) were no mean carpenters and always carried a set of tools'. Before the start Lucas decided to reduce the weight of their boat by removing what he deemed to be unnecessary timber. On the first stroke Nickalls broke his stretcher and cracked the skin. Despite what amounted to a 'slow puncture' Nickalls and Lucas led at once. Then the Magdalen pair ran into the booms and Nickalls and Lucas waited for them to catch up. The loss of time rather than distance proved fatal, for although they were soon well ahead again they were beginning to sink. Hampshire and Philipps, plodding on like the legendary tortoise, were amazed to come up with the two hares, *nantes in gurgito vasto* near the mile post. After stopping to offer assistance they paddled on to the finish and offered a re-row. But the Committee ruled that the race had ended as soon as one boat passed the winning post.

1925–1927 Radley College reached the final of the Ladies' Plate for the fifth time in 1925, only to fail once more at the last fence; Lady Margaret were the winners by two lengths. In a David and Goliath relationship Radley had always aspired to beat Eton in the Ladies' Plate, but had never had the good fortune to meet them on the occasions when they might have succeeded. This year was one such, for in their semi-final Radley defeated Shrewsbury by a length and three-quarters, Shrewsbury having beaten Eton by two lengths and three-quarters.

In 1926 the Grand entries dropped to four, Leander winning for the third year in succession. Three inches of rain fell during Regatta week in 1927, but that certainly did not dampen the enthusiasm for Thames Rowing Club, who won the Grand, Stewards', Thames and Wyfold Cups. In the Grand final Thames beat London, and this, surprisingly, was only the second occasion when these great tideway rivals met in the final of Henley's premier trophy.

Kent School, U S A, came to Henley for the first time this year and went near to robbing Thames Rowing Club's second crew of their victory in the Thames Cup. In the opening round Kent were level at the mile post before Thames got away to win by a quarter of a length.

1928–1929 Thames R C had another good year in 1928, retaining the Grand, Stewards' and Thames Cup, losing the Wyfold Cup and gaining the Goblets through G. C. Killick and J. Beresford Jr. The Stewards' final was the race of the year, Thames beating London by two feet.

Two dead-heats compensated for bad weather in 1929, London beating the Argonaut Rowing Club of Canada by a quarter of a length in the re-row of the first heat of the Grand Challenge Cup, and Killick and Beresford beating H. R. Carver and T. R. B. Sanders in a re-row of a first-round Goblets heat. Killick and Beresford went on to win the event, but London lost to Leander.

Browne and Nichols School, USA achieved what Kent School had narrowly missed two years before, becoming the first of many American winners of the Thames Cup.

1930–1931 London Rowing Club came into their own in the early 1930s, winning the Grand in 1930, 1931 and 1933, the Thames Cup in 1931, 1932, and 1935, the Stewards' in 1930 and 1931, and the Wyfold Cup in 1930, 1932, 1933 and again in 1936–38.

One of London's greatest races came against the Berliner Ruder Club in 1931. In the Grand semi-final both crews started at 40. London had half a length lead at the Barrier, but Berlin came through at Fawley to lead by a third of a length at the mile. London, spurting at 40, seemed to be making no impression when the German crew came to a standstill, rowed out opposite the grandstand. In the final London had another hard race to beat Thames.

H. R. A. 'Jumbo' Edwards, partnered by L. Clive, narrowly beat the Kingston brothers, Dick and Jack Offer, to reach the final of the Goblets – the Offers hitting the booms near the mile post – but went on to win the final comfortably from W. A. T. Sambell and L. Luxton. This gave Edwards his third Henley medal, for he was also rowing in the London eight and four. Though three and even more wins had been achieved in the Regatta's early days, when entries were far fewer, this was, and indeed still is, the only instance in modern times of an oarsman winning three Henley events. In three days Edwards had beaten Harvard University, Berlin and Thames RC in the Grand, Brasenose and Piacenza, Italy, in the Stewards', and the Offers and Sambell and Luxton in the Goblets.

But that was not the end of the excitement in 1931. Bob Pearce, of Canada, an outstanding sculler who later turned professional, found himself matched in the first round of the Diamond Sculls against T. A. Brocklebank, better known as a Cambridge University stroke. With a weight advantage of three and a half stone Pearce was a 'dead cert', and it was said that some of the professional watermen had suggested that he should not beat the popular Tom Brocklebank by an excessive margin. Perhaps he took this advice without realizing that whilst Brocklebank was not in his class as a single sculler he was nevertheless a formidable racer. Having taken an early lead Pearce was content to scull a couple of lengths in front until, half-way along the enclosures, Brocklebank suddenly unleashed a spurt which him on level terms – before Pearce realized his danger. He countered – but only just in time.

C. T. Steward commented in his *Henley Records* that 'Pearce won comfortably by half a length'. This race is probably my earliest clear Henley memory for I had been taken, as a schoolboy, into the Stewards' Box on the finishing line. It may technically have been an 'easy' race, but I can vouchsafe that Bob Pearce looked anything but 'comfortable' during those last few strokes. One wonders what might have happened if Brocklebank had delayed his attack for a few strokes – a 'comfortable defeat' perhaps?

1932   Selections for the Los Angeles Olympics were at stake in 1932. Leander, represented by the Cambridge Boat Race crew, fought off desperate attacks by Thames Rowing Club to win the Grand by half a length. Thames won comfortably in the Stewards'. In the Goblets Edwards and Clive forced a dead heat with the Offer brothers on Thursday, won the re-row which took place on Friday, and the final, without difficulty, on Saturday.

Shrewsbury won the Ladies' Plate for the second time in their history, and it is worth looking at the situation in the Ladies' at that time. Entries were limited to sixteen, with elimination races on the Saturday before the Regatta. In 1931 there had been twenty-one entries of which one-third were from schools. Two schools and three Oxbridge colleges were eliminated, Eton and Bedford reached the quarter-finals, Monkton Combe reached the semi-finals, and Shrewsbury lost the final by a third of a length to Jesus. In 1932 there were twenty-three entries of which three schools and four colleges were eliminated. Monkton Combe reached the quarter-final and Shrewsbury were the winners. The stronger school crews certainly reckoned themselves to be at no disadvantage against colleges in that era.

1933–1934   In 1933 eliminating races were abandoned except for the Diamond Sculls.

Kent School became the second American school to win the Thames Cup, and the Diamonds, which had been dominated by foreign scullers since Beresford's last win in 1926, produced an all-British final, won by T. G. Askwith from H. L. Warren. This was the only home final in thirty-seven years (1926–1962).

A dry summer and a light following breeze during Regatta week triggered a spate of records in 1934. But perhaps the most impressive performance was in an event in which the course record was not broken. Dr Buhtz of Berliner Ruderclub was suffering from lumbago, and sparing his back as far as possible. He cleared every opponent before the top of Temple Island, and in the final was two lengths clear of W. Rutherford of the United States at the end of the first minute. Leading by four lengths, and paddling, he was 5 seconds inside F. S. Kelly's 1905 record of 3 min. 55 sec. at Fawley. Unpressed he went on to equal Kelly's 8 min. 10 sec. overall.

1935–1936   Having won the Stewards' Cup for two years, Pembroke College, Cambridge, took the Grand in 1935, the first college crew to do so since Magdalen in 1921. The Stewards' Cup went to one of the all-time great coxless fours, FC Zurich, who knocked no less than ten seconds off the record set by Pembroke in the previous year. This was the only record set in 1935, indicating Zurich's exceptional quality.

Zurich cruised to victory in both the Grand and the Stewards' in 1936, and set tongues wagging in the enclosures with a vengeance. The orthodox hailed them as the finest crews they had seen in decades. But the truth was that FC Zurich was a football club, with a rowing section, and claimed to have learned their rowing by reading Fairbairn's books and studying a film of recent Pembroke crews.

Among Zurich's victims in the Grand was the Tokyo Imperial University crew, en route to the Berlin Olympic Games. At Marlow Regatta, two weeks before Henley, the Japanese impressed by winning with rates of striking well into the 50s. At Henley they beat Quintin in their first heat of the Grand, spurting to 56 at the finish. Was there to be a sensation? Next day they started at 48, but Zurich, at 43, rowed right away from them, winning in the end by a humiliating six lengths.

Three American schools reached the semi-finals of the Thames Cup, and this was the start of a long period of domination of this event by crews from across the Atlantic. Tabor Academy were the winners this year, and their Henley debut caused something of a furore, just as Royal Chester's had when they first arrived eighty years before. For if Zurich were per-fection to English eyes, Tabor were the opposite. To quote what I wrote in *Henley Regatta* in 1956, they 'seemed to do almost everything that it is possible to do wrong in a boat. They had no balance, and could not keep their blades off the water; they scarcely even kept time. How we all laughed – until they romped away with the Thames Cup. We had to keep on laughing, too, for they did the same thing three times in the next four years'.

1937–1938   There were few excitements in 1937, though Jesus, Cambridge, put up a spir-ited defence of the Grand Challenge Cup, losing by half a length to Rudergesellschaft

Wiking. In the Ladies' Plate Magdalen rowed a dead heat with Clare, who won the re-row by a quarter of a length, and the final by a length from First Trinity.

Radley at last achieved their ambition of winning the Ladies' Plate in 1938, but once again the draw deprived them of a chance of beating Eton, who fell to Pembroke, Cambridge, by a length in the semi-final. In the final Radley took a length off Pembroke along the enclosures to win by a length and a quarter.

After thirty-three years F. S. Kelly's Dia-monds record of 8 min. 10 sec. finally fell. J. W. Burk of Pennsylvania, who had evolved his own unique style of sculling at an exceptionally high rate of striking, was never pressed. In the final, against L. D. Habbits of Reading, he started at 44 and never dropped below 39. Leading by four lengths at Fawley he saw that his time of 3 min. 51 sec. was only one second outside Dr Buhtz's best, and went on for the course record, finishing in 8 min. 2 sec.

1939   To celebrate the Centenary in 1939 the Stewards sent invitations to all the Dominions and to all foreign countries which had signed Agreements with the Regatta. They also offered for competition a pair of silver cups as pres-entation prizes for a special event to be called the Centenary Double Sculls. This was the first time Henley had ever solicited foreign entries. Numerically the response was not great, three each for the Grand, Thames, Wyfold and Double Sculls, five for the Diamonds and one for the Stewards'. But it was sufficient to bring about the discomfiture of British rowing.

Harvard University beat Argonaut RC of

Canada in the final of the Grand; Zurich beat Oriel in the Stewards'; and Tabor beat Kent School in the final of the Thames Cup. Burk returned to defend his Diamonds title, complaining that he had missed two weeks training since the previous Henley. But he did not have it all his own way this time. Two lengths down to R. Verey of Poland at the quarter-mile signal, he touched the booms near the Barrier and was still a length down at Fawley, striking 36. Spurting to 40, Burk then took the lead to win by just over a length.

The race of the Regatta, however, came in the final of the new Double Sculls event. Jack Beresford and Dick Southwood, veteran winners of the Olympic Double Sculls in 1936, were giving away twenty-four years and three stone in weight to G. Scherli and E. Broschi of Italy, and against a head wind in the final. Beresford and Southwood led by half a length at the Barrier but the Italians came through at Fawley and led in turn by half a length at the mile. In a tremendous finishing spurt along the enclosures Beresford and Southwood fought back to force a dead-heat.

As this was a special event, with no challenge trophy, the Committee decided against ordering a re-row and gave presentation cups to all four scullers. Perhaps they were not uninfluenced, too, by the fact that Beresford was forty-one years of age, and Southwood thirty-six.

It was a fitting climax to the Centenary Regatta. Two months later Europe was once again engulfed in war and the Royal Regatta in abeyance for the second time in its history.

11 Back in Business: 1940–1953

1940–1945   A limited Schools Regatta was planned in July 1940, but cancelled in view of the serious war situation after the evacuation of the British army from Dunkirk. Oxford and Cambridge rowed boat races at Henley in 1940 and 1945, and School Regattas were organized by Eton in 1941, 1942 and 1943.

In 1945 a 'Royal Henley Regatta' – so called to distinguish it from the regular 'Henley Royal Regatta' – was organized two months after the end of hostilities in Europe and whilst the war in the Far East was still in progress. Inevitably it was on a makeshift two-day basis, and rowed three-abreast over a course starting at the Remenham Barrier. Imperial College, London, won the Danesfield Cup for Eights from the Royal Australian Air Force and Jesus College, Cambridge. In the Hedsor Cup for Schools Radley won from Eton and Bedford, whilst the Barrier Cup for Scullers was won by W. E. C. Horwood from H. P. Henry.

1946–1947   By 1946 the Royal Regatta was back in business in earnest. There were 110 entries, compared with 127 in 1939, and gratifyingly the Grand, Goblets, Double Sculls and Diamonds all produced international finals. Leander beat RC Zurich in the Grand, and their spares, the eighteen-year-old twins, J. F. and C. G. Burgess, raced O. Secher and P. Paerregaard of Denmark to a standstill at the mile to win the Goblets. The exhausted Danish pair capsized.

The Double Sculls became a permanent event this year, but, being a new event in Britain, only two home entries were received, one of which withdrew. Then J. H. Neame, stroking the Trinity Hall double, injured his hand a few days before the Regatta. The only foreign entry came from R. E. Panelo and E. D. Chafuen from Buenos Aires. Substitutes are not permitted in the individual Henley events, but on this occasion, to give the Argentinians a race, the Committee invited H. L. Warren, who had sculled for Britain in the Berlin Olympics but had not raced at Henley since 1936, to take Neame's place. This he sportingly did, but Panelo and Chafuen inevitably won with some ease.

Five English crews entered for the Grand Challenge Cup in 1947, indicating the resurgence of rowing after the war. Leander were favourites but it was Jesus's year. They slipped Leander at the mile in a heat, and Delftsche Sport, Holland, at Remenham Club, in the final.

Kent School and Tabor Academy, who had been absent in 1946, quickly restored the pattern of American domination in the Thames Cup, Kent beating Tabor by two lengths in the final.

The Princess Elizabeth Cup, introduced in 1946 to encourage school rowing, attracted only six entries in 1947, Eton, Monkton Combe, Radley, St Edward's and Bryanston all preferring the Ladies' Plate, in which Eton beat

Monkton Combe in the semi-final but lost to First and Third Trinity in the final. Stroking this Eton eight was C. G. V. Davidge, destined to become one of the most successful Henley oarsmen of the post-war era.

1948   In 1948 Henley became the first town in the world to stage two Olympic Regattas. Unlike 1908, when there had been only a fortnight between the Royal and the Olympic Regattas, there was a full month this time. The Royal Regatta was not closed to foreign entries, and although not many were received there was added interest from the fact that Olympic selection was at stake for many of the British crews.

Thames Rowing Club had a struggle with Leander in a heat of the Grand, just edging ahead in the last quarter of a mile to win by half a length. The final they won comfortably from a combined Jesus and Pembroke crew.

W. G. R. M. Laurie and J. H. T. Wilson returned from their jobs in the Sudan, after a ten-year absence from Henley, to take the Goblets title which they had won in 1938. The Diamond Sculls were dominated by the Australian, Mervyn Wood, but he was hard pressed in a heat by A. D. Rowe. In the Double Sculls B. Piessens and W. A. Collet, of Belgium, beat two of the British Olympic aspirants, R. F. Winstone and R. D. Burnell, and W. E. C. Horwood and D. C. H. Garrod, by the same margin of two lengths.

Four schools entered for the Ladies' Plate, and Eton, the only one of the four not to enter also for the Princess Elizabeth Cup, were the winners. Bryanston won through the Ladies' Plate heats to make it an all-schools final for the first time since 1893, pressing Eton to two-thirds of a length at the finish. Bryanston withdrew from the semi-final of the Princess Elizabeth Cup because they had qualified for the quarter-final of the Ladies'. Bedford also had a fine crew and won the Princess Elizabeth Cup with some ease.

So far as Olympic selections were concerned, Henley had not been very helpful. Thames had an ineligible Swiss national rowing in their eight, and opted to go for the Olympic Coxless Fours. The Leander eight, based on Cambridge University, proved also to have an ineligible oarsman, but won the Olympic nomination with two changes in their order. In the Double Sculls Burnell had to take a new partner, B. H. T. Bushnell, and sculled and won a trial against Horwood and Garrod. Only Laurie and Wilson in the pair, single sculler Tony Rowe, and Thames Rowing Club in the four could be said to have proved themselves beyond a peradventure in the Royal Regatta.

Henley Regatta racing, of course, is on a 'sudden death' knockout basis. International racing is on a 'repêchage' system, which, without going into the small print, means that no competitor is eliminated until beaten twice. For the 1948 Olympic Regatta the Henley course was widened to provide three lanes. To avoid having corners this entailed moving the start to the top of Temple Island. The distance was then about twenty metres short of the official distance of 2,000 metres. The repêchage system cannot work satisfactorily with only three racing lanes. But the fact was that the resumption of the Olympic Games so soon after the war, and the faith which international sportsmen had in Britain's ability to organize the Games, and in Henley's ability to stage the Olympic Regatta, was such that everyone accepted such problems in good part.

Twenty-seven nations competed in the Olympic rowing which produced many hotly contested races. America's University of California were dominant in the Eights, with Great Britain as runners-up. Laurie and Wilson in the Coxless Pairs, and Bushnell and Burnell in the Double Sculls provided welcome gold-medal victories for the home crowd. The Coxless Fours fell to Italy, and the Coxed Fours to the United States. Denmark took the Coxed Pairs, and Australia the Single Sculls.

1949–1951 'After the turmoil of the Olympic year, 1949 brought a welcome return to the old order of things' was my own verdict in *Henley Regatta – A History* (OUP 1957). On reflection I might have added 'for the last time', for Henley was now approaching momentous changes in the pattern of foreign competition. So perhaps the years 1949–53 should be seen as 'the last session' of the old order of things.

However that may be, 1949 was a successful and entertaining year. There was a record of 156 starters, and with the lowest flow of water in the river since 1921, and favourable wind conditions, race records tumbled on every side.

Trinity, winning the Stewards' Cup in record time, became the first Oxford college to win a Henley event since Magdalen in 1921. In the Grand they beat Delftsche Sport, Holland, by three feet, and fell to Leander in the semi-final. In this race Leander, easing up at the finish, equalled the course record of 6 min. 44 sec. A few minutes earlier Lady Margaret had

achieved 6 min. 43 sec. in the Ladies' Plate. The pity was that Lady Margaret had entered for the second event, for they would certainly have had a fine race against Leander.

Lensbury scored their first Henley victory in winning the Wyfold Cup, and in the semi-final lowered the record by 11 seconds to 7 min. 24 sec.

The Committee limited the Ladies' Plate – and indeed all events except the Thames and Wyfold Cups – to sixteen crews this year, hoping to encourage some of the stronger schools to remain loyal to the Ladies' Plate. The result was that only five schools entered for the new Princess Elizabeth Cup, whilst of the seven which went for the Ladies', three were eliminated before the Regatta started.

No doubt as a result of this experience all the schools except Eton switched to the Princess Elizabeth Cup in 1950. It was not a happy year for British rowing, for Leander were put out of the Grand by Njord, Holland, who lost to Harvard in the final, whilst in the final of the Stewards' Cup they damaged an outrigger in hitting one of the piles, losing to Hellerup, Denmark. There was however a sculling compensation when A. D. Rowe became the first Englishman to win the Diamonds since 1933.

Cambridge had great success in 1951. Against foreign entries from Holland, Spain and Italy, Lady Margaret were comfortable winners of the Grand, Pembroke won the Ladies' Plate from Jesus, whilst C. B. M. Lloyd, Lady Margaret's stroke, and J. G. P. Crowden, no. 7 for Pembroke, together won the Goblets. Trinity Hall won the Visitors' from First and Third Trinity, Caius won the

Wyfold Cup from Clare, and T. A. Fox, of Pembroke, won the Diamonds from A. E. Larsen of Denmark. Finally, P. Bradley, lately of Pembroke, won the Double Sculls in partnership with R. D. Burnell, who thus enjoyed the doubtful distinction of being the only Oxford man to appear in the finals.

Administratively, 1951 demonstrated the difficulties – some may think partly self-inflicted – which the Committee were encountering in their effort to balance and rationalize the Ladies' Plate and Thames Cup entries. The limitation recently imposed on the Ladies' Plate drove many Oxbridge crews into the Thames Cup. This resulted in a record entry of forty-nine, including twenty from Oxford and Cambridge. Two crews scratched, and thirty had to take part in eliminating races before the Regatta opened.

1952–1953 In 1952 the impending Olympic Regatta in Helsinki reduced the number of foreign entries but brought a welcome compensation in entries from Australia, Canada and the first-ever from New Zealand.

In the final of the Grand, Leander Club faced Sydney Rowing Club, just as they had before the Stockholm Olympics in 1912. But this time the roles were reversed. At Henley, after leading the Australians by a length and a quarter after half a mile, Leander was almost caught at the mile post before drawing away again to win by half a length, setting a new record of 6 min. 38 sec. In Helsinki the Australians beat Leander, rowing for Great Britain, but this time, unfortunately, their placings were

third and fourth, not first and second as they had been forty years earlier.

The New Zealanders proved to be not quite good enough in the Stewards'. Mervyn Wood was too strong for Fox in the Diamond Sculls; but his Australian compatriots, J. Rodgers and M. Riley, lost the Double Sculls final to R. M. A. George and J. Van Stichel of Antwerp.

In the Goblets it fell to H. C. I. Bywater and T. H. Christie, of Westminster Hospital, to lower the record set in the famous dead-heat of 1911. In the semi-final Bywater and Christie won easily in 8 min. 5 sec; in the final next day they were one second slower.

Soon after the 1952 Regatta came the sad news of the death of Sir Harcourt Gold, OBE, the President of Henley Royal Regatta.

If 1953 was the end of an era, or 'sub-era' in Henley history – 'Henley before the Russians' one might label it – it was nevertheless a vintage year in its own right.

A very fine Leander eight won the Grand, safely if not easily, from the Union Sportive Metropolitaine des Transports, France, and made it a double with a win over First and Third Trinity in the Stewards'. More remarkably perhaps, because of the number of races involved, the Royal Air Force achieved the double in the Thames and Wyfold Cups, this being the first time that the same four men had won these two events since Trinity Hall in· 1901. Furthermore it was the first time since 1936 that the Thames Cup did not cross the Atlantic, with the exception of 1946 when no American crews were at Henley. There were no less than forty-one entries of which eighteen had to take part in the eliminating races. The problem of eliminating races was well illustrated, for four of the nine winners had easier races in the first round of the Regatta itself: Corpus Christi, Cambridge, went on to reach the semi-finals; Maidenhead, Peterhouse and St Catharine's all reached the quarter-finals; whilst Queen's College, Oxford, and Jesus, Cambridge, survived to the third round. Undoubtedly there were some unlucky crews amongst those who failed to qualify this year. The R A F ensured a British victory by holding on to win by a third of a length from Princeton University in the semi-final. Altogether the R A F raced ten times to win the two events.

The individual events, though less closely contested, produced outstanding performances. In the Goblets R. Baetens and M. Knuysen of Antwerp clipped seven seconds off the record set in 1952, and on the next day lowered the record by a further seven seconds, to 7 min. 51 sec., without any significant opposition. R. George, a 14-stoner from Liège, became the first man to scull over the Henley course in 8 minutes, but in the final was cracked by T. A. Fox. And a new Double Sculls record of 7 min. 21 sec. – only one second slower than the Wyfold record – was set by E. Schriever and P. Stebler of Zurich.

The only event which was in some measure disappointing in 1953 was the Ladies' Plate, which attracted only eleven entries. And that had the compensation of a school crew, Radley, in the final. They led Jesus by three feet at the mile, but lost in the end by three-quarters of a length.

12 A New Era – Challenge from the East: 1954–1974

1954 The new era to which we have already referred, and which began in 1954, may be described as the 'Russian era'. In the ensuing ten years they won the Grand and Stewards' five times, the Goblets twice and the Double Sculls three times. But the significance for Henley went beyond the winning of these events. Leander Club, after all, had been more dominant during previous decades than the crews from half a dozen clubs in the Soviet Union were during this decade. What changed the pattern at Henley, and arguably worldwide, in 1954, was the advent of a fully integrated 'national team'. For the first time we see a team covering all the open events, arriving complete with coaches, team managers, doctors, and physiotherapists. Inevitably the standard required to win the open events had to rise dramatically. Later, to meet this challenge, the West Germans, followed by the East Germans and ultimately the British themselves, followed suit. And there were casualties along the way. Top clubs and universities from both sides of the Atlantic found it increasingly frustrating to enter for events in which they would face national crews preparing for European, World and Olympic Championships.

Unfortunately British rowing was at a low ebb this year. Thames Rowing Club lost by half a length to Krylia Sovetov in the semi-final of the Grand. But the Russians looked to have something in hand, and easily beat Leander in the final. A record entry of eleven fours, five of them from overseas, produced some unusually poor steering, and only mediocre competition in the Stewards' Cup. The only verdict under one length was between two Soviet fours, Krylia Sovetov and Avangard. But the Royal Air Force, conceding more than a stone a man, raced gallantly to hold Krylia Sovetov to a length and a quarter in the final.

Due to two withdrawals, S. L. Blom and R. Gitz, of Holland, reached the Goblets final without a race; but they were no match for I. Buldakov and V. Ivanov who gave Russia her third victory. In the Diamond Sculls P. Vlasic of Yugoslavia, the European Single Sculls champion, raced the Russian Y. Tukalov, the 1952 Olympic champion, to a standstill just beyond Fawley. In the final Vlasic, showing signs of cumulative fatigue, several times encroached on the water of his Swiss opponent, A. Colomb. In the end he won by six feet and the umpire rejected a Swiss appeal for interference, that not being an offence under the then Henley code. T. A. Fox, partnered by the veteran A. J. Marsden, unexpectedly despatched the Russians, G. Zhilin and I. Emchuk, in the Double Sculls, but the trophy was retained quite easily by the holders, E. Schriever and P. Stebler, of Zurich.

With the only other event open to foreign competition – the Thames Cup – going to the Massachusetts Institute of Technology, this was statistically the worst Regatta to date for the home crews.

1955 Despite the discomfiture of the British, the first visit of Soviet crews to Henley had been an undoubted success. One or two less reputable newspapers tried to manufacture a dispute over national anthems and flags, which some of the Russians expected but which Henley, of course, have never used. Unhappily their return in 1955 was a different story. One hastens to add that this had nothing to do with the oarsmen. For once Henley Regatta was caught up in a political row of major proportions.

The trouble arose from a strike in the London Docks, which held up the arrival of boats for a number of overseas competitors. The Russians' boats were on board a Russian freighter which was lying thirty-seventh in the queue of ships waiting to dock. Every effort was made by the Regatta Committee, and in the end by the Dock Union too, to overcome this problem, and by the Thursday before the Regatta clearance was obtained for the Russian freighter to dock ahead of her turn, and a volunteer team of oarsmen members of the National Dock Labour Board Sports Association were standing by to unload. But the Soviet shipping agent insisted that the entire cargo, and not just the racing boats, should be unloaded, to which there was not the slightest chance that the Union would agree. In the meantime the Russians, along with several other foreign crews, were practising in borrowed boats. Then, at 10 a.m. on the opening day of the Regatta, there came a bombshell from Henley, in the form of an announcement which read: 'We, the Soviet oarsmen, having discussed the situation which is the result of the fact that the Secretariat of the Henley Royal Regatta has failed in getting our boats off the ship, have decided to withdraw from all events and not to participate in the Henley Royal Regatta.'

Not many people believed that the Russian oarsmen had been allowed much of a say in this decision, and many were prepared to accept that the use of the word 'failed' was a result of bad translation rather than an intentional accusation. But by any mature reckoning the decision was, as *The Times* put it, 'incomprehensible, since, rowing in borrowed boats, it seemed that they had everything to win, and very little to lose'. But perhaps the Russian officials had other thoughts, for the public announcement of their crews' scratchings did have the effect of concentrating the mind of the shipping agent, who swiftly withdrew his unacceptable demands in the docks. The boats came ashore, and at 6.15 p.m. on the same day the Committee issued a statement:

> The Soviet crews have requested that they may be allowed to cancel their withdrawal from the Regatta. In the exceptional circumstances the Committee of Management have agreed to the readmission of crews competing in those events which have not yet begun.

So at the end of the day the price was paid only by the unfortunate Yuri Tukalov whose opening heat in the Diamond Sculls had already gone by default.

Rowing still in a borrowed boat, Krasnoe Znamia opened with a hard race against Jesus in the Grand, winning by half a length. Next day they reverted to their own boat, which some thought too small for them. After a quarter of a mile they led Vancouver by three-quarters of a length, but the Canadians took the lead at Fawley and stormed ahead along the enclosures to win by a length and a quarter amidst scenes of wild enthusiasm. The Henley crowd would have loved to see the Canadians go on to their first Grand victory, but it was not to be. University of Pennsylvania, who incidentally had circumvented the strike by persuading the US Air Force to fly their boat across the Atlantic, just had the edge in the final, and beat Vancouver by a third of a length.

Russia retained the Goblets title, and won the Double Sculls by the narrow margin of half a length from Switzerland. Bowman in the Swiss pair was T. Keller, destined to become President of the International Rowing Federation and a Steward of Henley Royal Regatta.

1956–1957 The year 1956 was not a vintage one, and not only because the Russians stayed away. The Olympic Games were due to take place in Australia, in the winter, and this probably affected the entries in the open events. There was however one first-rate challenger for the Grand, the French Army crew which was the heaviest crew (av. 13 st. 2 lb) yet to row at Henley. In the semi-final, against Jesus, who had unexpectedly despatched Leander, the French crew lost about two and a half lengths when their stroke man came off his seat at the start, yet caught Jesus at Fawley, and in the final had no difficulty in beating Roddklubben Three Towns, Sweden.

For the first time since 1861 Eton did not enter for the Ladies' Plate, but went for the Princess Elizabeth Cup which they duly won, but only after hard races against Shrewsbury,

and, in the final, an excellent St Paul's crew. It would be rash to deduce that they might have won the Ladies' more easily from the fact that their winning time was 16 seconds faster than the time in which Peterhouse won that event, for this was a year of variable headwind conditions. But it certainly did suggest that the best of the school crews were still very much a match for most of the colleges.

British prospects were bleak in 1957. *The Times* commented:

> The British have the reputation of being good losers – some say because they have so much practice at it . . . Henley permits only one chance . . . and to be frank it looks as though that will be sufficient to put an end to most British hopes.

This gloomy forecast would have been depressingly correct if it had not been for a super-human performance by two veterans of a decade of Henley racing, D. A. T. Leadley and C. G. V. Davidge, in the Goblets. In the semi-final M. Plaksin and S. Soldatov of the Soviet Union led them by half a length at the Barrier, 4 seconds inside the record. At Fawley the Russians still had half a length, but then Leadley and Davidge began to fight back. Spurting to 35 they came within a canvas at the mile. Then, at the bottom of the enclosures, Plaksin and Soldatov stopped dead, completely rowed out. In the final the Leander pair went for a lead, well aware of the finishing power of their opponents, A. Kloimstein and A. Sageder of Austria. At Fawley Leadley and Davidge led by just under two lengths. Then the Austrians began to close. Davidge fought them off, at 36, but it was desperately close, and the exhausted

British pair actually hit the booms on their last stroke – but they were home with a third of a length to spare.

In the Grand, Cornell University caught Krasnoe Znamia of the Soviet Union at the mile and an eighth, to win by a length, and then beat Yale by the same margin in the final. In the Diamond Sculls a new star was born when the youthful Australian, S. A. Mackenzie, reversed the result of the previous year's Olympics by beating the Russian, V. Ivanov, by four feet. It was a dramatic and controversial victory, as many of Mackenzie's subsequent successes were to prove. For, snatching an early lead, the Australian sculled in front of Ivanov for most of the distance, and when Ivanov suddenly spurted to 40 at the finish Mackenzie had no time to give way, and instead of running into him which would have given him the verdict on a foul, Ivanov touched the booms.

The Thames Cup was still the preserve of the Americans at this time, but the 1957 final deserves special mention. National Provincial Bank were attempting the Thames–Wyfold Cup double, as was not unusual with British clubs, but would no doubt have been regarded as insanity by our American friends. So, with four of their crew members rowing their ninth race, National Provincial faced the Princeton University lightweights, rowing their fifth race, in the Thames Cup final. Princeton led for most of the way, but the Bank drew almost level at the enclosures before the Americans drew away to win by a length. Inevitably some said that this was not a sensible way to meet foreign challengers. But for NPB their 'insurance' did pay off, for their four, in their tenth race, won the Wyfold Cup with some ease.

1958   To say that the prelude to the 1958 Regatta was inauspicious would be something of an understatement. At the draw Chairman Harold Rickett declared that on the previous day 10,000 gallons of water had been pumped out of the crews' changing tents. Nor were the prospects for the home crews at all rosy. But despite the abominable weather the racing turned out to be magnificent.

'Thunder and lightning signified the clash of the giants in the first round of the Grand' reported *The Times* Rowing Correspondent. But the University of Washington could not match Trud Club, Leningrad, who led all the way, and went on to overwhelm London Rowing Club next day, and Leichardt, Australia, in the final. But a welcome British revival saw Barn Cottage hold off Washington in one semi-final of the Stewards', whilst in the other National Provincial Bank caught Leningrad along the enclosures. In the final Barn Cottage had to rate 40 from the mile signal to beat National Provincial.

In the Goblets Leadley and Davidge retained their title with some ease, despatching Buldakov and Ivanov, winners in 1954 and 1955, in a heat, and R. Streuli and G. Kottmann of Switzerland in the final. And this time Mackenzie won the Diamonds final convincingly from Ivanov. Though with the same initial this, of course, is not the same Ivanov who rowed in the Russian pair.

1959–1960   Occasionally Henley seems to have a quiet year for no obvious reason, and 1959 was one such. However there was a touch of historical interest, as Oxford ended the hundred years' spell during which neither

Oxford nor Cambridge entered a representative crew at the Regatta. Perhaps one should say 'almost', for they labelled this one 'Isis'. Harvard were the only overseas entry, and they arrived with a boat named *Grand Challenge Cup 1914*, proclaiming their intent to repeat their first success at Henley. Oxford countered by painting *1869* on their bows, recalling the only occasion when Oxford and Harvard had clashed, albeit at Putney. They met in the semi-final, when Harvard won a hard race by half a length, going on to beat Thames with some ease in the final.

Oxford had some compensation when an excellent St Edmund Hall crew beat Nereus, Holland, and then Moto Guzzi, Italy, to win the Stewards' Cup. And a remarkable pair, R. B. Norton and H. H. Scurfield, of Hertford College, Oxford, who had not been considered for places in the University crew, romped away with the Goblets. The Australian, S. A. Mackenzie, scored his third Diamonds win, and in partnership with C. G. V. Davidge became the first and indeed the only man to win both sculling events in the same year at Henley.

The lull in the onslaught of foreign challengers continued in 1960. Apart from the Thames Cup, which had become the preserve of American universities – only one home win since 1946 – the only trophy to go abroad this year was the Grand. Even the Diamond Sculls, which Mackenzie won for the fourth time, stayed at home, since he sculled under Leander colours.

Oxford tried again for the Grand, this time under their University title. They despatched Yale in a heat and pushed Molesey to a third of a length in the final. Molesey at this time were as near to being a 'national' crew as it was possible to be before a national squad was set up. The members of their winning Grand eight split into two fours in the Stewards' Cup, four of them losing in the semi-final to the holders, St Edmund Hall, whilst the other four, as Barn Cottage Boat Club, dismissed the only overseas challengers, Belvoir, Zurich, in the other semi-final, going on to beat St Edmund Hall by four lengths in record time in the final.

Two members of the Oxford crew, I. L. Elliott and D. C. Rutherford, won the Goblets. In the first round of the Thames Cup, Harvard had to set new records all over the course to beat Isis by three-quarters of a length, and in the semi-final they held off Tideway Scullers School by only a quarter of a length. In the final they won fairly easily from Detroit Boat Club. During the week, in the Ladies' Plate, Eton twice covered the course in 6 min. 50 sec., which was the fastest time hitherto recorded by a school crew. In the final they just had the legs of Jesus to win by half a length.

1961 The Russians returned to Henley in 1961, winning two and losing two events. But pride of place this year surely went to S. A. Mackenzie, back in his Australian Mosman Rowing Club colours. History records that he won each of his Diamonds heats by only half a length. But this was a measure of his confidence and guile rather than an indication of close racing. In the final he was never in the slightest difficulty against O. Tjurin of Leningrad. This was Mackenzie's fifth Diamonds, equalling the record of J. Lowndes in 1879–83.

The Russians' second defeat came in the Double Sculls. A. Berkutov and Y. Tukalov, winners in 1957 and 1958, started as favourites but met their match in G. C. Justicz of Birmingham RC and N. J. Birkmyre of Aerial RC, who led all the way to win the final impressively by nearly two lengths.

The Russians' success came in the Grand and Stewards'. This year Molesey concentrated on their eight, and were widely fancied. But they were decisively beaten in their first race by Leander, with a crew drawn from recent Oxford crews. In the final Leander, though always close, could not quite match the strength of the USSR Navy Club.

Finland made their first entries at Henley this year and their excellent pair, V. Lehtela and T. Pitkanen, were easy winners in the Goblets. The Finnish double fell in a heat to Berkutov and Tukalov; and in the Thames Cup their eight lost narrowly to Eliot House, Harvard, who in turn lost the semi-final by only a third of a length to London University, winners of the final from Jesus College, Cambridge.

1962 Entries reached 200 for the first time in 1962. The quality was exceptional too, and favourable conditions led to the setting of many new records. Yet at the end of the week *The Times* reported 'Golden Henley spoiled by dull finals … every final won easily except one which was lost easily. This, the final of the Grand, was the only race in which the boats were overlapping at the finish'. *The Times* correspondent explained that this race was not won easily because the Soviet Navy crew had to fight all the way: but it appeared to have been 'lost easily' because the Italian Moto Guzzi

crew, immaculate and looking even better than the Russians, lost by a third of a length without any noticeable finishing spurt, and apparently scarcely out of breath.

But that was at the end of a dramatic week. The Grand semi-finals had seen Molesey against the Russian Navy, and Pennsylvania, USA against Moto Guzzi, Italy. Molesey had previously forced their way past Leander to reach that semi-final. And the Molesey men were attempting a quite unrealistic Grand–Stewards' Cup double. Predictably both halves of the eight failed too in the Stewards', in which Trud Leningrad gave Russia their second victory.

Once again the Russians won two and lost two, in the same events as in the preceding year. Justicz and Birkmyre disposed of O. Tjurin and B. Dubrovsky in the Doubles. Dubrovsky beat Birkmyre in the Diamonds, but then fell to W. L. Barry; his partner Tjurin fell to the Pole, E. Kubiak. Mackenzie, sculling for Leander, beat Barry in the final for his sixth Diamonds title. But this was not a happy story. Sculling in the semi-final against E. Kubiak of Poland, Mackenzie was several times warned for his steering. When he gave way, near the mile, the Pole moved across with him as often happens when scullers, and indeed coxless crews, are under pressure. Mackenzie seemed to falter, Kubiak in turn was warned, but before he could give way Mackenzie closed up, and caught a crab when his left scull went into the puddle left by Kubiak's right scull. Kubiak crossed the line several lengths ahead, and Mackenzie claimed and was awarded a foul. Passing the press box the Australian called out, 'If you can't beat them, fool them,' thus clearly proclaiming that he had deliberately engineered the foul. That is legitimate, but not very popular.

Public sympathy was with Kubiak, but not for long, for the Polish team manager then issued a statement criticizing the umpire, and withdrawing the other Polish entry, M. Siejkowski and K. Nasrecki, who by this time had reached the semi-final of the Goblets, on the grounds that he no longer trusted the fairness of Henley umpiring. That ill-advised and futile gesture, whilst not dispersing the feeling against Mackenzie, effectively destroyed any sympathy for the Poles.

1963 Henley 1963 had the unfortunate distinction of being the wettest for thirty-nine years. But the gloom was dispersed by some fine performances by home crews, only two trophies going abroad.

University of London were outstanding in the Grand. There were no Russians, but a good Cornell crew disposed of Nassovia Hochst, Germany, and London Rowing Club after a hard race, to reach the final on one side of the draw. On the other side, London University had no difficulty against Leander or Thames. London University started in the final at 46 against Cornell's 41, and at the Barrier led by half a length. Each time Cornell attacked, the Londoners countered, and in the end won convincingly by three-quarters of a length.

Another fine British performance came from W. L. Barry in the Diamonds, against G. Kottmann of Switzerland. Barry was closing with every stroke at the finish and lost by only two feet. New Zealand won their first Henley trophy in the newly founded Prince Philip Cup. They were pushed hard by Nereus, Amster-

dam, in the first heat, but had no difficulty thereafter.

1964 The 125th anniversary of Henley's founding came in 1964. For one crew at least the celebrations were unique, for the same nine men who had won the Grand Challenge Cup in 1914 returned to Henley for a reunion outing on the same course, and by way of gratitude presented to the Regatta a replica of the Grand Challenge Cup, by this time ready for retirement to ceremonial use only.

On 2 July, the Harvard party were entertained by the Stewards at a dinner at Leander Club. Proposing the toast to the Harvard crew of 1914, Harold Rickett, Chairman of the Committee of Management, addressed the assembled guests as follows:

> Senator Saltonstall, Members of the 1914 Harvard Crew, Ladies and Gentlemen –
> Tonight is an historic occasion, and I think that every one of us here must feel that we are personally taking part in history in the making.
> We are here this evening first to do honour to a crew famous in the rowing world – the Harvard crew of 1914. A crew famous in its own time as the first from America to be inscribed on this ancient trophy. A crew whose fame, moreover, has grown over the years. A crew who have organized their later careers with that same care as prompted them in 1914 to bring over their own drinking water. And a crew who have remained together as a crew long after it has fallen to others to have to disband.
> They have always put their crew interests

before all else. Even in public affairs crew interests come first. Through the person of their captain, Senator Saltonstall, for many years they were self-governing in the State of Massachusetts, and they can still command the election of their own crew representative in the Senate.

We salute this crew tonight. And in saluting them, we should salute also their wives, whom we now see to be just those same treasures as British rowing wives, whose delight it is to keep their husbands fit and ensure that they need never grow up.

I am delighted that the initials 'HRR' should this year stand for 'Harvard's Reunion Regatta'.

Secondly, we are here to receive, and give thanks for, the new 'Grand'. I cannot think of a more generous or appropriate gift, and I am sure that its presentation will not lead to the misunderstanding that occurred when after the last war an American, out of his outstanding generosity, offered to restore one of the City of London churches destroyed by bombing. Unfortunately, he could not come over to attend the rededication service of the restored church and so the service was recorded and the record sent to him. But the party to listen to the recording broke up suddenly when they heard the Bishop say, 'and now let us give thanks to God for this succour from America'. We tonight can be in no doubt of how the word 'succour' should be spelt.

Of course Harvard brought a younger crew along to try to repeat their success of fifty years earlier, but this visit coincided with the presence of the fastest Grand eight yet to have been seen at Henley, Club Zjalghiris Viljnjus,

USSR. I specify 'USSR' because this crew from Lithuania did not appreciate being referred to as 'Russians'. Unfortunately the old Grand Challenge Cup, traditionally used for the Henley draw, saw fit to express her disapproval of retirement by matching Harvard and Viljnjus in the first round. Suffice it to say that in this, the first of their three rows, Viljnjus equalled the record of 6 min. 30 sec. Next day against Thames they lowered it to 6 min. 23 sec., and in the final against London University they lowered the Barrier record by 1 second and the Fawley record by 3 seconds, finishing in 6 min 25 sec. All the verdicts were 'Easily'. *The Times* correspondent pointed out that if the five British crews entered had been permitted to race as a quarter-mile relay team they would probably not have won.

There were no other Russian entries. The Polish pair and sculler entered again, despite their experience in 1963, but this time were forced to withdraw because of a motor accident. An American, S. Cromwell, became the first single sculler to cover the Henley course inside 8 minutes. In the first round he beat M. P. Watkinson of New Zealand by two and a quarter lengths in 7 min. 54 sec. His hardest race came in the semi-final, when H. A. Wardell-Yerburgh pushed him to a length and a quarter.

In the Double Sculls G. C. Justicz and N. J. Birkmyre achieved their fourth win in five years. Pembroke College, Cambridge, sharing the anniversary with Harvard for they had won the Ladies' Plate in 1914, went one better in 1964, pulling off the Ladies' Plate and Visitors' Cup double.

1965   Being the largest country in Europe, well endowed with rivers and lakes and with a long sporting tradition, Germany has always been a considerable force in rowing, but it was the political factor which pushed 'Germany' into a position of dominance in the 1960s. Politically there were two Germanies, the Federal and the Democratic Republics, but rowing-wise they were not recognized as separate countries until 1965. Up to and inclusive of that year only one German team had access to the European and World Championships. East Germany were already aspiring to achieve pre-eminence in international sport, and so each year East and West Germany had to hold their own private selection trials to choose their national teams. I well recall asking an acquaintance from one or the other 'Germany' how they managed to produce such crews – it matters not which, as the reply would have been the same either way – 'Because we have to beat the second fastest crew in the world just to get here,' was the reply.

And so it came about that German crews, at first mostly from the Federal Republic, but later more often from the Democratic Republic, provided the same sort of 'super-élite' opposition at Henley during this decade as the Soviet Union had provided after 1954.

The prospects for the Grand Challenge Cup in 1965 were exciting, albeit non-existent for the British entries. There were the customary groans at the draw when the reigning Olympic champions, Vesper BC, were paired with Harvard, reported to be the fastest American university on record; Ratzeburger Ruderclub, twice European champions and runners-up to Vesper in Tokyo, were drawn against Turn und

Sportsclub, from East Berlin, whilst the four home entries were drawn against each other. But in the event this was a good draw. At 46 to Vesper's 44, Harvard led by two feet at the Barrier, Harvard continued at 40 but Vesper had a few feet at Fawley, 4 seconds inside the record. Thereafter Vesper just had the edge, winning by two-thirds of a length. TSC Berlin withdrew, presumably reckoning it not worth the cost of travelling to Henley to be beaten by Ratzeburg. Vesper and Ratzeburg easily beat Nautilus and London University in the semi-finals. In the finals, Ratzeburg, at 45 to Vesper's 42, gained a precious half-length up to Temple Island. They never dropped below 39 whilst the Americans never dropped below 38. In one of the greatest races ever seen at Henley Ratzeburg held that half-length, no more and no less, all the way to the finish, setting a record of 6 min. 16 sec. which was to stand for ten years. Quintin were clocked at 50 at the start of the Stewards' final, winning easily, 6 seconds inside the record. Four Yale members of the Oxford crew, rowing under Leander colours, lowered the Prince Philip record by 22 seconds during the week. But no performance at this Regatta was more remarkable than that of the American D. M. Spero, who, on the opening day, sculled past the German Achim Hill to clip 8 seconds off the Diamonds record, and on the final day administered the same treatment to Bristol's H. A. Wardell-Yerburgh to lower the record by a further 4 seconds.

1966–1967   The Democratic Republic of East Germany was recognized as a separate team for the first time in the World Championships in 1966, and this no doubt gave them the incentive to bring a full team to Henley Regatta. Only in the Stewards' Cup were they thwarted, and that by a bare quarter of a length by a gallant Danish four. In the Grand, Tideway Scullers were probably as fast as any British crew before them, and never rating below 39 they battled their way back from a deficit of nearly a length at Remenham to finish only half a length behind TSC Berlin. The only event open to foreign crews which was successfully defended this year was the Princess Elizabeth Cup, which Emanuel School won from St Paul's School, USA. Once again in 1967 it fell to a school, this time Eton, to score Britain's only 'international' success at Henley, over Tabor Academy in the Princess Elizabeth Cup. Emanuel, winners in 1966, this year made a bid to join Eton, Shrewsbury and Radley, the only schools ever to have won the Ladies' Plate. Emanuel reached the final without difficulty, and were only a third of a length behind First and Third Trinity at the bottom of the enclosures when they were stopped by a crab. In fairness one must say that it was the pressure applied by Trinity which brought this about. The East Germans did not defend the Diamond Sculls title but again failed to win only one of the events in which they started. This time it was the Double Sculls, in which M. Studach and M. Bürgin of Zurich easily beat K. Shäritz and J. Böhmer of Potsdam. The Tideway Scullers School reached the Grand final but were no match for Leipzig. It was a disappointing year, and four days' racing brought only nineteen races in which the verdicts were less than a length.

1968   The year 1968 was something of a nightmare for the Committee of Management. Because of problems over school examination dates Henley was held a week later than usual. It then clashed with both the North American Olympic Trials and Lucerne International Regatta, so that overseas entries fell to fourteen, the lowest number since 1949. Additionally the strongest flood-stream since records were started in 1883 rendered racing conditions unfair. Humphrey Playford, as the official Henley Regatta historian, tried to discount ninety-four races won off the Berks Station against fifty-two off Bucks, by claiming that many races were already won by Fawley, inferring that a preponderance of the faster crews happened to draw the Bucks Station. The truth was that the disadvantage of the Berks Station in the last quarter of a mile was obvious to all with eyes willing to see. On the other hand, suggestions that the Regatta ought to have been postponed were equally ill founded. Unless there was a strong possibility of an imminent reduction in the current, postponement would always be ruled out on practical and economic considerations. The only possible option in such circumstances would be to move the finishing post downstream. As often happens when conditions are unfair, it was apparent that determination plays at least as much part as the luck of the draw. There were only two international finals at Henley this year and both were won off the unfavoured Berks Station. In the Thames Cup final Leander romped away from Cornell; and in the Princess Elizabeth Cup JEB Stuart High School, USA, just held off Eton to win by a canvas.

1969–1970 Henley returned to its traditional date in 1969. The Princess Elizabeth entry fell from twenty-eight to thirteen, but overseas entries increased to a record fifty-three of which forty-six actually started, and that was more than double the average over the preceding twenty years. East Germany entered for only two events. They won the Grand from University of Pennsylvania, and the Diamonds through H. J. Böhmer, from W. B. Tytus of USA; but it was pleasing to note that in five Grand races there was only one in which the crews were not overlapping all the way. The Ladies' Plate went abroad for the first time to Nereus, Amsterdam, but Leander were comfortable winners in the Thames Cup over Pennsylvania. Unable to bring an eight because of examinations, Eton College became the first school to win the Visitors' Cup and that with some ease.

There was not much excitement in 1970 and the *Sunday Times* commented, 'Too few British crews were contesting the final stages and too many finals were won by uncompetitive margins . . . of the first six finals only the Grand Challenge Cup produced a verdict of less than three-and-a-half lengths'. Tideway Scullers earned some glory in the Grand when they held Vorwarts Rostock, who had six gold medallists on board, to half a length in the semi-final of the Grand. Rostock won the final by the same margin against Aegir, Holland. The East Germans suffered one of their rare Henley defeats in the Prince Philip Cup when Potsdam, despite starting at 46 and rowing 41 in the second minute, found themselves unable to hold Konstanz-Wetzlar, West Germany's 'Bulls of Konstanz', averaging $15\frac{1}{2}$ stone and

dominant in international Coxed Fours over a number of years. The Regatta ended on an unhappy note when Thames Tradesmen were disqualified in the final of the Wyfold Cup. Leading all the way from Trident Rowing Club, South Africa, Tradesmen were several times warned for their steering. Then, when Trident challenged along the enclosures, the crews collided in neutral water. Had they been able to disengage and race on to the finish the umpire might well have let them go, but they did not, and Thames Tradesmen were disqualified on the basis of their previous and repeated infringements. There followed an unseemly protest by the crew and some spectators, who were evidently ignorant of the Laws of Boat Racing.

1971 After suffering what had seemed to be the flood of the century in 1968, Henley had a double repetition of that experience in 1971. On 11 June a sudden spate washed away many of the Regatta installations, and when repairs were nearing completion the same thing happened again six days later. In both those floods the flow of water down the course was reckoned to be ten times the normal. Qualifying races on the Friday and Saturday before the Regatta were rowed over a shortened course of approximately 2,000 metres. The Thames Conservancy managed to reduce the flow during the four days of the Regatta to about twice the normal, and by superhuman efforts the contractors, in the words of the *Sunday Times*, 'produced Henley on time almost complete except for a somewhat hazardous access to the press box, in its usual immaculate form'. The Fourth Estate however enjoyed some compensation for the contractors had not had time to put the roof on the Stewards' Box, which had long cut off some seats in the press box from a full view of the course.

The entries were poor with the exception of the Diamond Sculls. There were only three for the Grand, Tideway Scullers winning the heat well from Leander, and the final as they liked from the Cairo Police. In the Stewards', the same Thames Tradesmen's four as in the previous year beat the same Trident four, this time without incident, and went on to beat Cambridge University by a length in the final. The Prince Philip had four contenders, and the Double Sculls only two. The Diamond Sculls was the exception, with seven overseas scullers in a field of twelve. D. P. Sturge, of London Rowing Club, did well to beat the selected sculler, J. Hellebrand of Czechoslovakia, and then N. H. Secher of Denmark, but fell to the reigning world champion, Alfredo Demiddi of the Argentine. Demiddi went on to beat the American, J. W. Dietz, rather easily in the final. In the Princess Elizabeth cup the holders and favourites, Ridley College, Canada, at an average weight of 14 st. 2 lb., lost their chance in the first heat when no. 6's outrigger snapped, and no. 5 caught a crab and was catapulted out of the boat. Ridley's coach, Neil Campbell, seemed pained that the race was not re-rowed, but it has always been a principle that crews must stand by their accidents after the start. Ridley's bad luck must not detract from the performance of Pangbourne College, who beat St Paul's School, USA, and Eton College, both selected in the draw, and then, in the final, led all the way from another selected crew,

St Andrew's School, USA, winning by two lengths.

1972 Without doubt 1972 was a memorable Henley year, but not all the memories were happy ones. Overseas entries held up well considering it was an Olympic year, but it was a lean period for British rowing. To take the happy memory first, the outstanding performance of the Regatta was the success of P. G. R. Delafield and T. J. Crooks in the Double Sculls. The Americans, L. Klecatsky and J. W. Dietz, could not hold them at the start, and Delafield and Crooks set a record of 2 min. 3 sec. at the Barrier, already leading by a length and a half. Thereafter they were in full control.

In the Grand, Tideway Scullers could not match Northeastern University, USA, and they in turn could not quite match WMF Moscow in the final. The Ladies' Plate produced a 'Double Dutch' final, DSR Laga winning easily from GSR Aegir. The Stewards' Cup has to be described as a non-event. There were only three entries and Thames Tradesmen withdrew after the draw. The final, which was the only race therefore, lasted just forty seconds before University of British Columbia steered into Spartak Moscow, breaking the Russian bowman's blade. Columbia were disqualified, Spartak offered a re-row which, of course, was not permissible under the rules. One wonders in such cases, when crews have travelled from afar, whether it would not be a good idea to arrange a private match. That was only the beginning of 1972's bad luck stories. In the final of the Diamond Sculls, the Irish sculler, Sean Drea, lost his fin soon after the start, and in a cross wind could not do himself justice against V. Butkus of the Soviet Union, losing by three and a half lengths. And, almost incredibly one may think, Ridley College, Canada, lost their chance of winning the Princess Elizabeth Cup for the second year in succession through losing a man overboard. This time a swivel came undone, and the no. 3 man went swimming opposite the enclosures. It was a semi-final, and Ridley still crossed the line well ahead of their Canadian compatriots, Brentwood College School, who next day lost the final to Kent School by only a canvas; but Ridley were disqualified for finishing with an incomplete crew. The implications of this ruling are discussed elsewhere (see page 33).

To end the saga, though it actually occurred before the 1972 Regatta opened, we must record a letter which appeared in *The Times*, under the heading, 'No Etonians at Henley':

From the Head Master of Eton College

Sir, It is indeed sad that having rowed at Henley since 1861, without a break apart from the War years, the clash of concurrent 'A' level examinations has finally compelled us to stop sending crews there. Last year, marking the 100th of Eton's appearances at Henley, seemed an appropriate moment to close the series.

Yours faithfully,

M. McCrum,
Eton College, Windsor.
June 28th

Whatever may have seemed appropriate to the Head Master of Eton in 1972, it would clearly not be appropriate for the Sesquicentennial

History to criticize his decision. Suffice it to say that he thereby achieved a unique sort of immortality in the annals of the Royal Regatta.

1973 'So the old lady has done it again', commented the *Sunday Times* after the 1973 Regatta: 'Just as we were getting ready for the final count out, Henley Royal Regatta has come up with a record home entry, a record foreign entry, increased attendances on every day of the regatta, and a completely new record book of fast times.' And incredibly only one of Russia's six entries reached the finals. That was Trud Kolomna who won the Grand from Northeastern University. In fairness it must also be said that their sculler, A. Timoschinin, was unable to defend the Diamonds title which he won in 1972, owing to an injury. The best result from a British point of view was the victory of M. J. Hart and C. L. Baillieu in the Double Sculls. In the semi-final Hart and Baillieu trailed G. Korschikov and J. Malischev of the Soviet Union by a length and a half at Fawley. Gradually hauling the Russians back, the British double were still half a length behind at the mile and an eighth signal, when they started a sustained spurt at 40, finally cracking the Russians opposite the grandstand. Mr Samsamov, the Russian coach, sportingly commented later, 'the British were sculling for the Queen . . . it is, after all, a Royal Regatta.' Hart and Baillieu went on to overwhelm U. Isler and H. Ruckstuhl of Switzerland in the final.

No British crew entered for the Grand. London University took the Stewards' Cup, helped by Potomac Boat Club running into the buoys. A Leander and London University combination put Trud Moscow out of the

Prince Philip Cup with a surprise finishing spurt which took them over the line with just six feet to spare. They just failed to achieve the same against Northeastern University in the semi-final. At the lower level, no British eight reached the Ladies' Plate semi-final, and only Thames Tradesmen and Emanuel School did so in the Thames and Princess Elizabeth Cups. Tradesmen were attempting the gruelling Thames and Wyfold Cup double, and like many before them won in the four but lost in the eight to Princeton.

1974   1974 marked the end of a Henley decade in which first Germany, and later the Soviet Union, had dominated the international events. Perhaps rowing's two superpowers were reaching the conclusion that the opposition scarcely justified the expenditure. But also British rowing was beginning to learn the lesson that only national squads can expect to succeed at international level in modern conditions. This was borne out in the Grand Challenge Cup. Leander and Thames Tradesmen, Britain's national eight for the forthcoming World Championships, easily won their heat against Tideway Scullers. In the other heat Trud Club held off a gallant challenge by a joint Vesper and Potomac crew from the United States. Leander and Tradesmen went down to the start

of the first Sunday finals to be held at Henley, with instructions from Britain's new professional coach, Bob Janousek, to attack all the way. And that is what they did. After half a mile, rating 38 to Trud's 36, the British led by three-quarters of a length. When Trud pulled them back to half a length at Fawley Leander-Tradesmen attacked again, and edged ahead to two-thirds of a length. But at the mile and an eighth the Russians forced their bows in front for the first time. Leander-Tradesmen sprinted to 40, but conceding half a stone a man they could not quite make it, and lost by half a length. This time the Russians were making no mistakes and took the other three events in which they competed, the Stewards', Goblets and Double Sculls, with some ease.

Drea had no difficulty in retaining his Diamonds title, and the only international event to be secured for Britain was the Prince Philip Cup, won by a joint Lady Margaret and Trinity, Cambridge, crew from the University of London. The Britannia Cup this year attracted an enormous entry of thirty-three, so that all had to take part in the qualifying race before the draw, and one, Thames Tradesmen, had to row twice to qualify. Wallingford School, bronze medallists in the 1973 World Youth Championships, were the outstanding crew, winning the Britannia Cup easily.

13 Fighting Back: 1975–1988

1975–1976 By 1975 British rowing was beginning to square up to the challenge of 'national squad' crews – representative composite crews preparing for the World Championships. Though the entry for the Grand was small there were six individual United States world champions shared between Harvard and the Union Boat Club, and six silver medallists in the Leander and Thames Tradesmen British eight, whilst Ridley Boat Club had six of Canada's national eight in the Grand this year. Union BC beat Ridley by half a length; Harvard beat Union by a third; and Leander–Tradesmen beat Vesper by a length. But in the final, Leander–Tradesmen proved to be much the fastest, leading Harvard by three lengths at the mile, and winning by two lengths.

Vesper, attempting a 'triple', were unfortunately disqualified after clashing with Potomac in the first heat of the Stewards' Cup, Potomac going on to win comfortably from Lady Margaret, Cambridge. In the final of the Prince Philip Cup Vesper lost to London University by about two lengths, after being level at Remenham Club.

In the absence of any significant foreign challenge, M. J. Hart and C. L. Baillieu won their second Double Sculls title with ease. G. A. S. Locke and F. J. Smallbone might well have kept the Goblets at home, but left their finishing spurt too late, so that H. A. Droog and R. J. Luynenburg of Holland got home with a third of a length to spare.

Sean Drea won his third Diamond Sculls for the Republic of Ireland, beating the rising West German star, P-M Kolbe, in the semi-final rather more easily than expected. Garda Siochana, probably the strongest crew yet to come from Ireland, took the Thames Cup. And in the Visitors' Cup Ealing joined the ranks of schools which have won adult events at Henley with a crew which was to go on to many international successes in subsequent years.

The standard was relatively low in 1976, with all Britain's national team preparing elsewhere for the Olympic Games. Indeed the only Olympic competitors present were Australia's I. F. Luxford and C. D. Shinners in the Goblets, and E. O. Hale in the Diamond Sculls. Both these trophies fell to Australia with minimal resistance.

The racing in the Grand Challenge Cup, however, made up in excitement for what it lacked in quality. There was no moment when any Grand eight was clear of its opponent. In the closest verdict, London Rowing Club, though conceding 2 stone a man, pushed Thames Tradesmen to a third of a length in the semi-final, whilst Tradesmen beat Leander in the final by two-thirds of a length.

In a strong Thames Cup the local Henley Rowing Club were the only British survivors to the semi-finals. They almost foundered when a swivel flew open on the eighteenth stroke, but recovered miraculously to beat the selected

University of Pennsylvania by a length and a half.

In the other semi-final, selected Harvard beat Christiania Roklub, Norway. In the final Henley led Harvard by a third of a length at Fawley, but the Americans drew level at the mile. Henley spurted to 41, but Harvard, at 43, just came home with a canvas to spare. Three of the oarsmen I. McNuff, J. M. Beattie and M. P. Cross, who had won the Visitors' Cup for Ealing Schools in 1975, this year won the Wyfold Cup for London Rowing Club, beating Trident RC, South Africa, and Potomac BC, USA, in the process.

1977–1978   There is no doubt that in the latter half of the 1970s the pattern of the open rowing events was changing, as a result of the impact of national crews both domestic and foreign. The entry lists for the Grand, Stewards' and Prince Philip Cups were falling, and the quality was fluctuating according to whether international crews did or did not happen to enter from year to year. Since there was no way of knowing this until the entries were published, the better club and university crews, good enough to have a realistic chance in the 'non-international' years but not when fully fledged national crews were competing, were also becoming reluctant to invite a hopeless defeat.

Thus in 1977 there were no entries in the Grand deemed worthy of selection in the draw. But the competition, perhaps for that very reason, was keen. University of Washington were the winners from Leander and Thames Tradesmen. In the Stewards' Cup the holders, London RC, were the sole entry, whilst in the

Prince Philip Cup the stern four men, who had won the Thames Cup for Garda Siochana two years before, were now the Ireland national four, and won as they liked. In the Goblets two pairs were far better than any others. Selected in the draw to meet in the final, J. Clark and J. Roberts, who were Great Britain's nominated coxless pair for the forthcoming World Championships, and J. Macleod and A. N. Christie, the British coxed pair designate, won all their heats easily. In the final Christie and Macleod were still overlapping at the mile signal but Clark and Roberts then drew away to win by three lengths.

Bulgaria sent their first entries in 1978. They were decisively the best of a field of five Grand crews, but had to work hard against University of Washington in the final. In the Stewards' there were only two entries, and unfortunately the holders, London RC, were forced to withdraw through illness, leaving Trakia Club to row over for Bulgaria's first Henley trophy. The Prince Philip Cup had seven contestants but Trakia were easy winners.

Bulgaria's fourth event was the Diamond Sculls, with M. Nikolov selected to meet T. J. Crooks, a member of Britain's 1976 silver medal eight, on one side of the draw, and West Germany's P-M Kolbe, selected to reach the final on the other side. Crooks sculled past Nikolov after the mile to win his semi-final. In the other, H. P. Matheson, another member of the 1976 British Olympic eight, unexpectedly left Kolbe standing at Fawley. Crooks won the final, 'Easily' according to the official verdict, but actually after a hard race as far as the three-quarter mile signal, where he finally got away from Matheson.

1979 It was the turn of the Great Britain national eight, this time rowing under Thames Tradesmen and London Rowing Club colours, to dominate the Grand in 1979. In the final Yale hung on gamely as far as Fawley, but, scarcely dropping below 40, Tradesmen–London rowed away from them over the second half of the course.

Once again there were only two entries for the Stewards', the same London four which rowed in 1977 winning easily from Oxford University. So in three years there had been two row-overs and only one race in this event. It was a different story in the Goblets, in which the 1979 entry was more notable for quantity than for quality, so that eight pairs had to be eliminated in the qualifying race before the Regatta opened. At the end of the week A. C. D. Wiggin and M. D. A. Carmichael were good winners, and went on to finish fourth in the World Championships. But the official *Regatta Records* pointed out that reckoning a margin of at least four lengths for a verdict of 'Easily', Wiggin and Carmichael were four lengths faster than the losing finalists, S. W. Woodhouse and J. S. Pearson of Cambridge University, who in turn were four lengths faster than their semi-final victims, who won their quarter-final by four lengths from a pair who had won their previous heat by three and a quarter lengths. At least eight pairs must have been still slower, having failed to qualify, so that the margin between the fastest and slowest entries must have been of the order of twenty lengths. Charity precludes naming the tail-enders.

In the sculling events, C. L. Baillieu, with a new partner, J. Clark, had no difficulty in winning the Doubles for the fifth time. In the Diamonds it was Matheson's turn. In all his heats he had led by three lengths or more at the Barrier. In the final the Belgian, J. T. Ghoos, was no match for him. Matheson was clear at the quarter-mile and won as he liked.

Wallingford Rowing Club won their first Henley trophy in the Wyfold Cup. And Wallingford School, in combination with Strode's College, beat Lady Margaret, Cambridge, in the final of the Visitors'.

1980 By any reckoning 1980 was something of a freak year at Henley. The fact that the Olympic Regatta was to take place only two weeks after the Royal Regatta meant that no Olympic contestants were at Henley – and that unfortunately included the whole of the Great Britain team. At the same time the Moscow boycott meant that there were a lot of world-class competitors around looking for consolation prizes.

So in the Grand Challenge Cup the four entries consisted of the United States, New Zealand and Norwegian national crews, and a West German crew comprising individually frustrated star performers. In the first heat the Norwegians, though not quite in the same class, hunted America's Charles River crew all the way. A strong stream precluded records, but this heat was won by two-thirds of a length in 6 min. 24 sec. The West German crew led New Zealand to the Barrier and held them to half a length at the mile, but, as might be expected of a relatively scratch crew, could not match the Kiwis' finish, losing by a length, the time for this heat being 6 min. 25 sec. The final was something of an anti-climax, with Charles River over-rating Waikato and Wairau by two or three strokes a minute until the final stages of the race, which the Americans had well in hand after Fawley.

It was a similar story in the Stewards' Cup, in which the most remarkable performance was perhaps that of the Wallingford lightweights, who, despite a weight deficit of more than $3\frac{1}{2}$ stone a man, somehow overlapped the New Zealanders all the way to the mile signal. In the final Avon and Petone, New Zealand, held Charles River and Dartmouth College to Fawley, after which the Americans were safe.

The Prince Philip Cup was expected to produce the best race of all between New Zealand and the United States, but tragically this never took place, as New Zealand's North Shore and Hawkes Bay composite were disqualified for two false starts in their opening heat against the Ridley Graduate Boat Club of Canada. A glance at Henley's starting installation (see Plates 69–70) shows why it is virtually impossible for a false start to go undetected, and a second infringement means mandatory disqualification.

Kingston, who had been unsuccessful candidates for a place in the British Olympic team, put up a great battle against Yale and Potomac, USA, in the semi-final. Yale and Potomac in turn pushed Charles River, USA, to two-thirds of a length in the final.

In the Goblets the American twins, M. and F. Borchelt, won all their races with ease. Olympic selection robbed C. L. Baillieu of a sixth Double Sculls title, which this time went to P. Walter and B. Ford of Canada. A record entry of thirty-seven in the Diamond Sculls caused the Henley Committee to include an extra round in this event, a decision then unique

in Henley's history of adhering strictly to the rule book. The standard was low, and of the four scullers selected in the draw only the Argentinian R. D. Ibarra reached the semi-finals. But he was a worthy winner in the end.

1981–1982 Henley's improving financial position in 1981 meant that the course could be fully boomed for the first time in twenty years, reducing interference from river traffic.

Two of Britain's three entries in the Grand were aiming at selection for the World Championships. Three of the four United States entries were selected in the draw, along with the Leander and Tyrian composite which was the Amateur Rowing Association's national squad crew. Leander–Tyrian outclassed Boston University, and then the selected University of Washington. The other selected crews, Yale and Cornell Universities, were respectively despatched by the unselected Oxford University and Thames Tradesmen composite, and University of London, also unselected. Oxford and Tradesmen then proved to be too strong for London University though they did not get away until after the mile.

The final was a magnificent race. London–Tyrian led by three-quarters of a length at the Barrier. Oxford–Tradesmen drew level at Remenham Club. London–Tyrian counterattacked desperately, but Oxford–Tradesmen were the winners. As a postscript, this verdict was reversed at the National Championships a few weeks later, and the two crews then combined to win a silver medal in the World Championships.

The Stewards' and Prince Philip Cups

40. *Above* The USSR Navy beating Leander Club by 1 length in the final of the Grand Challenge Cup in 1961. The USSR Navy: S. Derbyshev (bow), V. Schipunov, G. Borishov, V. Rozhkov, D. Semenov, A. Tkachuk, V. Khatuntsev, I. Andreev (str.), A. Luzgin (cox). Leander Club: P. C. D. Burnell (bow), R. L. S. Fishlock, J. O. B. Sewall, C. P. M. Gomm, I. L. Elliott, D. C. R. Edwards, J. R. Chester, C. M. Davis (str.), J. M. Howard-Johnston (cox).

41. Ratzeburger Ruderclub, Germany: H. Meyer (bow), D. Schreyer, G. Prey, K. Behrens, D. Thomatschek, J. Schroder, H. J. Wallbrecht, A. Aeffke (str.), P. Mainka (cox) beating Vesper BC, USA: J. B. Amlong (bow), H. M. Foley, J. F. Abele, P. A. Johnson, E. P. Ferry, H. B. Budd, F. Thompson, W. A. Stowe (str.), R. Zimonyi (cox) in the final of the 1965 Grand Challenge Cup.

42. *Above* Eton College: J. F. S. Hervey-Bathurst (bow), G. D. R. Oldham, Hon. J. P. F. Walston, P. H. Straker, H. P. Matheson, R. C. Floyd, E. H. N. Kenneil, A. R. E. Perceval (str.), R. A. Taylor (cox) beating Tabor Academy, USA: W. S. Wakeman (bow), K. H. Foster, W. D. Reed, G. H. Linzee, W. T. Rogers, R. S. Laing, D. Borden, T. S. Sanders (str.), L. S. Wolfe (cox) in the final of the Princess Elizabeth Cup in 1967.

43. Although they finished first in this heat of the Princess Elizabeth Cup in 1972, Ridley College, Canada were ruled not to have completed the course because they lost a man overboard. Ridley College were represented by S. Dorland (bow), T. Weinstein, O. Crassweller, D. McElheny, T. Powell, P. Szczucinski, R. MacLachlan, F. MacKay (str.), H. Watlington (cox). Their opponents, Brentwood College School, Canada, who went on to lose the final by a canvas from Kent School, USA, were represented by J. Burns (bow), D. Van Eeuwen, M. Moran, D. Lovell, J. Henniger, M. Bayles, R. Friedli, J. Allester (str.), K. Gray (cox).

44. *Above* Leander Club and Thames
Tradesmen RC pushed Trud Club, USSR to
half a length in the final of the Grand Challenge
Cup in 1974. The Trud Club were represented
by V. Riconen (bow), G. Nikurodze, B.
Vorobjor, S. Kiljaskin, V. Savelov, A. Shitov,
N. Surov, A. Olkhovik (str.), A. Jarov (cox).
Leander Club and Thames Tradesmen RC were
represented by W. G. Mason (bow), L. D.
Robertson, F. J. Smallbone, J. Clark, H. P.
Matheson, D. L. Maxwell, J. C. Yallop, T. J.
Crooks (str.), P. J. Sweeney (cox).

45. The local Henley Rowing Club came within
a canvas of winning the Thames Cup from
Harvard University in 1976. Harvard: T.
McGee (bow), P. Templeton, D. Wood, M.
Moore, R. Wiley, W. Perkins, H. Porter, G.
Gardiner (str.), H. You (cox). Henley RC: A. C.
Maffre (bow), C. F. Bushnell, D. M. Smith,
P. C. Allen, P. J. Marsden, I. Pankhurst, A. A.
Glenn, A. Richardson (str.), R. Woodford (cox).

46. S. G. Redgrave (Marlow RC) beating T. J. Crooks (Kingston RC) in the final of the Diamond Sculls, 1983.

47. Leander Club and University of London: R. Stanhope (bow), P. R. K. Beaumont, G. B. Stewart, S. F. Hassan, T. G. Dillon, A. M. Obholzer, S. Turner, N. J. Burfitt (str.), S. M. Jeffries (cox) beating the Australian Institute for Sport: J. C. S. Galloway (bow), H. B. McLachan, S. G. Patten, M. S. McKay, R. C. Finlayson, J. B. Tomkins, I. Popa, S. F. Evans (str.), D. Caterson (cox) by 1 foot in the final of the Grand Challenge Cup in 1988.

48. The Chairman makes the draw for Regatta heats from the old Grand Challenge Cup in the Town Hall.

49. Swan Upping: each year the swans are removed from the Henley Reach before the Regatta.

50a&b. Sometimes the elements are unkind: 1963 (*below*) and 1988 (*right*).

51. Some coxswains are chaired . . .

52. . . . and some are less fortunate.

53. 'You may not be able to read this one.'
(I. Ivanov of the USSR signs autographs.)

54. 'What big feet you have!' Wes Coker of
Washington-Lee High School has an admirer
in young David Allen of Maidenhead.

55. *Below* Crowds in the Stewards' Enclosure,
1979.

attracted only three entries each, once again demonstrating the inhibiting effect of the presence of national squad crews. Both were won easily by Great Britain's representative crews. The new event for Quadruple Sculls, the Queen Mother Challenge Cup, was dominated by the West German national quad, Ingleheim and Ulm.

The Goblets produced only one interesting race, the final between J. Macleod and N. Christie and T. F. F. Mossop and C. J. Jones, which the latter pair won by a length despite hitting the booms. The Double Sculls were dominated by E. R. Sims and S. G. Redgrave, and the Diamonds by C. L. Baillieu.

Women's Invitation Races for Coxed Fours and Double Sculls resulted in easy wins for the United States and Canada. The standard was good, but it was reckoned that the course, starting from the Barrier and so considerably longer than the 1,000 metres used internationally for womens' events at that time, contributed to there being no close verdicts.

In 1982 the German Democratic Republic made their first entries since 1970, but withdrew, which was a pity as the home crews might have given them a run for their money this year. Yale University, selected in the draw, were well beaten by University of London and Tyrian, whilst the British national eight, in Leander and London Rowing Club colours, paddled home against University of California, Berkeley. In the final, London University and Tyrian raced most gallantly to hold Leander–London to half a length at the finish.

The open fours events reached their nadir this year, not as regards quality but as regards competition. The reigning world champions

in coxless fours, Schaffhausen and Thalwil, Switzerland romped away with the Stewards' Cup in the only race in that event. The Prince Philip Cup produced one heat, won easily by Queensland and Mosman, Australia, who were no match for the University of London and Tyrian four in the final. And the Queen Mother Cup for Quadruple Sculls also provided only one race, which was won easily by Marlow and Thames Tradesmen.

Twenty-five pairs entered for the Goblets, many of them very bad, but the winners, M. Ivančić and Z. Celent, of Yugoslavia, had to fight hard in their semi-final against Macleod and Christie, who overlapped at the finish. In the final they were led for half a mile by P. D. Wensley and P. L. Reynolds. Poor steering let the British pair down, and Ivančić and Celent got away to win by a length and a half.

One of Henley's rare dead-heats occurred this year in a Thames Cup semi-final. Yale were leading by two-thirds of a length at Fawley, but University of London drew level along the enclosures. An immediate re-row was ordered as the final was scheduled later in the day. London University then seized the initiative at the start, gaining three-quarters of a length in the first quarter-mile, which proved to be decisive. Later London just managed to stave off Isis to win the final by a quarter of a length.

1983 There were six entries for the Grand in 1983, including three American Universities – Harvard, Cornell and Brown. These three raced in Cincinnati to decide which should come to Henley. Unfortunately Harvard, the winners, were then unable to make the trip, so that there remained only the three home crews in the

Grand. London RC and University of London, made up at short notice from members of the national squad, were easy winners.

For London University it was a good year, for in addition to having two men in this winning Grand crew they also won the Thames and Visitors' Cups and Silver Goblets.

The Stewards' and Prince Philip Cups also produced only three entries each. In the former the current world champions, Schaffhausen and Thalwil, Switzerland, won as they liked. In the Prince Philip final Kingston just got home in front of an Oxford and London Universities combination. Kingston made it a double with a win in the closely contested but rather mediocre standard Queen Mother Cup.

Sculling at no. 3 in this Kingston quad, the veteran T. J. Crooks was trying for a personal double, which led to the most interesting race of the Regatta. Tim Crooks made his Henley debut in 1966 rowing for Radley, and had many international and Henley successes behind him, including the Double Sculls in 1972 and the Diamonds in 1977 and 1978. Facing him in the final of the 1983 Diamonds was the rising young star, Steven Redgrave, Double Sculls winner in 1981 and 1982. Crooks had the technique, experience and pace, and should have had the guile. Redgrave had youth and strength. Starting at 38 to Crooks's 39, Redgrave had two-thirds of a length at the quarter-mile signal, but could get no more, and the positions remained unchanged past Fawley. Then Crooks began to inch back, until, at the mile, Redgrave led by only a quarter of a length. Crooks spurted to 34 and was almost level opposite the enclosures when he stopped, exhausted. The question for the connoisseur, of course, was what would have happened if Crooks had delayed his attack until he was within reach of the finish.

1984 Entries exceeded 300 for the first time in 1984, and a dry summer with favourable breezes during the Regatta resulted in twenty-three of the total of thirty-nine Henley records being equalled or lowered. It was an Olympic year, with the British team, but no others, competing in the Royal Regatta, so predictably all bar one of the open trophies stayed at home.

The British Olympic eight, rowing under Leander and London Rowing Club colours, were in a class of their own in the Grand Challenge Cup. Despite being clear of University of Pennsylvania at the quarter-mile in their heat, they became the first crew ever to reach Fawley inside 3 minutes (2 min. 57 sec.), and set a new course record of 6 min. 10 sec. in windless conditions. They had to work harder against a good University of Washington crew in the final, when a headwind made further records impossible.

The nominated Olympic coxless four, Nottinghamshire and Tyne, also set new records, but had to race hard for their victory, first against Kingston and Leander, and then against University of London Tyrian, both of whom believed that they should have had the Los Angeles nomination. Without doubt the British coxed four, Marlow and University of London Tyrian, would have broken the record in the only race in the Prince Philip Cup had there been any opposition, for under no pressure at all they were only one second slower than Northeastern University in 1973. This Marlow–London Tyrian four went on to win Britain's first Olympic gold medal since 1948.

The Goblets was not of a high standard, but was enlivened by personal rivalries and by selection frictions. In the final E. M. G. Pearson and C. D. M. Riches, who had been denied an Olympic trial, had the satisfaction of rowing the selected pair, J. M. Beattie and R. C. Stanhope, to a standstill, just short of the finishing post in the final. W. J. Lang and A. M. Genziani, who claimed that they should have been nominated for the Olympic coxed pairs, withdrew from the Goblets. It seems that Olympic selections move in a mysterious way, for Lang and Genziani, who had rejected the chance to prove their point at Henley, subsequently got their Los Angeles tickets, whilst Pearson and Riches did not.

Another disgruntled competitor, C. L. Baillieu, who also had been rejected as a candidate for Los Angeles, won the Diamonds with some ease.

The Americans, inevitably absent from the open events on account of the Olympic Regatta being held in California, came in strength for the Ladies' Plate. No less than seven of their university crews entered and five reached the quarter-finals, Brown University being the winners from Temple University.

1985 The year 1985 was a milestone in Henley history, with the long overdue abandoning of the student status limitations on the Ladies' Plate, which thus regained its rightful place as the 'no. 2' eight-oar event. In a high quality field eight crews were selected in the draw, and all but one reached the quarter-finals. After good racing in the heats Leander and Garda Siochana were well matched in the final. Leading by half a length at the Barrier, Leander could not get away, and the Irish crew drew level at the final signal before Leander somehow found new reserves, drawing away to win by a canvas.

With no British national eight involved this year the Grand was dominated by Harvard and Princeton Universities. Harvard's winning time was only one second slower than Leander's time in the 'new-look' Ladies' Plate, but one must add that they were not hard pressed.

The new qualification arrangements, effectively down-grading the Thames Cup, had the inevitable result of attracting a huge entry to this event, so that no less than thirty-eight crews were eliminated before the draw. London Rowing Club, Molesey, and Leander's lightweight crew entered, but were drafted into the Ladies' Plate on the basis that the 'third-class' event was no longer appropriate for 'first-class' clubs. This left Ridley College, Canada, in a class above the rest of the Thames Cup entry, and they duly won without being much extended.

1986 The Regatta was extended to five days in 1986, partly to ease the programme and cut down the hours of racing on the first two days, and partly to reduce the need to race two rounds of some events on the same day.

Great Britain's national squad eight, rowing as Nautilus, were much the strongest of the four Grand entries. University of Pennsylvania managed to lead them by half a length at the top of Temple Island in the final, but Nautilus rowed past them at Fawley and were well in control.

There were only three crews in the Stewards' Cup. Hansa Dortmund and Witten, the West

German reigning world champions, unfortunately had to row a substitute stroke, and lost the only heat to Ridley Boat Club, Canada. In the final Ridley just managed to stave off a finishing spurt at 41 by University of London Tyrian, to win by half a length. The Prince Philip Cup produced unusually close racing in the heats, but in the final Szczecin and Wroclaw, Poland, were too fast for Thames Tradesmen. A field of six quads suggested that the Queen Mother Cup was gaining popularity, but there were no overseas challengers and the standard was modest. In the semi-final, Tideway Scullers and Northampton scraped home by a quarter of a length from Nottinghamshire County, but in the final won as they liked from Rob Roy.

The most interesting feature this year was a double, or perhaps one should say an involuntary treble, attempt, originating with Steven Redgrave who set out to hold his Diamonds title and, in partnership with Andrew Holmes, to win the Goblets, a combination last achieved in 1894 by Guy Nickalls. This double bid became an indirect treble when Holmes was drafted into the Nautilus eight as substitute.

To accommodate this bid the finals of the Grand and Diamonds were raced in the morning. But, five minutes after Holmes had won the Grand, the Diamonds went terribly wrong for Redgrave. Racing against the Danish lightweight, B. Eltang, Redgrave went out for a quick kill, and led by two and a half lengths at the Barrier. But Eltang, twice world champion in lightweight sculls and clearly unimpressed by the fact that he was conceding 3 stone to the giant Englishman, had no intention of offering himself as a quick victim. On the

contrary he methodically worked his way back into the race. Just beyond the three-quarter mile signal he gained an overlap, and at Remenham Club Redgrave stopped, no doubt beaten psychologically rather than physically, but emphatically beaten none the less.

The only pairs of any real quality in the Goblets were Holmes and Redgrave, and the holders for the past two years, Pearson and Riches. But any prospect of an exciting final quickly disappeared when Holmes and Redgrave went clear at the top of the Island. Four or five lengths ahead at Fawley they won as they liked, so Holmes, but not Redgrave, achieved his double.

1987 The Russians returned to Henley in full force in 1987, entering for all seven open events, and winning four of them. Unfortunately the British World Championship team, with the exception of Holmes and Redgrave in the pair, were not on hand to meet this challenge, having opted to race in Amsterdam over the previous weekend.

One must recognize that there is a dilemma here. The Amateur Rowing Association coaching director has the primary task of producing crews for the international championships, and with Lucerne Regatta a week after Henley, the Royal Regatta may not always fit in well with training plans. On the other hand Henley is the shop window for rowing in Britain, and supporters, sponsors and press find it difficult to understand why Britain's representative national crews absent themselves from Britain's premier regatta. What the Russians and other national crews feel when they make their costly journey to beard the British on their home waters, only to find that their hosts have gone off to the barbers elsewhere, one can only guess.

However that may be, the undoubted highlight of Henley 1987 was not to be lost. This was the clash, in the Silver Goblets, between Holmes and Redgrave, the holders of the title and reigning world champions in coxed pairs, and Yuri and Nikolai Pimenov of the Soviet Union, thrice world champions in coxless pairs.

This epic confrontation was all but frustrated when, with the pairs racing level at the Barrier, a canoe was pushed on to the course and run down by Holmes and Redgrave. The race was stopped, the Pimenovs, misunderstanding the umpire's instruction to return to the start, began racing again and had to be recalled. At the second attempt the Russians led by a length at the quarter-mile. Holmes and Redgrave closed to three-quarters of a length at Fawley. At the mile the Pimenovs led by a length again, but could not get clear. Then the British pair renewed their attack and had closed to half a length, when the Russians suddenly stopped. Holmes and Redgrave paddled on to the finish, waving to the crowd which was not universally well received by the British public who like their losers to be cheerful and their winners to be unobtrusive.

Another world star achieved his Henley ambition this year. At his third attempt in thirteen years, West German Peter Kolbe, five times world champion, won the Diamond Sculls from V. Jakusha of the Soviet Union with some ease. Russia's third defeat came in the Queen Mother Cup, when the Soviet Army, reigning world champions in quadruple sculls, were held off in a desperate finish by the Ridley

Boat Club of Canada, 1985 world champions, by a third of a length.

In all their other events the Soviet crews deservedly triumphed. They took their revenge on Ridley in the final of the Grand, though never able to ease up. Dinamo Moscow were bravely but unavailingly chased by University of London Tyrian in the only race in the Stewards' Cup. In the Prince Philip Cup the Soviet Army caught the holders, Szczecin and Wroclaw of Poland at the final signal, winning by a third of a length. And in the Double Sculls N. Chouprina and V. Dosenko won all their races with some ease.

These were the great events of 1987, but it must also be recorded that the Irish put three crews into the semi-finals of a closely contested Thames Cup, Durham University filling the fourth place. University College Galway and Neptune Rowing Club went through to the final, which Galway won by two and a quarter lengths.

1988 The Princess Royal, presenting the prizes after the 1988 Regatta, remarked that time would tell whether she would for longer remember the magnificent racing or the appalling weather. It was fair comment for some of the world's fastest crews were demonstrating two-lane racing at its best, and at its best the confrontation of two well-matched crews racing on a boomed two-lane course is unique; whilst on shore – one could hardly say 'on dry land' – the spectators were engulfed in a sea of mud.

The entry of 386 crews including forty-two from the United States was a record, and the participation of Olympic crews, already nominated or seeking selection, from Great Britain,

Australia, Canada and the United States, provided the quality.

In the Grand Challenge Cup the young Great Britain eight, rowing as Leander and London University, snatched victory from the Australian Institute of Sport by one foot in the last few strokes. No finer race has ever been witnessed at Henley, for the Australians led by two-thirds of a length at the Barrier, only three seconds outside the record on a day which was certainly not fast, and held their advantage, give or take a few feet, until the last quarter-mile. Then the British crew launched a sustained attack which carried them to victory.

The disappointment of the Regatta was that the holders of the Goblets, A. J. Holmes and S. G. Redgrave, were forced to retire after their first race due to injury. The event was then won with some ease by T. S. Swinford and J. P. Riley of the United States. But the biggest surprise in the open events came in the final of the Diamond Sculls when the American Olympic sculler, A. H. Sudduth, was caught and comprehensively beaten by G. H. McGlashan from Melbourne, who had come to Henley as spare man for the Australian Olympic quad.

The quad duly won, too, but only by one length from Nautilus, seeking Olympic selection for Great Britain.

One of the most distinguished performances was by the Leander coxswainless four, fourth in the 1987 World Championships, who won as they liked from Penn Athletic of the United States, equalling the Barrier record of 1 min. 55 sec. before they eased off.

Of the four semi-finalists in the Ladies' Plate, Mercantile Rowing Club of Australia, Leander, and Tideway Scullers' School would all have made a good showing in the Grand in many years, while Nautilus, Britain's World Championship lightweight eight, were not far behind. In the final, Mercantile rowed through Leander in the last quarter-mile to win by a length in equal record time.

Unhappily, University College Galway, holders of the Thames Cup, were disqualified after a clash of blades with Thames Rowing Club towards the end of their semi-final. But Thames could not match Tideway Scullers in the final later in the day, so the end result was probably not affected.

PART THREE

Facts and Figures

Appendix 1 Ambition and Success

Ambition and success always have a fascination in athletics, but the statistics can be misleading. For sheer ambition at Henley W. B. Woodgate had no equal. In 1863 he entered for six events and carried home two trophies. But the truth is that during that two-day Regatta he won only one contested race – a heat of the Grand Challenge Cup. He lost the final of that event, a heat of the Ladies' Plate, and the final of the Stewards' Cup in which his crew, Brasenose College, had not been required to row in the challenge round because they were the holders from 1862. His two 'wins' came in the Visitors' and Goblets, both of which were unopposed 'row-overs'.

W. H. Milman and M. Haggard entered for five events in 1848 and won them all. But here again two were not contested and one was won on a foul. J. R. Selwyn also entered for five events in 1865 and won three, one on a row-over. It was not unusual to make multiple entries and to win three events in the early days because the number of entries was small. But the last man to achieve this feat, in 1931, did so in much more demanding circumstances. This was H. R. A. (Jumbo) Edwards, who had three races in the Grand, two of them hard-fought, two relatively easy wins in the Stewards', and two in the Goblets of which the first, against the brothers T. and J. S. Offer of Kingston, was a close one; the three finals were rowed in the space of five and a half hours.

Success in any particular year may be due to weak opposition. But sustained success over a number of years must indicate unusual prowess. On this basis the Top Twenty Winners table shows the twenty most consistently successful oarsmen and scullers in Henley's open events.

That the Nickalls family were in a class of their own is beyond dispute, with Guy, his brother Vivian, and his son Gully (Guy Oliver) winning forty-two events between them. But it would be wrong to regard this table as a definitive order of merit of all who have competed in the Royal Regatta. For example, Casamajor, unbeaten as a sculler, died a few weeks after his victory in 1861, and by all contemporary evidence could have gone on winning for several years more; and Stuart Mackenzie lost only one race at Henley before returning to his native Australia after only seven years competition at Henley. Many outstanding performers did not compete often enough to figure in the list of multiple winners.

Some victories have been more easily gained than others. Casamajor was so dominant as a sculler in his day that few of his contemporaries thought it worthwhile to challenge him. Coupled with the small entry lists that meant that Casamajor's fourteen trophies cost him on average only 1.29 races. Twenty years later Guy Nickalls had to row on average 2.27 races, and his son G. O. Nickalls in the 1920s, an average 2.8 races to win. Christopher Baillieu, more recently, required an average of 3.75 races for each of his sculling victories.

One of the questions perennially asked is how the stars of the past would have fared today. It is a question to which there is no satisfactory answer. One could not match Casamajor in his fixed-seat 'toothpick' against Mackenzie in his modern racing shell. Jack Beresford once replied to the question that since he disliked losing he supposed he would do whatever is necessary to win today. But Beresford was also apt to remark that 'a good big-un must beat a good little-un'. True – but that does not prove him to be the better man.

Top Twenty Winners in Open Events

	[1]	[2]				[3]		[4]	[5]		
		Open Events Won				Total Events		Races per Event Won	Total		
		Eights	Fours	Pairs	Sculls	Entered	Won		Races	Won	Lost
Guy Nickalls	1885–1907	4	7	6	5	32	22	2.27	70	60	10
F. S. Gulston	1868–1880	5	11	5		32	21	1.66	50	39	11
A. de L. Long	1867–1877	5	9	4		28	18	1.61	43	33	10
A. A. Casamajor	1855–1861	2	3	4	5	20	14	1.29	24	18	6
S. Le Blanc Smith	1865–1878	4	7	1		21	12	1.83	35	26	9
V. Nickalls	1888–1896	1	3	5	1	15	10	2.2	32	27	5
G. O. Nickalls	1920–1928	7	1	2		22	10	2.8	49	37	12
J. Beresford Jr	1920–1939	2	1	2	5	18	10	2.8	46	38	8
F. L. Playford	1873–1888	3	5		1	24	9	2.0	38	23	15
J. Lowndes	1878–1884		2	2	5	16	9	1.77	28	21	7
C. L. Baillieu	1967–1984				9	11	9	3.75	33	31	2
H. H. Playford	1852–1861	2	3	1	2	20	8	1.5	26	14	12
W. B. Woodgate	1861–1868	1	1	5	1	22	8	1.37	31	17	14
C. G. V. Davidge	1947–1963	2	2	3	1	23	8	2.75	50	35	15
S. A. Mackenzie	1957–1963			1	7	9	8	3.12	26	25	1
S. G. Redgrave	1980–		1	2	5	11	8	3.25	35	32	3
C. W. H. Taylor	1898–1904	2	3	2		10	7	1.71	18	14	4
J. Hastie	1872–1885	2	2	3		31	7	1.85	45	21	24
C. D. Burnell	1894–1902	4	3			12	7	2.63	28	23	5
F. S. Kelly	1899–1906	3	1		3	10	7	2.71	24	21	3

[1] Dates cover full span of Henley competition including school years where applicable.

[2] Figures in col. 2 refer only to wins in the Grand, Stewards' and Prince Philip Challenge Cups, the Silver Goblets, the Queen Mary and Double Sculls Challenge Cups and the Diamond Sculls.

[3] Summarizes col. 2.

[4] Shows the number of times competitors had to race for each win.

[5] Summarizes total number of races in open events. Thus Guy Nickalls won sixty races altogether of which fifty were in the twenty-two events which he won, giving the figure in col. 4 (50 ÷ 22 = 2.27).

Appendix 2 The Record Breakers

Record times are part of the sporting scene these days, no doubt because they are popular with the media ever hunting for 'news' on which to hang their 'views'. In the early days timekeeping at Henley was a chancy business. John Cooper commented on the system in his youth:

> ... there was a long telescope [in the Stewards' Stand]. Mr. Towsey, the Secretary was looking through it watching for the start but one of the Stewards coming up to him he was called away and I was turned on to watch. Almost immediately they started and I called 'They're off', but Mr. Towsey apparently moving a vote of no confidence in my youthful experience, came back to the telescope to confirm my opinion. Having done so to his own satisfaction he started furiously flagwagging a white pennant which was used to signal to the man who fired the gun in the Lion Meadow opposite (where the garden of Leander now is). The man in charge of the gun was not looking and the flagwagging must have gone on for at least a minute before the gun went off. Then the race was officially timed, the crews being nearly at Remenham Rectory before the clocking began.

Perhaps it is not surprising that H. T. Steward often did not bother to record the times in his History, and offered no Table of Records. Until 1874 there were not even official judges. Not until 1906 did the Regatta formally appoint timekeepers, though most recorded times were probably reliable from 1890 onwards. But the Straight Course as used today did not come in until 1924, so that strictly comparable records can be considered only from that year.

There is no questioning the fact that there is a keen sense of anticipation on a Henley morning when conditions look to be suitable for record-breaking. But rowing records are not in the same category as, for example, records on the running track. A mile is a mile on any running track in the world – unless someone has blundered badly – and within reason the statutory oval track means that a helpful wind in one direction is a hindering wind in the other direction. At Henley the finish is one mile and 550 yards from the start, but the distance which crews actually travel through the water depends on the speed at which the current is flowing. And the course is straight so that if there is any wind it must be either helping or hindering, and certainly not self-compensatory. In athletics there can be few days in the year when a track meeting is not in progress somewhere. At Henley there are just five days racing in each year, and with only two crews in each race the winner is more often than not under no pressure.

There are three requirements for breaking a record at Henley; firstly the conditions must be favourable, which means a minimal stream and a following wind – but not so strong as to cause rough water; secondly there must be motivation, which usually means effective opposition, though occasionally it may be the ambition to earn a place in the record book; and finally there must be a crew or sculler capable of achieving a record.

A glance at the tables of Record Times indicates how frequently, or infrequently, there is a conjunction of the required factors. In most years the opportunity to set new records simply does not occur. Once or twice in a decade records tumble like ninepins, indicating optimum conditions. But the impressive records are those which are set in years when other crews are not breaking records, or records which survive for a long time.

Of all the Henley records the most remarkable, surely, is F. S. Kelly's time of 8 min. 10 sec. in the Diamond Sculls in 1905. No other record fell that year, and Kelly, who was incidentally a composer and a talented concert pianist, not only sculled over the course four times to win the Diamonds, but also rowed three times in the Leander eight to win the Grand Challenge Cup, beating the Vesper Boat Club of Philadelphia, and Sport Nautique de Gand, in the process. Kelly's record stood for thirty-three years before falling to the redoubtable Joe Burk in 1938.

My father used to say that 'Cleg' Kelly was a bad trainer and a dirty eater! He was also reputed to be a poor judge of pace, apt to run out of steam before the end of a race. Certainly it is true that in the preceding year, 1904, he stopped short of the finish, after leading the Canadian Scholes by two lengths at the Barrier. In 1905 his Leander crew mates were positioned at strategic points along the bank to exhort him to ease up, which indeed he did, allowing H. T. Blackstaffe to scull past him at the Barrier. Three-quarters of a length behind at Fawley, Kelly was then allowed to have a go at his man, gaining three lengths before the mile and winning by a quarter of a minute. There could be a lesson in this story, indicating that the fastest times are not necessarily achieved under the most intense pressure.

In the tables that follow, times prior to 1924 (the first year in which the Straight Course was used) are shown in *italics*. (All times are shown in minutes and seconds.)

The following should also be noted:

(1) Times prior to 1906 were taken without a flag at Fawley. Such times are indicated by (1) in the tables.

(2) Official times to the Barrier were first taken in 1929.

(3) Where the same crew achieved the same time more than once in the same Regatta it is not repeated.

(4) Where the same crew has set more than one new record in the same year only the fastest time is shown (for example, in 1934 Leander lowered the Grand record to 6.45, and then to 6.44).

(5) Times shown on the same line were set in the same year but not necessarily in the same heat (for example, in the Grand in 1952 Leander set records to the Barrier and to Fawley in a heat, and to the finish in the final).

These abbreviations are used throughout the tables:

Clubs:
ASZ, BC, BSGM, CN, KSR, RC, RF, RG, RK,
RN, RSC, SC, SCN, SCW, SGD, SN, SP, UN,
USM, WMF all equate with 'Club'
AKZ – Akademicki Zwinzcz
A'naut – Argonaut
ASR, DSR, GSR (HOL) – Amsterdamsche, Delft-
sche, Groningen Studenten Roeivereniging
BA – Buenos Aires
Bags. – Bagsvaerd
BNC – Brasenose College, Oxford
CCC – Corpus Christi College
CRA – County Rowing Association
CSFA – Centre Sportif des Forces de l'Armée
DFFR – Danske Foreniging For Rosport
D'mouth – Dartmouth
DSR – Danske Studenter Rokclub
Ein. Dres. – Einheit Dresden
Ex. Coll., Oxf. – Exeter College, Oxford
FAV – Favorite Hammonia
1 & 3 Trin., Cam. – First & Third Trinity,
Cambridge
G'hopper – Grasshopper
H. Sch. – High School
IT – Institute of Technology
Kr. Znamia – Krasnoe Znamia
KRC – Kingston Rowing Club
L'boro' – Loughborough
LMBC – Lady Margaret Boat Club (St John's
College, Cambridge)
LRC – London Rowing Club
Mann. – Mannheim
Melb. – Melbourne
M'man. – Mosman
Nass. Hochst – Nassovia Hochst

NC – Nautical College
N'eastern – Northeastern
Nep. – Neptune
Not. Brit. – Nottingham Brittania Rowing Club
PBD – Poplar, Blackwall & District Rowing Club
Penn. – Pennsylvania
RMA – Royal Military Academy
Sc. – Scullers
Sch. – School
Schaf'en – Schaffhausen
SCVDF – SC Vittorino da Fettre, Piacenza
Seattle TC – Seattle Tennis Club
SEH – St Edmund Hall, Oxford
Strode's & Wall. Schs. – Strode's and Wallingford
Schools
Sub. Rms. – Subscription Rooms
Thames T'men – Thames Tradesmen
TRC – Thames Rowing Club
U. Brit. Col. – University of British Columbia
Vanc'r – Vancouver
Westminster H. – Westminster Hospital

Foreign crews:
Foreign crews are identified by the standard
international abbreviations except for USSR (URS).
The German Federal and Democratic Republics
signed separate Agreements with Henley before
the 1970 Regatta; previously all German crews were
identified 'GER'.

General:
L – Length; E – Easily; Disq. – Disqualified; NTT –
No Time Taken; NRO – Not rowed out; RO – Row-
over; CAN – Canvas; 1 – Berks Station; C – Centre
Station; 2 – Bucks Station.

The Grand Challenge Cup

		Barrier	Fawley	Finish
1891	Leander Club		(1)3.17	6.51
1929	Leander Club	2.01		
1934	Leander Club	1.55	3.15	6.44
1952	Leander Club	1.53	3.11	6.38
1957	Cornell Univ., USA			6.30
	Krasnoe Znamia, USSR	1.51	3.08	
1962	USSR Navy	1.49		
1964	CZ Viljnjus, USSR	1.48	3.05	6.23
1965	Ratzeburger RC, GER	1.46	3.00	6.16
1975	Harvard Univ., USA			6.13
1984	Leander Club & London RC	1.45	2.57	6.10
1987	USSR Army		2.56	

The Ladies' Challenge Plate

		Barrier	Fawley	Finish
1911	Eton College		3.19	6.56
1921	Pembroke Coll., Cam.			6.55
1929	First Trinity, Cam.	2.04		
1933	Trinity Hall, Cam.	2.03		
	First Trinity, Cam.	2.02		
	Lady Margaret BC, Cam.	2.01		
1934	Trinity Coll., Dublin	1.59	3.18	
	Jesus Coll., Cam.			6.48
1949	Lady Margaret BC, Cam.	1.56	3.13	6.43
1965	Jesus Coll., Cam.	1.54		
1970	GSR Aegir, HOL			6.42
1973	Harvard Univ., USA	1.53	3.10	
	University Coll., Dublin			6.37
	DSR Laga, HOL	1.52		6.36
	Harvard Univ., USA		3.09	6.34
	Univ. of Wisconsin, USA			6.32
1975	Durham Univ.	1.51		
	Isis BC	1.48		
	Univ. of London		3.08	6.30
1976	Trin. Coll. Hartford, USA			6.24
1982	Univ. of London		3.05	
	Brown Univ. USA			6.23
1987	Tideway Scullers		3.04	

The Thames Challenge Cup

		Barrier	*Fawley*	*Finish*
1886	London RC			7.08
	Wadham Coll., Oxf.		3.26	
1921	Corpus Christi Coll., Cam.		3.25	7.06
1926	Kingston RC		3.24	
1929	Thames RC	2.07		
1930	Vesta RC	2.04		
1933	Thames RC	2.03		
	Bedford RC	2.01		
1934	Westminster Bank RC	2.00	3.22	
	London RC			6.58
1949	Lady Margaret BC, Cam.	1.59	3.19	6.51
1958	Princeton Univ., USA	1.57	3.18	6.45
1960	Harvard Univ., USA	1.55	3.13	6.39
1962	National Provincial Bank	1.53	3.11	6.37
1965	Isis BC			6.35
	Derby RC	1.52	3.09	
1968	Leander Club	1.51		
1973	Princeton Univ., USA		3.08	6.33
1975	Garda Siochana, IRL	1.50		
	Quintin BC	1.49	3.05	
1976	Henley RC			6.32
	Christiania, NOR		3.04	6.25
1984	Vesta RC			6.24
	Leander Club		3.03	6.18
	Cantabrigian RC	1.48	3.00	6.16

The Princess Elizabeth Challenge Cup

		Barrier	*Fawley*	*Finish*
1947	Bedford School	2.06	3.33	7.25
1948	Bedford School	2.03	3.26	7.04
1951	Radley College	2.02	3.25	7.03
1952	Radley College		3.21	6.57
	Bryanston School	2.00		
1957	Shrewsbury School	1.59		6.56
1960	Shrewsbury School		3.18	6.53
	St Edward's School	1.57		
1962	Radley College			6.48
	Shrewsbury School	1.56	3.17	
1965	Emanuel School	1.55	3.14	6.44
1973	Ridley College, CAN	1.53	3.11	6.38
1975	St Paul's, Concord, USA	1.52		6.36
	Ridley College, CAN		3.10	6.32
1986	Hampton School		3.09	

The Stewards' Challenge Cup

		Barrier	*Fawley*	*Finish*
1908	Magdalen Coll., Oxf.		3.36	7.28
1925	Third Trinity, Cam.			7.27
1929	First Trinity, Cam.	2.14		
1930	London RC	2.08	3.35	
1934	Pembroke Coll., Cam.		3.33	7.24
1935	Zurich RC, SUI	2.04	3.28	7.14
1949	Trinity Coll., Oxf.			7.13
1960	Barn Cottage BC			7.10
	St Edmund Hall, Oxf.	2.03		
1962	Molesey BC	2.02	3.27	7.01
1965	Quintin BC	1.59	3.22	6.55
1973	Trud Leningrad, USSR	1.58	3.18	
1975	Lady Margaret BC, Cam.	1.57		
	Potomac BC, USA			6.50
1984	Notts. CRA & Tyne	1.55	3.13	6.44
1986	Ridley BC, CAN			6.41
1987	Dinamo Moscow, USSR			6.40

The Prince Philip Challenge Cup

		Barrier	Fawley	Finish
1963	Nereus, HOL	2.08	3.36	
	Auckland RC, NZL			7.27
1964	Molesey BC			7.25
1965	Thames RC	2.04	3.31	
	Tideway Scullers		3.30	7.16
	Leander Club	2.02	3.25	7.03
1973	Northeastern Univ., USA	1.58	3.21	7.00
1987	Soviet Army, USSR			6.51

The Queen Mother Challenge Cup

		Barrier	Fawley	Finish
1981	Ingleheim & Ulm, GFR	1.59	3.22	7.00
1982	Marlow & Thames T'men		3.19	6.57
1984	Nottinghamshire CRA	1.55	3.15	
	Maidenhead & Bewdley	1.53	3.12	6.37
1987	Ridley BC, CAN	1.49	3.05	6.22

The Visitors' Challenge Cup

		Barrier	Fawley	Finish
1908	Magdalen Coll., Oxf.		3.41	7.30
1911	Third Trinity, Cam.		3.39	
1925	Third Trinity, Cam.		3.37	
1929	Third Trinity, Cam.	2.35		
1930	Trinity Coll, Dublin	2.34		
	Brasenose Coll., Oxf.	2.14		
1934	First Trinity, Cam.	2.12		
1938	Oriel Coll., Oxf.	2.08	3.31	7.18
1952	Trinity Coll., Oxf.	2.04		
	Pembroke Coll., Cam.		3.30	7.15
1965	St Edmund Hall, Oxf.			7.13
1973	University of London	2.02	3.26	7.09
	Exeter University	2.01		
1975	Ealing High School		3.24	
	Hampton School			7.08
1976	Salisbury Sch., USA	2.00	3.23	
	University of London			7.04
1984	Imperial College, Lon.	1.59		
1986	University of London	1.58	3.21	
1987	Imperial College, Lon.			6.58

The Wyfold Challenge Cup

		Barrier	Fawley	Finish
1921	Jesus Coll., Cam.		3.39	7.35
1929	Jesus Coll., Cam.	2.16		
1933	Selwyn Coll., Cam.	2.15		
1934	Liverpool Victoria	2.12		
	Reading RC	2.09	3.38	
1949	Lensbury RC			7.24
1952	Corpus Christi Coll., Cam.	2.08	3.36	
1953	Royal Air Force	2.06	3.31	7.20
1960	Crowland RC	2.04	3.30	7.16
1962	University of London			7.13
	Nottingham & Union BC	2.03	3.28	
1965	Derby RC	2.01	3.25	7.06
1973	Tideway Scullers	2.00		
	Thames Tradesmen	1.53		7.02
1975	Nott. & Union BC		3.20	
	Leander Club			7.00
	Thames Tradesmen			6.57
1976	Univ. Coll. and Hosp., Lon.		3.18	
	Potomac BC, USA			6.54
1984	Nottinghamshire CRA		3.16	
1987	Nottinghamshire CRA			6.49

The Britannia Challenge Cup

		Barrier	Fawley	Finish
1968	Thames RC	2.05	3.36	7.34
1969	Kingston RC			7.32
1973	Univ. of London	2.03	3.29	7.22
	Isis BC		3.28	7.15
1975	Leander Club	2.00	3.25	
1976	Tideway Scullers			7.11
1982	Molesey BC			7.08
1984	Neptune RC, IRL			7.02
	Tideway Scullers	1.59	3.21	7.00

The Silver Goblets and Nickalls' Challenge Cup

		Barrier	*Fawley*	*Finish*
1906	Johnstone & Powell		*3.51*	
1911	Beresford & Cloutte dead			*8.08*
	Logan & Rought heat			
1929	Killick & J Beresford Jr	2.29		
1933	Powell & Gilmour	2.24		
1934	Braun & Moller, GER	2.21	3.55	
1952	Bywater & Christie	2.18	3.54	8.05
1953	Baetens & Knuysen, BEL	2.14	3.46	7.51
1957	Plaksin & Soldatov, USSR	2.10	3.42	
1962	Lecky & Budd			7.49
1964	Kiely & Lecky			7.48
1965	Gorny & Bergau, GER		3.41	7.35
1966	Lucke & Boethe, GER	2.08		
1973	Borchelt & Adams, USA		3.40	
1976	Luxford & Shinners, AUS		3.39	7.30
1984	Beattie & Stanhope	2.03	3.34	
1987	Holmes & Redgrave	2.02	3.30	7.18

The Double Sculls Challenge Cup

		Barrier	*Fawley*	*Finish*
1939	J. Beresford Jr & Southwood	2.20	3.58	8.27
1946	Panelo & Chafuen, ARG	2.19	3.52	8.08
1948	Piessens & Collet, BEL	2.15	3.47	7.54
1949	Parsner & Larsen, DAN	2.12	3.39	7.27
1953	Schreiver & Stebler, SUI	2.04	3.32	7.21
1960	Justicz & Birkmyre		3.28	7.17
1965	Studach & Bürgin, SUI		3.27	7.01
1972	Delafield & Crooks	2.03		
1973	Isler & Ruckstuhl, SUI	2.02		
	Hart & Baillieu		3.23	6.59
	Hart & Baillieu with Isler & Ruckstuhl, SUI (level)	2.01		
1982	Clift & Redgrave	1.58		

The Diamond Sculls

		Barrier	Fawley	Finish
1905	Kelly		(1)3.55	8.10
1929	Gunther, HOL	2.28		
1930	Pearce, CAN	2.25		
1933	Zavrel, TCH	2.24		
	Buhtz, GER	2.15	3.50	
1938	Burk, USA			8.02
1953	George, BEL			8.00
1958	Ivanov, USSR	2.13		
1960	Mackenzie		3.48	
1962	Mackenzie		3.47	
1964	Cromwell, USA			7.54
1964	Hill, GER		3.43	
	Spero, USA			7.42
1973	Drea, IRL	2.11	3.42	
1975	Dietz, USA	2.10		
	Drea, IRL	2.09	3.41	7.40
1987	Kolbe, GFR	2.06	3.39	

Appendix 3 Winners and Trophies

The Grand Challenge Cup 1839

As has been remarked elsewhere, the early Henley rulemakers started from scratch. There were no Rules for Regattas, no Laws of Boat Racing, and no Amateur Status Rules to follow.

The Henley Grand Challenge Cup was offered as an eight-oared event open to all comers, though the founders can have had no expectations of entries from abroad. The published qualifications stated:

> That any crew composed of members of a College of either of the Universities of Oxford, Cambridge, or London, the schools of Eton and Westminster, the officers of the two Brigades of Household Troops, or of members of a club established at least one year previous to the time of entering, be considered eligible.

Since any 'established club' was admissible, it may at first sight seem illogical that certain categories of oarsmen were mentioned specifically. But there was a differentiation. A 'club' had to be 'established'. But any group of Guards officers, any Etonians or Westminsters, Oxonians or Cantabs, could make up a crew without necessarily having a formal 'club'.

Examples would be 'Cambridge Subscription Rooms, London', Westminster and Eton (Oxford)', 'Grenadier Guards', and 'Oxford Aquatics'. Effectively the Stewards were indicating that these categories were automatically regarded as eligible 'amateurs'.

Over the years, there have been minor alterations to the wording, adding other schools, branches of the armed forces and so on, and even today members of universities (no longer confined to Oxford and Cambridge), schools (no longer specified), and the armed forces (no longer 'officers') are specified as eligible, irrespective of whether or not they enter under the colours of an 'established club'. In 1970 'composite' crews were admitted: but individually the oarsmen must be members of established clubs. Although a composite crew can consist of members of nine different clubs, only two may be named. This is solely a matter of programme convenience.

In essence the Grand Challenge Cup was and is Henley's premier eight-oared event, 'open to the world'.

Throughout this Appendix † applies to the time over the Shortened Course in 1923.

Grand Challenge Cup

Year	Winner	Station	Loser	Lengths	Time
1839	Trinity College, Cam.	I	Etonian Club, London	$\frac{1}{2}$	8.30
1840	Leander Club	I	Trinity College, Cam.		9.15
1841	Cam. Sub. Rms., Lon.	I	Leander Club	Disq.	
1842	Cam. Sub. Rms., Lon.	I	Cambridge Univ. BC	Feet	8.30
1843	Oxford University BC	2	Cam. Sub. Rms., Lon.	I	9.00
1844	Etonian Club, Oxf.	2	Caius College, Cam.	3	8.25
1845	Cambridge University BC	2	Oxford University BC	2	8.30
1846	Thames Club, London	I	First Trinity, Cam.	$3\frac{1}{2}$	8.15
1847	Oxford University BC	2	Thames Club, London	3	8.00
1848	Oxford University BC	2	Thames Club, London	E	9.11
1849	Wadham College, Oxf.	C	Second Trinity, Cam.	Disq.	
1850	Oxford University BC			RO	
1851	Oxford University BC	2	Cambridge Univ. BC	6	7.45
1852	Oxford University BC	I	Oxford Aquatic Club		
1853	Oxford University BC	I	Cambridge Univ. BC	18in.	8.30
1854	First Trinity, Cam.	I	Wadham College, Oxf.	2	8.15
1855	Cambridge University BC.	2	Oxford University BC	$2\frac{1}{2}$	8.32
1856	Royal Chester RC	I	Lady Margaret BC, Cam.	E	
1857	London RC	I	Oxford University BC	$1\frac{1}{4}$	7.55
1858	Cambridge University BC	I	London RC	$\frac{1}{2}$	7.26
1859	London RC	2	Cambridge Univ. BC	$\frac{1}{4}$	7.45
1860	First Trinity, Cam.	I	London RC	3	8.45
1861	First Trinity, Cam.	I	Trinity College, Oxf.	$2\frac{1}{2}$	8.10
1862	London RC	C	Trinity College, Oxf.	3	8.05
1863	University College, Oxf.	C	Brasenose College, Oxf.	2	7.42
1864	Kingston RC	I	University College, Oxf	$1\frac{1}{2}$	7.43
1865	Kingston RC	C	London RC	$2\frac{1}{2}$	7.25
1866	Etonian Club, Oxf.	I	Kingston RC	$\frac{1}{4}$	8.29
1867	Etonian Club, Oxf.	I	London RC	$1\frac{1}{2}$	7.54
1868	London RC	I	Eton College	$1\frac{1}{4}$	7.20
1869	Etonian Club, Oxf.	I	London RC	2	7.28
1870	Etonian Club, Oxf.	I	London RC	$1\frac{1}{4}$	7.18
1871	Etonian Club, Oxf.	I	London RC	$1\frac{1}{2}$	8.05
1872	London RC	I	Kingston RC	6	8.27
1873	London RC	C	Eton College	3	7.52
1874	London RC	I	Eton College	$\frac{2}{3}$	7.41
1875	Leander Club	I	Molesey BC	2	7.19
1876	Thames RC	2	Jesus College, Cam.	I	7.26
1877	London RC	I	Thames RC	$1\frac{1}{4}$	8.02
1878	Thames RC	I	Jesus College, Cam.	2	7.42
1879	Jesus College, Cam.	C	Kingston RC	2	8.39
1880	Leander Club	I	London RC	$1\frac{1}{2}$	7.03

Grand Challenge Cup

Year	Winner	Station	Loser	Lengths	Time
1881	London RC	2	Leander Club	1	7.23
1882	Exeter College, Oxf.	c	Thames RC	5	8.11
1883	London RC	1	Twickenham RC	1	7.51
1884	London RC	1	Twickenham RC	NRO	7.27
1885	Jesus College, Cam.	1	Twickenham RC	2	7.22
1886	Trinity Hall, Cam.	2	Etonian Club, Oxf.	$\frac{1}{2}$	6.53$\frac{1}{2}$
1887	Trinity Hall, Cam.	2	Thames RC	4ft	6.56
1888	Thames RC	2	Leander Club	$\frac{3}{4}$	7.01
1889	Thames RC	2	New College, Oxf.	1	7.04
1890	London RC	2	Brasenose College, Oxf.	$1\frac{3}{4}$	7.04$\frac{1}{2}$
1891	Leander Club	1	London RC	1	6.51
1892	Leander Club	2	Thames RC	3	7.48$\frac{1}{2}$
1893	Leander Club	1	London RC	$1\frac{3}{4}$	7.12
1894	Leander Club	2	Thames RC	$\frac{1}{2}$	7.22
1895	Trinity Hall, Cam.	2	New College, Oxf.	$\frac{1}{3}$	7.30
1896	Leander Club	2	Thames RC	$2\frac{1}{4}$	7.43
1897	New College, Oxf.	2	Leander Club	2ft	6.51
1898	Leander Club	1	First Trinity, Cam.	$\frac{3}{4}$	7.13
1899	Leander Club	2	London RC	$1\frac{1}{4}$	7.12
1900	Leander Club	2	Trinity College, Cam.	$\frac{1}{2}$	7.06
1901	Leander Club	2	Univ. of Penn., USA	1	7.04
1902	Third Trinity, Cam.	1	Leander Club	$1\frac{1}{2}$	7.17
1903	Leander Club	2	Third Trinity, Cam.	6ft	7.09
1904	Leander Club	2	New College, Oxf.	1	7.20
1905	Leander Club	1	S Nautique Gand, BEL	$2\frac{1}{4}$	6.58
1906	C Nautique Gand, BEL	2	Trinity Hall, Cam.	3	7.09
1907	S Nautique Gand, BEL	2	Christ Church, Oxf.	1	7.31
1908	Christ Church, Oxf.	1	Eton College	$1\frac{1}{2}$	7.10
1909	RC Nautique Gand, BEL	2	Jesus College, Cam.	1	7.08
1910	Magdalen College, Oxf.	1	Jesus College, Cam.	2	7.19
1911	Magdalen College, Oxf.	2	Jesus College, Cam.	$2\frac{1}{4}$	7.02
1912	Sydney RC, AUS	1	Leander Club	$\frac{3}{4}$	7.06
1913	Leander Club	2	Jesus College, Cam.	1	7.11
1914	Harvard AA, USA	2	Union BC, Boston, USA	$1\frac{1}{4}$	7.20
1920	Magdalen College, Oxf.	2	Leander Club	2	7.24
1921	Magdalen College, Oxf.	2	Jesus College, Cam.	1	6.54
1922	Leander Club	1	Thames RC	1	7.36
1923	Thames RC	1	Pembroke College, Cam.	$\frac{1}{3}$	6.45†
1924	Leander Club	1	Jesus College, Cam.	6ft	8.03
1925	Leander Club	1	Thames RC	$\frac{3}{4}$	6.53
1926	Leander Club	1	Lady Margaret BC, Cam.	2	6.56
1927	Thames RC	1	London RC	$\frac{3}{4}$	7.16

Grand Challenge Cup

Year	Winner	Station	Loser	Lengths	Time
1928	Thames RC	1	First Trinity, Cam.	$1\frac{1}{2}$	6.56
1929	Leander Club	2	Thames RC	2	7.00
1930	London RC	2	Leander Club	$1\frac{1}{2}$	6.59
1931	London RC	2	Thames RC	$\frac{1}{3}$	7.33
1932	Leander Club	2	Thames RC	$\frac{1}{2}$	7.19
1933	London RC	2	Berliner RC, GER	$\frac{1}{4}$	7.36
1934	Leander Club	1	Princeton Univ., USA	$\frac{3}{4}$	6.45
1935	Pembroke College, Cam.	1	Leander Club	$1\frac{3}{4}$	6.52
1936	Zurich RC, SUI	2	Leander Club	$1\frac{1}{4}$	7.25
1937	R G Wiking, GER	2	Jesus College, Cam.	2	7.33
1938	London RC	1	Trinity Hall, Cam.	$1\frac{1}{3}$	6.58
1939	Harvard Univ., USA	2	Argonaut RC, CAN	3	7.40
1946	Leander Club	2	RC Zurich, SUI	$\frac{3}{4}$	7.01
1947	Jesus College, Cam.	1	R Delftsche S., HOL	$1\frac{1}{4}$	7.14
1948	Thames RC	1	Jesus & Pembroke, Cam.	$2\frac{1}{2}$	7.02
1949	Leander Club	1	Thames RC	1	6.54
1950	Harvard Univ., USA	2	K S R Njord, HOL	$1\frac{1}{4}$	7.23
1951	Lady Margaret BC, Cam.	1	DSR Laga, HOL	1	7.16
1952	Leander Club	1	Sydney RC, AUS	$\frac{1}{2}$	6.38
1953	Leander Club	1	USM des Transports, FRA	$\frac{3}{4}$	6.49
1954	Krylia Sovetov, USSR	2	Leander Club	$2\frac{1}{2}$	7.16
1955	Univ. of Penn., USA	2	Vancouver RC, CAN	$\frac{1}{3}$	6.56
1956	CSFAF, FRA	2	RK Three Towns, SUE	1	7.06
1957	Cornell Univ., USA	1	Yale Univ., USA	$\frac{1}{2}$	6.53
1958	Trud Leningrad, USSR	2	Leichhardt RC, AUS	$2\frac{1}{2}$	6.40
1959	Harvard Univ., USA	1	Thames RC	$2\frac{3}{4}$	6.57
1960	Molesey BC	1	Oxford University BC	$\frac{1}{3}$	6.35
1961	USSR Navy, Moscow	1	Leander Club	1	6.43
1962	USSR Navy, Moscow	2	Moto Guzzi, ITA	$\frac{1}{3}$	6.40
1963	University of London	2	Cornell Univ., USA	$\frac{3}{4}$	6.38
1964	CZ Viljnjus, USSR	2	University of London	E	6.25
1965	Ratzeburger RC, GER	2	Vesper BC, USA	$\frac{1}{2}$	6.16
1966	TSC, Berlin, GER	1	Tideway Scullers Sch.	$\frac{1}{2}$	6.35
1967	SCW Leipzig, GER	2	Tideway Scullers Sch.	$2\frac{1}{2}$	6.46
1968	University of London	1	Oxford University BC	3	7.56
1969	Einheit Dresden, GER	2	Univ. of Penn., USA	$\frac{3}{4}$	6.28
1970	Vorwarts Rostock, GER	1	GSR Aegir, HOL	$\frac{1}{2}$	6.34
1971	Tideway Scullers School	2	Cairo Police, UAR	$2\frac{1}{3}$	6.46
1972	WMF Moscow, USSR	2	N'eastern Univ., USA	$\frac{2}{3}$	6.33
1973	Trud Kolomna, USSR	1	N'eastern Univ., USA	$2\frac{2}{3}$	6.23
1974	Trud Club, USSR	2	Leander & Thames T'men	$\frac{1}{2}$	6.34
1975	Leander & Thames T'men	1	Harvard Univ., USA	2	6.16

Grand Challenge Cup

Year	Winner	Station	Loser	Lengths	Time
1976	Thames Tradesmen	1	Leander Club	$\frac{2}{3}$	6.25
1977	Univ. of Washington, USA	1	Leander & Thames T'men	1	6.27
1978	Trakia Club, BUL	2	Univ. of Washington, USA	$\frac{3}{4}$	6.51
1979	Thames T'men & LRC	2	Yale Univ., USA	$2\frac{1}{3}$	6.35
1980	Charles River RA, USA	1	Waikato & Wairau, NZL	$1\frac{1}{4}$	6.35
1981	Oxf. Univ. & Thames T'men	2	Leander Club & Tyrian	$\frac{1}{2}$	7.15
1982	Leander Club & London RC	2	Univ. of Lon. & Tyrian	$\frac{1}{2}$	NTT
1983	London RC & Univ. of Lon.	2	Cambridge Univ. BC	4	6.26
1984	Leander Club & London RC	1	Univ. of Washington, USA	3	6.22
1985	Harvard Univ., USA	1	Princeton Univ., USA	$3\frac{2}{3}$	6.27
1986	Nautilus RC	2	Univ. of Penn., USA	$\frac{3}{4}$	6.18
1987	Soviet Army, USSR	1	Ridley BC, CAN	$1\frac{1}{3}$	6.11
1988	Leander Club & Univ. of Lon.	2	Aus. Inst. for Sport, AUS	1ft	6.17

The Ladies' Challenge Plate 1845

Originally offered as the New Challenge Cup, the trophy was not ready in 1845 and medals only were presented in the first year. The title is a mystery for when the trophy appeared in 1846 it turned out to be not a Plate but a handsome Ewer. It has been suggested that it was given by the 'Ladies of Henley', but there is no record of this.

Destined to be Henley's second-ranking eight-oar event it was originally 'open to college and other amateur clubs, except university clubs, subscription rooms, or clubs similarly constituted'. In 1848 the qualification was widened to include clubs of 'other public establishments, and clubs restricted to one particular profession, or class of persons, or to any particular town or place (distant at least seven miles from Westminster Bridge)', with the odd proviso that no member of the crews should at the same time be a member of any other club.

After being won by Royal Chester in 1856 the qualification was narrowed to admit only Oxford and Cambridge college crews, and Eton and Westminster schools. For the next 130 years the Ladies' Plate was a student event, though the connotation of 'student' was progressively widened.

In 1985 the Ladies' Plate was opened to all clubs, so that it is now similar to the Grand Challenge Cup except that, as the sole remaining concession to students, combined entries are accepted from schools or from college boat clubs within the same university, but not from clubs.

Ladies' Challenge Plate

Year	Winner	Station	Time	Year	Winner	Station	Time
1845	St George's Club, Lon.	I	8.25	1887	Trinity Hall, Cam.	2	7.10
1846	First Trinity, Cam.	I		1888	Lady Margaret BC, Cam.	I	7.18
1847	Brasenose College, Oxf.	I	9.00	1889	Christ Church, Oxf.	2	7.22
1848	Christ Church, Oxf.	2		1890	Balliol College, Oxf.	2	7.16
1849	Wadham College, Oxf.	I		1891	Balliol College, Oxf.	I	7.20
1850	Lincoln College, Oxf.	RO		1892	First Trinity, Cam.	2	7.43$\frac{1}{2}$
1851	Brasenose College, Oxf.	2	8.10	1893	Eton College	2	7.32
1852	Pembroke College, Oxf.	RO		1894	Eton College	I	7.36
1853	First Trinity, Cam.	I	8.15	1895	Eton College	I	7.25
1854	First Trinity, Cam.	2	7.55	1896	Eton College	2	8.06
1855	Balliol College, Oxf.		7.58	1897	Eton College	2	7.01
1856	Royal Chester RC	C		1898	Eton College	2	7.03
1857	Exeter College, Oxf.	2	7.57	1899	Eton College	I	7.20
1858	Balliol College, Oxf.	2	7.51	1900	New College, Oxf.	2	7.18
1859	First Trinity, Cam.	2	7.55	1901	University Coll., Oxf.	2	7.28
1860	First Trinity, Cam.	RO		1902	University Coll., Oxf.	2	7.16
1861	First Trinity, Cam.	I	8.10	1903	Magdalen College, Oxf.	I	7.33
1862	University Coll., Oxf.	C	8.17	1904	Eton College	I	7.20
1863	University Coll., Oxf.	C	7.23	1905	Eton College	2	7.12
1864	Eton College	RO		1906	First Trinity, Cam.	2	7.23
1865	Third Trinity, Cam.	C	Disq.	1907	Trinity Hall, Cam.	2	7.44
1866	Eton College	2	8.16	1908	Jesus College, Cam.	I	7.05
1867	Eton College	C	7.55	1909	St John's Coll., Oxf.	I	7.09
1868	Eton College	2	7.25	1910	Eton College	I	7.16
1869	Eton College	C	7.58	1911	Eton College	2	6.56
1870	Eton College	C	7.46	1912	Eton College	I	7.04
1871	Pembroke College, Oxf.	I	7.59	1913	First Trinity, Cam.	2	7.24
1872	Jesus College, Cam.	I	8.35	1914	Pembroke College, Cam.	2	7.24
1873	Jesus College, Cam.	2	7.53	1920	Christ Church, Oxf.	2	7.30
1874	First Trinity, Cam.	C	8.06	1921	Eton College	I	7.09
1875	Trinity Coll., Dublin	I	7.30	1922	Brasenose College, Oxf.	2	7.47
1876	Jesus College, Cam.	C	7.31	1923	Trinity College, Oxf.	2	6.55†
1877	Jesus College, Cam.	C	8.23	1924	Shrewsbury School	2	8.04
1878	Jesus College, Cam.	I	8.52	1925	Lady Margaret BC, Cam.	2	7.07
1879	Lady Margaret BC, Cam.	C	8.52	1926	Jesus College, Cam.	I	7.05
1880	Trinity Hall, Cam.	I	7.26	1927	First Trinity, Cam.	I	7.29
1881	First Trinity, Cam.	I	7.51	1928	Jesus College, Cam.	I	7.06
1882	Eton College	C	8.37	1929	First Trinity, Cam.	I	7.16
1883	Christ Church, Oxf.	I	7.51	1930	Lady Margaret BC, Cam.	2	7.10
1884	Eton College	2	7.37	1931	Jesus College, Cam.	2	8.07
1885	Eton College	2	7.21	1932	Shrewsbury School	2	7.40
1886	Pembroke College, Cam.	2	7.17	1933	Lady Margaret BC, Cam.	I	7.38
				1934	Jesus College, Cam.	I	6.48
				1935	Trinity Hall, Cam.	2	7.07
				1936	First Trinity, Cam.	2	7.48

Ladies' Challenge Plate

Year	Winner	Station	Time	Year	Winner	Station	Time
1937	Clare College, Cam.	1	7.38	1966	Lady Margaret BC, Cam.	1	7.04
1938	Radley College	1	6.56	1967	First & Third Trin., Cam.	1	7.03
1939	Clare College, Cam.	2	8.13	1968	Cherwell BC	1	8.23
1946	Jesus College, Cam.	2	7.08	1969	ASR Nereus, HOL	2	6.55
1947	First & Third Trin., Cam.	2	7.21	1970	GSR Aegir, HOL	2	7.00
1948	Eton College	2	7.15	1971	University of London	2	7.00
1949	Lady Margaret BC, Cam.	1	6.50	1972	DSR Laga, HOL	1	6.59
1950	New College, Oxf.	2	7.25	1973	Harvard Univ, USA	1	6.35
1951	Pembroke College, Cam.	2	7.25	1974	Univ. Coll., Dublin	1	6.58
1952	Lady Margaret BC, Cam.	2	6.50	1975	University of London	1	6.31
1953	Jesus College, Cam.	2	7.00	1976	Trin. Coll., Hartford, USA	2	6.49
1954	First & Third Trin., Cam.	2	7.33	1977	Trinity Coll., Dublin	1	6.53
1955	Queens' College, Cam.	2	7.26	1978	Imperial College, Lon.	2	6.59
1956	Peterhouse, Cam.	2	7.41	1979	Yale Univ., USA	1	7.14
1957	Pembroke College, Cam.	1	7.11	1980	Yale Univ., USA	1	6.37
1958	Jesus College, Cam.	2	6.51	1981	Univ. of Wash'ton, USA	2	7.18
1959	Lady Margaret BC, Cam.	1	7.13	1982	University of London	1	6.56
1960	Eton College	2	6.50	1983	Harvard Univ., USA	1	6.35
1961	Lady Margaret BC, Cam.	1	7.04	1984	Brown University, USA	1	6.42
1962	Queens' College, Cam.	2	6.54	1985	Leander Club	1	6.26
1963	RMA Sandhurst	2	6.55	1986	Neptune RC, IRL	2	6.29
1964	Pembroke College, Cam.	1	6.47	1987	University of London	2	6.23
1965	St Edmund Hall, Oxf.	1	6.49	1988	Mercantile RC, AUS	1	6.23

The Thames Challenge Cup 1868

The Thames Cup was instituted as the third-ranking eight-oared event. Amalgamations of college or club crews – which today we would call 'composites' – were barred, as also were individuals who had rowed for, or were entered for, the Grand or Stewards' Cups, or who had rowed Head of the River at Oxford or Cambridge.

The rule was simplified in 1869, and became 'the same as for the Grand but no crew or individual to enter for the Thames Cup and the Grand or Stewards' at the same Regatta'. This was modified in 1880 to exclude only winners of those events.

In 1910 doubles entries in the Thames and Ladies' were barred, and in 1950 the same proviso was extended to the Princess Elizabeth Cup. The prohibition on past winners of the Grand and Stewards' was withdrawn in 1951, and the ban on double entries in the Thames and Stewards' was removed in 1954. At this point the Thames Challenge Cup qualification was therefore the same as for the Grand, but barring double entries in the other eight-oar events.

The Thames Cup qualification was radically changed in 1985, and in 1987, to ensure a standard below that of the Ladies' Plate. Recent Henley winners and internationals are excluded, as also are crews, other than school crews, rated on the Amateur Rowing Association's points system above the equivalent of Senior II on 1 May of the year of entry.

Thames Challenge Cup

Year	Winner	Station	Time
1868	Pembroke College, Oxf.	C	7.46
1869	Oscillators Club		RO
1870	Oscillators Club	1	7.53
1871	Ino RC	2	8.36
1872	Thames RC	C	8.42
1873	Thames RC	C	8.02
1874	Thames RC	1	8.19
1875	London RC	1	7.33
1876	West London RC	1	7.36
1877	London RC	1	8.29
1878	London RC	C	7.55
1879	Twickenham RC	1	8.55
1880	London RC	C	7.24
1881	Twickenham RC	1	7.50
1882	Royal Chester RC	1	
1883	London RC	1	8.05
1884	Twickenham RC	1	7.48
1885	London RC	1	7.36
1886	London RC	2	7.08½
1887	Trinity Hall, Cam.	2	7.20
1888	Lady Margaret BC, Cam.	2	7.19
1889	Christ Church, Oxf.	1	7.16
1890	Thames RC	2	7.21½
1891	Molesey BC	2	7.18
1892	Jesus College, Cam.	2	8.10
1893	Thames RC	1	7.49
1894	Trinity College, Oxf.	1	7.58
1895	ASR Nereus, HOL	1	7.29
1896	Emmanuel College, Cam.	2	8.07
1897	Kingston RC	2	7.09
1898	Trinity College, Oxf.	1	7.19
1899	First Trinity, Cam.	2	7.25
1900	Trinity College, Cam.	2	7.24
1901	Trinity Hall, Cam.	2	7.23
1902	Trinity Hall, Cam.	1	7.34
1903	Trinity College, Dublin	1	7.37
1904	Caius College, Cam.	1	7.30
1905	Thames RC	1	7.28
1906	Christ's College, Cam.	2	7.23
1907	Christ's College, Cam.	2	7.45
1908	Wadham College, Oxf.	2	7.15
1909	Wadham College, Oxf.	2	7.21
1910	Anglian BC	2	7.36
1911	First Trinity, Cam.	1	7.13
1912	RC de Paris, FRA	2	7.33
1913	Oriel College, Oxf.	2	7.30
1914	Caius College, Cam.	1	7.27
1920	Thames RC	2	7.43
1921	Christiania RK, NOR	2	7.12
1922	Worcester College, Oxf.	2	7.56
1923	First Trinity, Cam.	1	7.12†
1924	Maidenhead RC	1	8.29
1925	First Trinity, Cam.	1	7.16
1926	Selwyn College, Cam.	1	7.09
1927	Thames RC	1	7.34
1928	Thames RC	1	7.23
1929	Browne & Nichols, USA	2	7.28
1930	Vesta RC	1	7.23
1931	London RC	1	7.43
1932	London RC	1	7.41
1933	Kent School, USA	1	7.30
1934	Thames RC	2	7.04
1935	London RC	1	7.05
1936	Tabor Academy, USA	1	7.44
1937	Tabor Academy, USA	2	7.31
1938	Kent School, USA	2	7.03
1939	Tabor Academy, USA	1	7.53
1946	Imperial College, Lon.	1	7.11
1947	Kent School, USA	2	7.22
1948	Princeton Univ., USA	2	7.20
1949	Princeton Univ., USA	2	6.58
1950	Kent School, USA	1	7.34
1951	Univ. of Penn., USA	1	7.19
1952	Univ. of Penn., USA	2	7.03
1953	Royal Air Force	2	6.59
1954	Massachusetts IT, USA	2	7.24
1955	Massachusetts IT, USA	2	7.21
1956	Princeton Univ., USA	1	7.10
1957	Princeton Univ., USA	1	7.08
1958	Harvard Univ., USA	1	6.57
1959	Harvard Univ., USA	2	7.13
1960	Harvard Univ., USA	1	6.47
1961	University of London	2	6.59
1962	Nat. Provincial Bank	1	6.46

Thames Challenge Cup

Year	Winner	Station	Time
1963	Queens' College, Cam.	I	6.53
1964	Eliot House, USA	2	6.55
1965	Isis BC	I	6.37
1966	Harvard Univ., USA	I	6.57
1967	Cornell Univ., USA	2	7.06
1968	Leander Club	I	8.08
1969	Leander Club	I	6.43
1970	Leander Club	2	7.01
1971	Harvard Univ., USA	2	6.48
1972	Harvard Univ., USA	2	6.55
1973	Princeton Univ., USA	2	6.37
1974	Antwerpse RV, BEL	2	6.52
1975	Garda Siochana, IRL	I	6.37

Year	Winner	Station	Time
1976	Harvard Univ., USA	2	6.39
1977	London RC	I	6.37
1978	London RC	2	6.54
1979	Leander Club	I	6.49
1980	University of London	2	6.26
1981	Charles River RA, USA	2	7.16
1982	Charles River RA, USA	2	6.47
1983	University of London	2	6.38
1984	Cantabrigian RC	2	6.30
1985	Ridley College, CAN	2	6.34
1986	Ridley College, CAN	I	6.35
1987	Univ. Coll. Galway, IRL	I	6.34
1988	Tideway Scullers Sch.	I	6.41

The Princess Elizabeth Challenge Cup 1946

The Princess Elizabeth Cup was instituted in 1946, over a shortened course of about one mile and with competition on the last two days of the Regatta only, being intended as an encouragement to the weaker schools who stood no chance in the Ladies' Plate.

The full course was used in the following year. In 1949 double entries in the Princess Elizabeth and Thames Cup were banned, and the same prohibition was extended to the Ladies' Plate in 1950. Foreign schools were admitted in 1964.

Year	Winner	Station	Time
1946	Bedford School	I	4.54*
1947	Bedford School	2	7.25
1948	Bedford School	2	7.20
1949	Winchester College	2	7.11
1950	St Paul's School	2	7.44
1951	Bedford School	2	7.27
1952	Radley College	2	7.00
1953	St Paul's School	2	7.06
1954	Winchester College	2	7.59
1955	Shrewsbury School	2	7.24
1956	Eton College	I	7.25

* Shortened course from Remenham Barrier

Year	Winner	Station	Time
1957	St Paul's School	I	7.19
1958	St Edward's School	I	6.59
1959	St Edward's School	2	7.15
1960	Shrewsbury School	I	6.53
1961	Shrewsbury School	2	7.07
1962	Radley College	I	6.58
1963	NC, Pangbourne	I	7.02
1964	Wash'ton-Lee H. Sch., USA	I	6.52
1965	Tabor Academy, USA	2	6.44
1966	Emanuel School	2	6.55
1967	Eton College	I	7.03
1968	J. E. B. Stuart H. Sch., USA	2	8.17

Princess Elizabeth Cup

Year	Winner	Station	Time	Year	Winner	Station	Time
1969	Wash'ton–Lee H. Sch., USA	1	7.00	1979	Ridley College, CAN	2	6.59
1970	Ridley College, CAN	1	7.06	1980	St Paul's Sch., Conn., USA	1	7.19
1971	Pangbourne College	1	7.04	1981	Holy Spirit H. Sc., USA	2	7.35
1972	Kent School, USA	2	7.02	1982	Eton College	2	7.09
1973	Ridley College, CAN	1	6.43	1983	Eton College	1	6.52
1974	Holy Spirit H. Sch., USA	1	7.10	1984	St Edward's School	1	6.48
1975	Ridley College, CAN	1	6.32	1985	Hampton School	1	6.45
1976	Holy Spirit H. Sch., USA	2	6.37	1986	Hampton School	1	6.37
1977	Ridley College, CAN	1	6.53	1987	Belmont Hill Sch., USA	2	6.34
1978	Eton College	2	7.10	1988	Hampton School	2	6.41

The Ladies' Challenge Plate

The Thames Challenge Cup

The Princess Elizabeth Challenge Cup

The Stewards' Challenge Cup 1841

Instituted in 1841 this was the premier event for coxed fours. The Challenge Cup was not ready until the spring of 1842 when it was presented to the 1841 winners. The Stewards' Cup was offered for coxless fours in 1873; the qualification has always been 'the same as for the Grand Challenge Cup'.

Year	Winner	Station	Loser	Lengths	Time
1841	Oxford Midge Club, Lon.	I	Cambridge Sub. Rms.	I	—
1842	Oxford Midge Club, Lon.	C	Dreadnought Club, Henley	2	9.16
1843	St George's Club, Lon.	I	Oxford Midge Club, Lon.	2	10.15
1844	Oxford University BC	C	Oxford Sub. Rms.	E	9.16
1845	Oxford University BC	2	St George's Club, Lon.	feet	8.25
1846	Oxford University BC		Guy's Club, London	E	—
1847	Christ Church, Oxf.			RO	
1848	Christ Church, Oxf.			RO	
1849	Leander Club	C	Second Trinity, Cam.	NRO	—
1850	Oxford University BC			RO	
1851	Cambridge Univ. BC		Brasenose College, Oxf.	4	—
1852	Oxford University BC		Argonaut Club	$2\frac{1}{2}$	—
1853	Oxford University BC	2	Argonaut Club	$2\frac{1}{2}$	8.57
1854	Pembroke College, Oxf.	2	Lady Margaret BC, Cam.		9.38
1855	Royal Chester RC		Lady Margaret BC, Cam.	E	—
1856	Argonaut Club, London			RO	
1857	London RC	I	Lady Margaret BC, Cam.	4	8.25
1858	London RC			RO	
1859	Third Trinity, Cam.	2	London RC	2ft	8.25
1860	First Trinity, Cam.	2	London RC	E	9.26
1861	First Trinity, Cam.	C	London RC	2	9.35
1862	Brasenose College, Oxf.	I	Third Trinity, Cam.	2	9.40
1863	University College, Oxf.	C	Brasenose College, Oxf.	I	8.24
1864	London RC	I	University Coll., Oxf.	$1\frac{3}{4}$	
1865	Third Trinity, Cam.	C	London RC	$\frac{2}{3}$	8.13
1866	University Coll., Oxf.	I	Kingston RC	4	9.28
1867	University Coll., Oxf.	I	Oxf. Radleian Club	I	8.45
1868	London RC	2	University Coll., Oxf.	NRO	8.22
1869	London RC	I	Oxf. Radleian Club	2	8.36
1870	Etonian Club, Oxf.	I	London RC	$\frac{2}{3}$	8.05
1871	London RC	2	Kingston RC	I	9.09
1872	London RC	I	Kingston RC	E	9.21

56. Upmarket – Fawley Bar.　　　　57. Downmarket – Remenham Farm.

58. Beer . . .

59. . . . or champagne.

60. 'I never eat when I am driving.'

Stewards' Challenge Cup

Year	Winner	Station	Loser	Lengths	Time
1873	London RC	C	Kingston RC	3	8.23
1874	London RC	C	Thames RC	3	9.00
1875	London RC	C	Leander Club	$2\frac{1}{2}$	7.56
1876	London RC	1	Thames RC	E	8.27
1877	London RC	C	Thames RC	E	9.07
1878	London RC	1	Shoe-Wae-Cae-Mette, USA	NRO	8.37
1879	Jesus College, Cam.	1	Lady Margaret BC, Cam.	2	9.37
1880	Thames RC	1	Molesey BC	2	7.58
1881	Hertford College, Oxf.	C	Thames RC	NRO	8.15
1882	Hertford College, Oxf.	1	Thames RC	E	—
1883	Thames RC	1	London RC	NRO	—
1884	Kingston RC	1	Twickenham RC	Disq.	—
1885	Trinity Hall, Cam.	1	Jesus College, Cam.	E	7.53
1886	Thames RC	1	Trinity Hall, Cam.	1	7.39
1887	Trinity Hall, Cam.	2	Leander Club	NRO	7.53
1888	Trinity Hall, Cam.	2	Brasenose College, Oxf.	NRO	8.25
1889	Thames RC	2	Third Trinity, Cam.	E	7.53
1890	Brasenose College, Oxf.	2	Thames RC	$\frac{3}{4}$	7.37
1891	Thames RC	2	Trinity Hall, Cam.	$1\frac{1}{4}$	7.45
1892	Royal Chester RC	2	Thames RC	$\frac{1}{4}$	8.38
1893	Magdalen College, Oxf.	2	Thames RC	$\frac{3}{4}$	7.45
1894	Thames RC	1	New College, Oxf.	E	8.20
1895	London RC	2	Thames RC	$1\frac{1}{4}$	7.43
1896	London RC	1	Thames RC	1	8.42
1897	Leander Club	2	New College, Oxf.	2	7.30
1898	Leander Club	2	New College, Oxf.	$1\frac{1}{4}$	7.42
1899	Magdalen College, Oxf.	2	Fav. Hammonia, GER	5	7.51
1900	Leander Club	2	Trinity College, Cam.	$1\frac{1}{4}$	7.55
1901	Third Trinity, Cam.	2	Leander Club	E	7.54
1902	Third Trinity, Cam.	1	Leander Club	E	7.45
1903	Third Trinity, Cam.	2	R Netherlands RSC, HOL	$1\frac{3}{4}$	8.05
1904	Third Trinity, Cam.	2	Winnipeg RC, CAN	$1\frac{1}{2}$	7.30
1905	Leander Club			RO	8.26
1906	Leander Club	1	Third Trinity, Cam.	2ft	7.36
1907	Magdalen College, Oxf.	2	Leander Club	3	8.42
1908	Magdalen College, Oxf.	1	London RC	$1\frac{1}{2}$	7.40
1909	Thames RC	2	Magdalen College, Oxf.	$1\frac{1}{2}$	7.38
1910	Winnipeg RC, CAN	2	Mainzer RV, GER	E	7.52
1911	Thames RC	2	Trinity Hall, Cam.	$1\frac{1}{4}$	7.35
1912	New College, Oxf.	2	Thames RC	$2\frac{1}{4}$	7.36
1913	New College, Oxf.	1	Mainzer RV, GER	Disq.	—
1914	Leander Club	1	Mainzer RV, GER	NRO	7.52

Stewards' Challenge Cup

Year	Winner	Station	Loser	Lengths	Time
1920	Magdalen College, Oxf.	1	Thames RC	E	8.03
1921	Magdalen College, Oxf.	2	Leander Club	3	7.32
1922	Eton Vikings Club	1	G'hopper, Zurich, SUI	E	8.25
1923	Third Trinity, Cam.	2	Magdalen College, Oxf.	E	7.30†
1924	Third Trinity, Cam.	2	Leander Club	3	8.37
1925	Third Trinity, Cam.	2	Leander Club	2	7.27
1926	Thames RC	2	Leander Club	E	7.34
1927	Thames RC	2	Leander Club	2	8.01
1928	Thames RC	1	London RC	2ft	7.43
1929	First Trinity, Cam.	2	London RC	1	7.32
1930	London RC	2	Leander Club	$1\frac{1}{2}$	7.34
1931	London RC	1	SCVDF, Piacenza, ITA	3	8.45
1932	Thames RC	2	Berliner RC., GER	2	8.09
1933	Pembroke College, Cam.	1	London RC	$1\frac{3}{4}$	8.16
1934	Pembroke College, Cam.	1	London RC	NRO	7.24
1935	FC Zurich RC, SUI	1	London RC	3	7.14
1936	FC Zurich RC, SUI	1	Leander Club	2	7.50
1937	Leander Club	2	Thames RC	1	8.32
1938	Leander Club	2	Trinity College, Oxf.	E	7.33
1939	RC Zurich, SUI	2	Oriel College, Oxf.	4	8.09
1946	Leander Club	2	Oriel College, Oxf.	$2\frac{1}{2}$	7.48
1947	Thames RC	1	London RC	E	8.04
1948	Thames RC	2	Isis and Granta Clubs	4	7.48
1949	Trinity College, Oxf.	2	London RC	3	7.13
1950	Hellerup Roklub, DAN	1	Leander Club	4	8.03
1951	Thames RC	2	Leander Club	$1\frac{1}{2}$	7.53
1952	Thames RC	1	London RC	2	7.24
1953	Leander Club	2	First & Third Trin., Cam.	$\frac{3}{4}$	7.25
1954	Krylia Sovetov, USSR	2	Royal Air Force	$1\frac{1}{4}$	8.26
1955	Krylia Sovetov, USSR	2	Leander Club	3	7.40
1956	Thames RC	2	London RC	$3\frac{1}{2}$	8.06
1957	Krylia Sovetov, USSR	1	London RC	E	7.35
1958	Barn Cottage BC	2	Nat. Provincial Bank	$\frac{1}{2}$	7.16
1959	SEH & Lincoln Coll., Oxf.	2	SP Moto Guzzi, ITA	E	7.39
1960	Barn Cottage BC	2	SEH & Lincoln Coll., Oxf.	4	7.10
1961	Trud Club, USSR	1	Thames RC	2	7.23
1962	Trud Club, USSR	2	ASR Nereus, HOL	$1\frac{1}{2}$	7.23
1963	Molesey BC	1	Thames RC	$\frac{2}{3}$	7.16
1964	Tideway Scullers School	2	Leander Club	E	7.11
1965	Quintin BC	2	Nautilus Club	E	6.55
1966	Roforeningen Kvik, DAN	1	Derby RC	1	7.17
1967	SGD Potsdam, GDR	1	ASR Nereus, HOL	2	7.31

Stewards' Challenge Cup

Year	Winner	Station	Loser	Lengths	Time
1968	Nautilus (Midlands) RC	1	London RC	4	8.53
1969	ASR Nereus, HOL	1	Nottingham & Union RC	E	7.06
1970	SGD Postdam, GDR	1	London RC	3	7.22
1971	Thames Tradesmen	2	Cambridge University BC	1	7.12
1972	Spartak Moscow, USSR	1	U. Brit. Columbia, CAN	Disq.	NTT
1973	University of London	1	Potomac BC., USA	$\frac{1}{2}$	7.03
1974	Dinamo Club, USSR	2	Leander & Thames T'men	E	7.12
1975	Potomac BC, USA	2	Lady Margaret BC, Cam.	$2\frac{1}{3}$	6.50
1976	U.Brit. Col. & Vanc'r, CAN	1	Thames Tradesmen	$\frac{1}{3}$	7.10
1977	London RC			RO	
1978	Trakia Club, BUL			RO	
1979	London RC	1	Oxford University BC	E	7.19
1980	Charles River & D'mth, USA	1	Avon & Petone RCs, NZL	2	7.04
1981	LRC & Thames T'men	2	Vesper BC, USA	E	7.48
1982	Schaf'en & Thalwil, SUI	1	Univ. of Lon. & Tyrian	$3\frac{2}{3}$	7.10
1983	Schaf'en & Thalwil, SUI	2	Cambridge University BC	E	7.02
1984	Notts. CRA & Tyne RC	2	Univ. of Lon. Tyrian	CAN	6.57
1985	Univ. of Lon. Tyrian	1	Bagsvaerd RK., DAN	3	7.08
1986	Ridley BC, CAN	2	Univ. of Lon. Tyrian	$\frac{1}{2}$	6.41
1987	Dinamo, Moscow, USSR	1	Univ. of Lon. Tyrian	1	6.40
1988	Leander Club	1	Penn Athletic RA, USA	E	6.44

The Prince Philip Challenge Cup 1963

For Coxed Fours; qualifications as for The Grand Challenge Cup.

Year	Winner	Station	Loser	Lengths	Time
1963	Auckland RC, NZL	1	Thames RC	E	7.32
1964	Molesey BC	1	Phillips Exeter, USA	$2\frac{1}{3}$	7.25
1965	Leander Club	1	Tideway Scullers School	$\frac{1}{2}$	7.03
1966	SGD Potsdam, GER	1	Kobenhavn, DAN	E	7.19
1967	ASK Vorwarts, GER	2	Tideway Scullers School	2	7.39
1968	Tideway Scullers School			RO	9.08
1969	DSR Laga, HOL	1	Hutt Valley, NZL	$\frac{1}{2}$	7.19
1970	Konstanz/Wetzlar, GFR	1	SGD Potsdam, GDR	$3\frac{1}{3}$	7.24

Prince Philip Challenge Cup

Year	Winner	Station	Loser	Lengths	Time
1971	London RC & Univ. of Lon.	2	Leander Club	$1\frac{2}{3}$	7.39
1972	St Catharine's RC, CAN	I	Oxford University BC	5	7.22
1973	Northeastern Univ, USA	I	Massachusetts IT, USA	E	7.13
1974	LMBC & Third Trin., Cam.	2	University of London	E	7.32
1975	University of London	I	Vesper BC, USA	$1\frac{2}{3}$	7.02
1976	Thames Tradesmen RC	2	Leander Club	RO	NTT
1977	Garda Siochana, IRL	2	Thames Tradesmen RC	$2\frac{3}{4}$	7.35
1978	Trakia Club, BUL	2	Quintin BC & Marlow RC	E	7.35
1979	Garda Siochana, IRL	I	University of London	I	7.37
1980	Charles River RA, USA	2	Yale Univ. & Potomac, USA	$\frac{2}{3}$	7.11
1981	Kingston RC	2	Garda Siochana, IRL	$3\frac{3}{4}$	7.45
1982	Univ. of London & Tyrian	I	Q'land U. & M'man, AUS	$2\frac{1}{2}$	7.32
1983	Kingston RC	2	Univ. of Lon. & Oxford Univ.	$\frac{1}{2}$	7.08
1984	Marlow RC & Univ. of Lon.	2	KSR Njord, HOL	E	7.01
1985	Tideway Scullers School	I	Thames T'men & Tyrian	3	7.11
1986	Szczecin & Wroclaw, POL	I	Thames T'men & Exeter	$2\frac{3}{4}$	7.12
1987	Soviet Army, USSR	I	Szczecin & Wroclaw, POL	$1\frac{1}{3}$	6.51
1988	Vancouver RC, CAN	2	Syracuse University, USA	E	7.16

The Queen Mother Challenge Cup 1981

For Quadruple Scullers; qualifications as for The Grand Challenge Cup.

Year	Winner	Station	Loser	Lengths	Time
1981	Ingleheim & Ulm, GFR	2	Maidenhead & Marlow RCs	E	7.23
1982	Marlow RC & Thames T'men	I	Lea RC	E	6.57
1983	Kingston RC	I	Hamburger & Germania, GFR	I	7.90
1984	Maidenhead & Bewdley	2	Quintin BC	E	6.56
1985	Bewdley & Thames T'men	2	Tideway Scullers School	$3\frac{3}{4}$	6.27
1986	Tideway Sc. & N'hampton	I	Rob Roy Club	4	7.03
1987	Ridley BC., CAN	I	Soviet Army, USSR	$\frac{1}{3}$	6.22
1988	Univs. of Melb. & Q'land, AUS	2	Nautilus RC	I	6.35

The Stewards' Challenge Cup   The Prince Philip Challenge Cup   The Queen Mother Challenge Cup

The Visitors' Challenge Cup 1847

In 1847 there were no entries for the District Challenge Cup, and only one for the Town Cup. According to newspaper reports St George's Club intended to enter for the Stewards' Challenge Cup but their entry was received too late. In the Stewards' Cup Worcester College withdrew, leaving Christ Church to row over. Thus there would have been no four-oar race at all this year. Herbert Steward comments, 'The Stewards, apparently with a view of making sport, and probably to give some consolation to St George's, offered a special prize at the last moment for a cup to be called "The Visitor's Challenge Cup", for any four-oar crew.' The District Cup trophy was allocated to this purpose.

The Visitors' Cup was advertised in the following year and placed under the same qualification rules as the Ladies' Plate. It became an event for coxless fours in 1874, and has remained as a restricted event for student crews.

Visitors' Challenge Cup

Year	Winner	Station	Time
1847	Christ Church, Oxf.	1	9.00
1848	Christ Church, Oxf.		RO
1849	Second Trinity, Cam.		RO
1850	Christ Church, Oxf.	1	
1851	Christ Church, Oxf.	2	9.00
1852	Argonaut Club, Lon.		
1853	Argonaut Club, Lon.	2	9.02
1854	Lady Margaret BC, Cam.	2	8.48
1855	Lady Margaret BC, Cam.		
1856	Lady Margaret BC, Cam.	1	
1857	Pembroke College, Oxf.	2	8.40
1858	First Trinity, Cam.		
1859	Third Trinity, Cam.		RO
1860	First Trinity, Cam.		RO
1861	First Trinity, Cam.	C	8.57
1862	Brasenose College, Oxf.	1	9.40
1863	Brasenose College, Oxf.		RO
1864	University College, Oxf.		RO
1865	Third Trinity, Cam.		RO
1866	University College, Oxf.	1	8.49
1867	University College, Oxf.		RO
1868	University College, Oxf.	1	8.15
1869	University College, Oxf.	C	9.05
1870	Trinity College, Dublin	1	8.36
1871	First Trinity, Cam.	C	9.08
1872	Pembroke College, Oxf.	C	9.28
1873	Trinity College, Dublin		RO
1874	Trinity College, Dublin	C	8.47
1875	University College, Oxf.	1	8.20
1876	University College, Oxf.	C	8.05
1877	Jesus College, Cam.	C	9.07
1878	Columbia College, USA	C	8.42
1879	Lady Margaret BC, Cam.	2	9.22
1880	Third Trinity, Cam.	1	8.16
1881	First Trinity, Cam.	1	8.22
1882	Brasenose College, Oxf.	1	9.23
1883	Christ Church, Oxf.	C	
1884	Third Trinity, Cam.	1	8.39
1885	Trinity Hall, Cam.	1	7.41
1886	First Trinity, Cam.	1	$8.20\frac{1}{2}$
1887	Trinity Hall, Cam.	1	8.08
1888	Brasenose College, Oxf.	2	7.59
1889	Third Trinity, Cam.	2	8.06
1890	Brasenose College, Oxf.	2	7.42
1891	Trinity Hall, Cam.	2	7.45
1892	Third Trinity, Cam.	2	8.23
1893	Third Trinity, Cam.	2	8.21
1894	New College, Oxf.		RO
1895	Trinity College, Oxf.	2	8.17
1896	Caius College, Cam.	2	8.29
1897	Trinity College, Oxf.	1	7.53
1898	New College, Oxf.	2	7.37
1899	Balliol College, Oxf.	2	8.01
1900	Trinity College, Cam.	2	7.53
1901	Balliol College, Oxf.	1	8.27
1902	Jesus College, Cam.	2	7.59
1903	University College, Oxf.	2	8.25
1904	Third Trinity, Cam.	2	7.36
1905	Trinity Hall, Cam.	1	7.53
1906	Third Trinity, Cam.	1	7.49
1907	Magdalen College, Oxf.	2	8.07
1908	Magdalen College, Oxf.	2	7.30
1909	Christ Church, Oxf.	1	7.53
1910	Trinity Hall, Cam.	2	7.56
1911	Third Trinity, Cam.	1	7.37
1912	Christ Church, Oxf.	2	8.19
1913	Pembroke College, Cam.	1	8.13
1914	Lady Margaret BC, Cam.	2	8.26
1920	Merton College, Oxf.	2	8.26
1921	Lincoln College, Oxf.	1	7.44
1922	Third Trinity, Cam.	1	8.28
1923	Magdalen College, Oxf.	1	7.44†
1924	Third Trinity, Cam.	1	9.14
1925	Third Trinity, Cam.	1	7.45
1926	Christ Church, Oxf.	1	8.15
1927	Christ's College, Cam.	2	8.16
1928	First Trinity, Cam.	1	7.54
1929	Third Trinity, Cam.	1	7.46
1930	Brasenose College, Oxf.	2	8.06
1931	Pembroke College, Cam.	2	8.45
1932	Jesus College, Cam.	1	8.21
1933	Christ's College, Cam.	2	8.16
1934	First Trinity, Cam.	1	7.38
1935	Jesus College, Cam	1	7.40

Visitors' Challenge Cup

Year	Winner	Station	Time	Year	Winner	Station	Time
1936	Jesus College, Cam.	1	8.34	1966	Lady Margaret BC, Cam.	1	7.31
1937	Trinity Hall, Cam.	1	8.16	1967	Magdalene College, Cam.	2	7.45
1938	Oriel College, Oxf.	1	7.18	1968	Imperial College, Lon.	1	9.25
1939	Trinity Hall, Cam.	1	8.09	1969	Eton College	1	7.22
1946	1 & 3 Trinity, Cam.	2	7.59	1970	Fitzwilliam Coll., Cam.	2	7.40
1947	Trinity Hall, Cam.	2	8.00	1971	University of London	2	7.34
1948	Magdalen College, Oxf.	1	7.51	1972	University of London	2	7.26
1949	Clare College, Cam.	2	7.31	1973	1 & 3 Trinity, Cam.	1	7.15
1950	Lady Margaret BC, Cam.	1	8.08	1974	Pembroke College, Cam.	1	7.25
1951	Trinity Hall, Cam.	2	8.09	1975	Ealing High Schools	1	7.12
1952	Pembroke College, Cam.	2	7.15	1976	University of London	2	7.21
1953	Magdalen College, Oxf.	1	7.29	1977	Univ. of Wash'ton, USA	1	NTT
1954	1 & 3 Trinity, Cam.	1	7.57	1978	Durham University	1	7.29
1955	Trinity Hall, Cam.	2	7.58	1979	Strode's & Wall. Schs	1	7.26
1956	Merton College, Oxf.	2	7.47	1980	University of London	1	7.26
1957	Pembroke College, Cam.	2	7.33	1981	University of London	2	NTT
1958	Keble College, Oxf.	1	7.32	1982	Durham University	2	7.50
1959	Pembroke College, Cam.	2	7.50	1983	University of London	1	7.17
1960	1 & 3 Trinity, Cam.	1	7.31	1984	Shiplake & Borlase's	1	7.27
1961	St Edmund Hall, Oxf.	1	7.27	1985	Imperial College, Lon.	1	7.15
1962	Keble College, Oxf.	2	7.53	1986	Reading University	2	7.07
1963	Christ's College, Cam.	2	7.32	1987	Imperial College, Lon.	2	6.58
1964	Pembroke College, Cam.	2	7.27	1988	Durham University	1	7.04
1965	St Edmund Hall, Oxf.	2	7.13				

The Wyfold Challenge Cup 1847

The cup was presented to the Regatta in 1847 by Mr Donkin of Wyfold Court, and, there being no event without a trophy already, was designated by the Stewards as a prize for the winners of the challenge heats of the Grand Challenge Cup, originally a 'challenge' event in which the preceding 'winner' became the 'holder', required to defend only in the final. If only one crew challenged they automatically took the Wyfold Cup, and if they also won the Grand they took both cups.

In this manner the Wyfold Cup was won by:
1847 Oxford University BC*
1848 Thames Club
1849 Wadham College, Oxf.*
1850 Oxford University BC*
1851 Cambridge University BC
1852 Oxford Aquatic Club
1853 Cambridge University BC
1854 First Trinity, Cam.*
* These crews also won the Grand.

In 1855 the Wyfold Challenge Cup was made over to a newly instituted race for coxed fours, for any club not composed of resident members of either Oxford or Cambridge Universities. The qualification was altered in 1857 to admit any amateur crew, but excepting those individual oarsmen who had previously entered for or were currently inscribed for the Stewards' Challenge Cup. In 1874 The Wyfold Cup became an event for coxless fours.

Over the years there have been numerous modifications barring double entries in the Wyfold Cup

and the Stewards', the Grand and the Visitors' Cups, and the participation of individuals who had rowed, or were rowing in various other events. In principle the Wyfold Cup has always been and remains a subsidiary event for fours, open today to any single university, college or club crew, or crews composed of members of the armed forces, with the requirements that at least two members of such crews must have won an event at Henley within the previous five years, or have achieved a status qualification based on wins elsewhere. The purpose of this proviso is to ensure an acceptable standard.

Year	Winner	Station	Time
1855	Royal Chester RC		–
1856	Argonaut Club, Lon.	1	–
1857	Pembroke College, Oxf.	2	8.30
1858	First Trinity, Cam.		RO
1859	First Trinity, Cam.	1	8.21
1860	London RC	1	10.08
1861	Brasenose College, Oxf.	1	9.43
1862	London RC	2	9.20
1863	Kingston RC	2	8.50
1864	Kingston RC		RO
1865	Kingston RC	1	8.23
1866	Kingston RC	1	–
1867	Kingston RC	C	–
1868	Kingston RC	1	8.32
1869	Oscillators Club	C	–
1870	Thames RC	1	8.34
1871	Thames RC	C	9.06
1872	Thames RC	1	8.42
1873	Kingstown Harbour BC	1	8.37
1874	Newcastle RC	C	9.00
1875	Thames RC	1	8.10
1876	West London RC	C	8.24
1877	Kingston RC		RO
1878	Kingston RC	1	8.44
1879	London RC	1	9.56
1880	London RC	1	8.04
1881	Dublin University BC	1	8.08
1882	Jesus College, Cam.	C	8.58

Year	Winner	Station	Time
1883	Kingston RC	1	8.51
1884	Thames RC	1	8.58
1885	Kingston RC	2	–
1886	Thames RC	2	8.04
1887	Pembroke College, Cam.	1	7.50
1888	Thames RC	1	7.59
1889	London RC	1	7.58
1890	Kingston RC	2	7.46
1891	Royal Chester RC	1	7.50
1892	Molesey BC	1	8.42
1893	Molesey BC	2	8.28
1894	Thames RC	1	8.16
1895	London RC	2	8.16
1896	Trinity College, Oxf.	2	8.41
1897	Kingston RC	1	8.00
1898	Kingston RC	2	8.28
1899	Trinity Hall, Cam.	2	7.57
1900	Trinity Hall, Cam.	2	8.14
1901	Trinity Hall, Cam.	1	8.09
1902	Burton-on-Trent RC	1	7.43
1903	Kingston RC	1	8.23
1904	Birmingham RC	2	8.01
1905	London RC	1	7.59
1906	London RC	1	7.58
1907	Magdalen College, Oxf.	2	8.49
1908	Thames RC	1	7.55
1909	Balliol College, Oxf.	2	7.44
1910	Trinity Hall, Cam.	1	8.09

Chris Smith looks at Henley

61–65.

Wyfold Challenge Cup

Year	Winner	Station	Time	Year	Winner	Station	Time
1911	Pembroke College, Cam.	1	7.40	1956	Royal Engineers	2	7.56
1912	Queens' College, Cam.	2	8.03	1957	National Provincial Bank	2	7.49
1913	Lady Margaret BC, Cam.	1	8.01	1958	Burton Leander RC	2	7.35
1914	London RC	2	8.35	1959	Molesey BC	2	7.45
1920	Thames RC	2	8.10	1960	St Thomas's Hospital	1	7.24
1921	Jesus College, Cam.	2	7.46	1961	National Provincial Bank	2	7.28
1922	Thames RC	2	9.06	1962	Force Navale, BEL	1	7.30
1923	Imperial College BC	1	7.50†	1963	Nottingham & Union	2	7.24
1924	Royal Chester RC	1	9.16	1964	Sons of the Thames RC	2	7.19
1925	Thames RC	1	7.35	1965	Derby RC	2	7.06
1926	London RC	1	7.59	1966	Norwich Union	1	7.28
1927	Thames RC	1	8.23	1967	Tideway Scullers Sch.	2	7.29
1928	Trinity Hall, Cam.	2	7.47	1968	Severn Scullers RC	1	9.06
1929	Thames RC	2	7.44	1969	London RC	1	7.16
1930	London RC	1	7.52	1970	Trident RC, SA	1	NTT
1931	Thames RC	2	9.13	1971	Harvard Univ, USA	1	7.37
1932	London RC	1	8.29	1972	Leander Club	1	7.25
1933	London RC	1	8.28	1973	Thames T'men	2	7.02
1934	Reading RC	1	7.36	1974	Porcellian Club, USA	1	7.37
1935	Reading RC	2	7.39	1975	Thames T'men	1	6.57
1936	London RC	1	8.26	1976	London RC	2	6.56
1937	London RC	1	8.20	1977	City Orient RC	2	7.15
1938	London RC	1	7.41	1978	Molesey BC	2	7.38
1939	Maidenhead RC	1	9.10	1979	Wallingford RC	2	7.35
1946	King's College, Lon.	2	7.57	1980	Nottingham BC	2	7.13
1947	Quintin BC	1	8.19	1981	Hanlan BC, CAN	2	7.54
1948	Victoria Lake RC, SA	1	7.55	1982	Nottingham BC	2	7.21
1949	Lensbury RC	2	7.41	1983	Lea RC	2	7.14
1950	Royal Engineers	2	8.13	1984	Nottinghamshire CRA	2	6.59
1951	Caius College, Cam.	2	7.55	1985	Molesey BC	2	7.03
1952	CCC, Cam.	1	7.28	1986	Charles River RA, USA	2	7.02
1953	Royal Air Force	2	7.38	1987	Nottinghamshire CRA	2	6.49
1954	Royal Engineers	2	8.06	1988	Nottinghamshire CRA	1	6.59
1955	Thames RC	2	7.51				

The Britannia Challenge Cup 1968

This second event for coxed fours, was instituted in 1968 as the 'Henley Prize'. Nottingham Britannia Rowing Club donated the trophy the following year, and the title of the event was changed accordingly.

It is restricted to crews from the United Kingdom and the Republic of Ireland. Composite crews are not permitted and there is the same status requirement as for the Wyfold Cup.

Year	Winner	Station	Time
1968	Crowland RC	1	9.32
1969	Kingston RC	1	7.32
1970	London RC	1	7.48
1971	Hereford RC	1	7.45
1972	Wallingford RC	2	7.39
1973	Isis BC	2	7.19
1974	Wallingford Schools	1	7.51
1975	Leander Club	1	7.18
1976	Tideway Scullers School	2	7.22
1977	Tideway Scullers School	1	7.28
1978	Kingston RC	2	7.44

Year	Winner	Station	Time
1979	City Orient RC	2	7.50
1980	Leander Club	2	7.24
1981	Vesta RC	2	8.13
1982	Neptune RC, IRL	2	7.45
1983	Lea RC	2	7.26
1984	Tideway Scullers School	1	7.22
1985	Maidenhead RC	1	7.22
1986	Bedford Star RC	1	7.19
1987	Lea RC	1	7.20
1988	University of London	1	7.07

The Visitors' Challenge Cup

The Wyfold Challenge Cup

The Britannia Challenge Cup

The Silver Goblets and Nickalls' Challenge Cup 1845

Instituted in 1845 as the 'Silver Wherries' for presentation prizes. In 1850 presentation goblets were given in place of the wherries and the name of the event was changed to the 'Silver Goblets'. The Nickalls' Challenge Cup was donated by Tom Nickalls in 1895 to celebrate two successive wins by his sons Guy and Vivian. It is 'Open to all Amateurs'.

Year	Winner	Station	Loser	Lengths	Time
1845	Mann & Arnold (Caius Coll., Cam.)	2	Chapman & Peacock (London)	2	—
1846	Haggard & Milman (Ch. Ch., Oxf.)	1	E. & T.H. Fellows (Exeter Coll., Oxf. & Leander Club)	3	—
1847	Falls & Coulthard (St George's, Lon.)	2	Pollock & T.H. Fellows (Cam. Sub. Rms. & Leander Club)	Disq.	—
1848	Haggard & Milman (Ch. Ch., Oxf.)		Bruce & Wallace (Thames Club, Lon.)	Disq.	—
1849	Peacock & Playford (Thames Club, Lon.)		Steward & Michell (Oriel Coll., Oxf.)	2	—
1850	Hornby & Chitty (BNC & Balliol, Oxf.)		Vaughan & Fellows (Oriel Coll., Oxf. & Leander Club)	E	—
1851	Aitken & Chitty (Ex. & Balliol, Oxf.)	C	Clarke & Vaughan (Wadham & Oriel Colls, Oxf.)		—
1852	Barker & Nind (Christ Church, Oxf.)		Short & Irving (New & Ball. Colls, Oxf.)	RO	—
1853	Gordon & Barlee (Christ's, Cam.)	2	Forster & Wright (St John's, Cam.)	2	10.00
1854	Short & Cadogan (New Coll. & Ch. Ch., Oxf.)		Swaine & Craven (St John's, Oxf.)	E	9.36
1855	Casamajor & Nottidge (Wandle Club)		Short & Cadogan (New Coll. & Ch. Ch., Oxf.)	E	—
1856	Casamajor & Nottidge (A'naut, Lon.)	C	Playford & Paine (Argonaut, Lon.)	E	—
1857	Ware & Lonsdale (Balliol Coll., Oxf.)	C	Halcombe & Jackson (Wadham, Oxf.)	E	9.22
1858	Playford & Casamajor (London RC)	1	Ware & Lonsdale (Balliol Coll., Oxf.)	$1\frac{1}{2}$	—
1859	Ware & Arkell (Ball. & Pemb., Oxf.)		Casamajor & Paine (London RC)	4	9.00
1860	Casamajor & Woodbridge (LRC)	2	Inglis & Royds (First Trinity, Cam.)	2	11.50
1861	Champneys & Woodgate (BNC, Oxf.)	1	Channel & Burney (1 Trinity, Cam.)	E	—
1862	Champneys & Woodgate (BNC, Oxf.)	2	Hawkshaw & Chambers (3 Trinity, Cam.)	1 RO	9.45
1863	Shepherd & Woodgate (BNC, Oxf.)				
1864	Selwyn & Kinglake (3 Trinity, Cam.)		L. P. & E. D. Brickwood (LRC)	E	9.29
1865	May & Fenner (London RC)	1	Snow & Warre (Eton College)	3	9.07
1866	Corrie & Woodgate (Kingston RC)	C	Kemble & Foster (New College, Oxf.)	E	9.23
1867	Corrie & Brown (Kingston RC)	2	Raikes & Woodgate (Oxf. Radleian Club)	E	9.49
1868	Crofts & Woodgate (BNC, Oxf.)	C	Muirhead & Phelps (Cambridge Univ.)	E	—

Silver Goblets and Nickalls' Cup

Year	Winner	Station	Loser	Lengths	Time
1869	Long & Stout (London RC)	I	Calvert & McClintock-Bunbury (Eton Coll.)	3	9.20
1870	Corrie & Hall (Kingston RC)	C	James B. & John B. Close (1 Trin., Cam.)	NRO	–
1871	Long & Gulston (London RC)	C	James B. & John B. Close (1 Trin., Cam.)	$1\frac{1}{4}$	10.17
1872	Long & Gulston (London RC)	I	Croskell & Thompson (Lancaster)	E	–
1873	Knollys & Trower (Kingston RC)	C	Long & Gulston (London RC)	E	9.22
1874	Long & Gulston (London RC)	C	Mair & Trower (Kingston RC)	E	10.03
1875	Chillingworth & Herbert (Ino RC)	I	Long & Gulston (London RC)	Disq.	–
1876	Le Blanc Smith & Gulston (LRC)	C	Campbell & Davey (Twickenham)	E	8.55
1877	Eyre & Hastie (Thames RC)	C	Le Blanc Smith & Playford (LRC)	NRO	–
1878	Edwards-Moss & Ellison (Eton Club, Oxf.)	C	Prior & Sandford (LMBC, Cam.)	E	9.14
1879	Labat & Gulston (London RC)	C	Eyre & Hastie (Thames RC)	E	11.16
1880	Eyre & Hastie (Thames RC)	C	Payne & Leader (Molesey BC)	5	8.45
1881	Eyre & Hastie (Thames RC)	I	Adcock & Playford (London RC)	4	9.04
1882	Brown & Lowndes (Hertford, Oxf.)	I	Adcock & Playford (London RC)	NRO	–
1883	Roberts & Brown (Twickenham RC)	I	Tween & Hastie (Thames RC)	E	9.22
1884	Lowndes & Brown (Twickenham RC)	I	G. R. B. & C. E. Earnshaw (LRC)	E	9.01
1885	H. & D. H. McLean (Eton Club, Oxf.)	I	G. R. B. & C. E. Earnshaw (LRC)	E	7.36
1886	Churchill & Muttlebury (3 Trin., Cam.)	2	H. & D. H. McLean (New College, Oxf.)	$\frac{1}{2}$	8.40
1887	Barclay & Muttlebury (3 Trin., Cam.)	I	H. & D. H. McLean (New College, Oxf.)	NRO	8.15
1888	Symonds & Buck (Cam. and Oxf. Univs.)	2	D. H. McLean & Muttlebury (Leander)	NRO	–
1889	Gardner & Muttlebury (Cam. Univ.)	I	Ampthill & G. Nickalls (Oxf. Univ.)	2 ft.	8.25
1890	Ampthill & G. Nickalls (Oxf. Univ.)	2	Francklyn & Muttlebury (3 Trin., Cam.)	$1\frac{3}{4}$	8.38
1891	Ampthill & G. Nickalls (Leander)	I	Wilkinson & Fletcher (Oxf. Univ.)	1 ft.	8.36
1892	V. Nickalls & Fletcher (Oxf. Univ.)	I	Clark & Muttlebury (Thames RC)	E	9.07
1893	V. Nickalls & Fletcher (Oxf. Univ.)	2	Kerrison & Lewis (3 Trinity, Cam.)	E	8.44
1894	G. Nickalls & V. Nickalls (Formosa)	2	Crisp & Smith (Kingston RC)	I	9.35
1895	G. Nickalls & V. Nickalls (LRC)	I	Broughton & Muttlebury (TRC)	NRO	9.11
1896	G. Nickalls & V. Nickalls (LRC)	2	Crum & Pitman (New College, Oxf.)	E	9.10
1897	Balfour & G. Nickalls (Leander Club)	I	Bell & Fernie (Trinity Hall, Cam.)	NRO	8.59
1898	Bogle & Fernie (Thames RC)	2	Hutchinson & Fairbairn (Jesus, Cam.)	E	8.41
1899	Phillips & Willis (Leander Club)	I	Orme & Pennington (St George's Hosp.)	$1\frac{1}{4}$	8.49
1900	Goldie & Maitland (Trinity, Cam.)	I	Dudley-Ward & Etherington-Smith (Trinity Coll., Cam.)	2 L	8.33
1901	Hale & Warre (Balliol College, Oxf.)	I	De Somville & Crombrugge (Ghent, BEL)	2	8.50
1902	Dudley-Ward & Taylor (3 Trin., Cam.)	2	Craven & Knight (London RC)	E	8.36
1903	Klaus & Ehrenberg (Berlin, GER)	2	Stuart & Steele (Kingston RC)	E	8.45
1904	Goldie & Taylor (3 Trinity, Cam.)	I	Beresford & Blackstaffe (KRC & Vesta)	$2\frac{1}{2}$	8.33
1905	Nelson & Thomas (3 Trinity, Cam.)	2	Stuart & Fox (London RC)	NRO	8.40
1906	Johnstone & Powell (3 Trin., Cam.)	2	Molmans & Visser (Ghent, BEL)	3	9.15
1907	Johnstone & Powell (Leander Club)	2	Beresford & Vernon (Thames RC)	E	8.52

Silver Goblets and Nickalls' Cup

Year	Winner	Station	Loser	Lengths	Time
1908	Barker & A. C. Gladstone (Ch. Ch., Oxf.)	1	Beresford & Vernon (Thames RC)	4	8.26
1909	Johnstone & Williams (Leander Club)	1	Beresford & Vernon (Thames RC)	3	8.30
1910	Burn & Thomson (Leander Club)	2	Wielsma & Croon (Amstel., HOL)	$\frac{3}{4}$	8.45
1911	Beresford & Cloutte (Thames RC)	2	Bruce & C. A. Gladstone (Ch. Ch., Oxf.)	$1\frac{1}{2}$	8.15
1912	Logan & Rought (Thames RC)	1	Beresford & Cloutte (Thames RC)	$1\frac{1}{4}$	8.36
1913	A. A. & S. E. Swann (Trin. Hall, Cam.)	1	S. D. Gladstone & Buxton (Old Etonians)	$1\frac{1}{2}$	8.39
1914	A. A. & S. E. Swann (Trin. Hall, Cam.)	2	Williams & Le Blanc Smith (Third Trin., Cam.)	1	9.02
1920	Nickalls & Lucas (Magdalen, Oxf.)	2	Fairbairn & Logan (Thames RC)	E	8.53
1921	Campbell & Playford (Jesus, Cam.)	2	MacIver & Johnson (Ch. Ch., Oxf.)	E	8.52
1922	Nickalls & Lucas (Magdalen, Oxf.)	1	West & Vernon (Thames RC)	E	9.19
1923	Godden & Eason (Trinity, Oxf.)	2	Nickalls & Playford (Leander Club)	5 ft.	8.12†
1924	Ely & Macnabb (3 Trinity, Cam.)	2	Gadsden & Pitman (Ch. Ch., Oxf.)	3	10.06
1925	Morrison & Hamilton-Russell (Third Trinity, Cam.)	2	Nickalls & Lucas (Leander Club)	4	8.17
1926	Carver & Hamilton-Russell (Third Trinity, Cam.)	2	Nickalls & Pearson (Leander Club)	$1\frac{1}{4}$	8.36
1927	Nisbet & O'Brien (London RC)	2	Nickalls & Boret (Leander Club)	E	9.23
1928	Killick & J. Beresford Jr (TRC)	2	Daniel & London (Quintin BC)	E	9.57
1929	Killick & J. Beresford Jr (TRC)	1	Graham & Morphett (BNC, Oxf.)	$1\frac{3}{4}$	8.32
1930	Prideaux & Rickett (3 Trinity, Cam.)	1	Graham & Johnston (BNC, Oxf.)	NRO	8.42
1931	Edwards & Clive (Ch. Ch., Oxf.)	2	Sambell & Luxton (Pembroke, Cam.)	4	9.57
1932	Edwards & Clive (Ch. Ch., Oxf.)	2	Migotti & Lascelles (Gorduli, Oxf.)	3	9.05
1933	Powell & Gilmour (Eton Vikings)	2	E. F. & T. S. Bigland (R Chester RC)	E	9.17
1934	Braun & Moller (RG Wiking, GER)	2	E. F. & T. S. Bigland (R Chester RC)	$1\frac{1}{4}$	8.09
1935	Cree & Burnford (Jesus Coll., Cam.)	2	Fidler & Newton (Thames RC)	$2\frac{1}{2}$	8.20
1936	R. F. & J. S. Offer (Kingston RC)	2	Wingate & Baddeley (Vesta RC)	$1\frac{1}{4}$	9.17
1937	Wingate & Baddeley (Vesta RC)	2	Kingsford & Lewis (London RC)	3	9.43
1938	Laurie & Wilson (Leander Club)	2	E. F. & T. S. Bigland (R Chester RC)	E	8.08
1939	Sanford & H. Parker (Trinity Hall, Cam.)	2	Carpmael & R. Parker (London RC)	$2\frac{1}{2}$	9.05
1946	J. F. & C. G. Burgess (Leander)	1	Secher & Paerregaard (DFFR, DAN)	NRO	8.47
1947	Pinches & Sturges (London RC)	2	Gleave & Jamison (Magdalen, Oxf.)	$2\frac{1}{2}$	8.46
1948	Laurie & Wilson (Leander Club)	1	Bromley & Grace (Mosman, AUS)	3	8.30
1949	Butcher & Christie (Thames RC)	1	Morris & Burrough (London RC)	$2\frac{1}{2}$	8.20
1950	Rosa & v Antwerpen (Antwerp, BEL)	2	Pinches & Sturges (London RC)	$\frac{3}{4}$	9.10
1951	Crowden & Lloyd (Pemb. Coll. & LMBC, Cam.)	2	Rosa & v Antwerpen (Antwerp, BEL)	E	8.52
1952	Bywater & Christie (Westminster H.)	1	Leadley & King (Emmanuel, Cam.)	$1\frac{1}{3}$	8.06
1953	Baetens & Knuysen (Antwerp SC, BEL)	2	Kesel & Hahn (Saarbrucken, GER)	4	8.10
1954	Buldakov & Ivanov (Khimik, USSR)	2	Blom & Gitz (Het Spaane, HOL)	2	8.44
1955	Buldakov & Ivanov (Khimik, USSR)	1	Gobbo & Davidge (Leander Club)	4	8.30

Silver Goblets and Nickolls' Cup

Year	Winner	Station	Loser	Lengths	Time
1956	Thompson & Wolfson (Pemb. Coll., Cam.)	1	Clay & Findlay (Marlow RC)	3	8.45
1957	Leadley & Davidge (Leander Club)	2	Kloimstein & Sageder (Donau, AUT)	$\frac{1}{3}$	8.17
1958	Leadley & Davidge (Leander Club)	1	Streuli & Kottmann (Zurich, SUI)	$3\frac{1}{2}$	8.04
1959	Norton & Scurfield (Hertford, Oxf.)	2	Beresford & Porter (London RC)	E	8.20
1960	Elliott & Rutherford (Keble & Magdalen Colls., Oxf.)	1	Nicholson & Marshall (Nott. Brit.)	$\frac{2}{3}$	7.58
1961	Lehtela & Pitkanen (Valk Vesiveikot, FIN)	2	Waite & Nicholson (Nott. Union & Brit.)	E	8.09
1962	Neuss & Jordon (Nass. Hochst, GER)	2	Farquharson & Nicholson (Univ. of Lon. & Middx Hosp.)	2	8.02
1963	Davidge & Mackenzie (Leander)	1	T. K. & J. B. Amlong (Vesper, USA)	4	7.55
1964	Kieley & Lecky (Leander Club)	1	Hall & Napier (Leander Club)	2	7.53
1965	Gorny & Bergau (Rostock, GER)	2	Boelen & Enters (Willem III, HOL)	$2\frac{1}{4}$	7.42
1966	Lucke & Bothe (TSC Berlin, GER)	2	Easterling & McCarthy (PBD)	2	8.31
1967	Gelpke & Jacob (Einheit Dres., GER)	1	Sutton & Sharp (Sons of the Thames)	E	8.18
1968	Sutton & Sharp (Sons of the Thames)	1	Hamilton & McCowen (Tideway Scullers Sch.)	E	NTT
1969	Bitterli & Fankhauser (Luzerne, SUI)	1	Wait & Sweeney (Nott. & Union BC)	E	7.56
1970	Schreiber & Schmorde (Dyn., Berlin, GDR)	1	Xouris & Watt (Corio Bay, AUS)	E	8.17
1971	Locke & Crooks (Leander Club)	1	Dalley & Winckless (Quintin BC)	E	8.07
1972	Broniec & Slusarski (Bydgoszcz, POL)	2	Vasiliev & Poljakov (Spartak, L'grad, USSR)	$2\frac{1}{4}$	7.59
1973	Borchelt & Adams (Potomac BC, USA)	1	Dedecker & de Weert (Antwerp, BEL)	NRO	7.42
1974	Ivanov & Eshinov (Dinamo, USSR)	2	Macleod & Christie (LMBC, Cam.)	E	7.59
1975	Droog & Luynenburg (Nereus, HOL)	1	Locke & Smallbone (Leander Club & Thames Tradesmen)	$\frac{1}{3}$	7.36
1976	Luxford & Shinners (Sydney Univ., AUS)	2	Lecky & Crooker (Boucherville, CAN)	E	7.30
1977	Clark & Roberts (Thames T'men)	1	Macleod & Christie (LMBC, Cam.)	3	7.54
1978	Clark & Roberts (Thames T'men)	1	De Veth & Vittenboogaard (V. Heel, HOL)	E	8.12
1979	Wiggin & Carmichael (Leander Club)	1	Woodhouse & Palmer (Cam. Univ.)	E	8.10
1980	M. & F. Borchelt (Potomac BC, USA)	1	Palmer & Laurie (Eton Vikings)	E	8.02
1981	Mossop & Jones (Kingston RC)	1	Macleod & Christie (London RC)	1	8.46
1982	Ivancic & Celent (Gusar, YOU)	1	Wensley & Reynolds (Univ. of Lon. & Kingston RC)	$1\frac{1}{2}$	8.11
1983	Field & Hill (Tyrian BC)	1	Whitwell & Knight (Notts. CRA)	E	7.48
1984	Pearson & Riches (Cambridge & Molesey)	1	Beattie & Stanhope (Thames T'men)	NRO	7.57
1985	Pearson & Riches (Molesey BC)	1	Moore & Brown (Neptune, IRL)	5	7.49
1986	Holmes & Redgrave (Leander Club & Marlow)	1	Pearson & Riches (Molesey BC)	E	7.39

Silver Goblets and Nickolls' Cup

Year	Winner	Station	Loser	Lengths	Time
1987	Holmes & Redgrave (Leander Club & Marlow)	1	Y. Pimenov & N. Pimenov (Dinamo, Moscow, USSR)	NRO	
1988	Swinford & Riley (Penn ARC, USA)	1	Chilmaid & Butt (London RC)	E	7.48

The Double Sculls Challenge Cup 1939

This Double-Sculling race for presentation goblets was instituted to mark the Centenary Regatta in 1939. The Challenge Cup and medals were added in 1946. This is open to all amateurs.

Year	Winner	Station	Loser	Lengths	Time
1939	J. Beresford Jr & Southwood (Thames RC)	with	Scherli & Brischi (SCN, Trieste, ITA)	DH	8.35
1946	Panelo & Chafuen (BA, ARG)	1	Newton & Warren (Trin Hall, Cam.)	4	8.08
1947	Horwood & Garrod (Quintin BC)	1	Vrba & Vavrena (Cesky AC, TCH)	4	8.23
1948	Piessens & Collet (Ant. & Bruss. BEL)	2	Horwood & Garrod (Quintin BC)	2	8.02
1949	Parsner & Larsen (DFDS, DAN)	2	Brown & Tinegate (L'boro' & B'ham)	2½	7.39
1950	Parsner & Larsen (DFDS, DAN)	1	Brown & Tinegate (L'boro' & B'ham)	E	8.21
1951	Bradley & Burnell (Leander Club)	1	Davies & Kemp (Reading RC)	2	8.41
1952	George & van Stichel (Liege & Antwerp, BEL)	1	Rodgers & Riley (Sydney RC, AUS)	E	7.37
1953	Schriever & Stebler (Zurich, SUI)	2	Poynter & Baker (Bedford RC)	E	7.37
1954	Schriever & Stebler (Zurich, SUI)	2	Beech & Tinegate (Birmingham RC)	E	8.46
1955	Zhilin & Emchuk (Burevestnik, USSR)	1	Vollmer & Keller (Zurich, SUI)	½	7.55

Double Sculls Challenge Cup

Year	Winner	Station	Loser	Lengths	Time
1956	S. C. & W. H. Rand (Royal Air Force)	2	Marsden & Melvin (London RC)	$1\frac{1}{2}$	7.47
1957	Berkutov & Tukalov (Kr. Znamia, USSR)	1	Baker & Spracklen (Marlow & RAF)	E	7.41
1958	Berkutov & Tukalov (L'grad, USSR)	1	Baker & Spracklen (Marlow)	E	7.21
1959	Davidge & Mackenzie (Leander)	2	Justicz & Birkmyre (B'ham & Ariel)	$2\frac{3}{4}$	7.55
1960	Justicz & Birkmyre (B'ham & Ariel)	1	Monnerau & Duhamel (Rouen, FRA)	$1\frac{3}{4}$	7.17
1961	Justicz & Birkmyre (B'ham & Ariel)	2	Berkutov & Tukalov (L'grad & Mos., USSR)	$1\frac{3}{4}$	7.38
1962	Justicz & Birkmyre (Leander Club)	1	Joyce & Maclehose (Ex. & CCC, Oxf.)	E	7.39
1963	Alwin & v.d. Togt (Will. III & R'dam, HOL)	2	Monnereau & Duhamel (Rouen, FRA)	2	7.30
1964	Justicz & Birkmyre (Leander Club)	1	Fredericksen & Kruse (DSR, DAN)	$\frac{3}{4}$	7.32
1965	Studach & Burgin (Zurich, SUI)	1	Haake & Bruckhandler (Berlin, GDR)	$1\frac{2}{3}$	7.01
1966	Haake & Bruckhandler (Berlin, GDR)	1	Cooper & Cooke (Leander Club)	$3\frac{3}{4}$	7.20
1967	Studach & Burgin (Zurich, SUI)	2	Schabitz & Bohmer (Potsdam, GDR)	$1\frac{1}{4}$	7.47
1968	Barry & Findlay (Tideway Sc. Sch. & Nat. Prov. Bank)	1	Cowley & Drake (St Ives RC)	2	9.18
1969	Oswald & Burgin (N'chatel & Zurich, SUI)	2	Cowley & Drake (St Ives RC)	3	7.35
1970	McKibbon & v. Blom (Long Beach, USA)	2	Webb & Cooke (Nott. & Union RC)	$3\frac{1}{2}$	7.43
1971	M.A. & C.A. Brigden (Walton RC)	1	Balmer & Parsonage (Scot. Argonauts)	1	8.21
1972	Delafield & Crooks (Leander Club)	2	Klecatsky & Dietz (NY AC, USA)	$1\frac{2}{3}$	7.24
1973	Hart & Baillieu (Leander Club)	1	Isler & Ruckstuhl (Stafa & Zurich, SUI)	$4\frac{1}{2}$	7.11
1974	Korchikov & Timoshinin (Din., USSR)	1	Isler & Ruckstuhl (Stafa & Zurich, SUI)	$2\frac{1}{2}$	7.23
1975	Hart & Baillieu (Leander Club)	1	Levy & Gee (Weybridge & Molesey)	E	7.23
1976	Prentice & Spencer (London RC)	2	Van Drooge & Nolet (Nereus, HOL)	2	7.22
1977	Hart & Baillieu (Leander Club)	2	Stone & Wood (Harvard Univ., USA)	E	7.20
1978	Hart & Baillieu (Leander Club)	2	Spencer & Prentice (PBD)	E	7.44
1979	Clark & Baillieu (Thames Tradesmen & Leander Club)	1	Rudkin & Gold (Bewdley & PBD)	E	7.32
1980	Walter & Ford (Victoria City, CAN)	2	Allsopp & Wood (Hartford BC & Univ. of Washington, USA)	2	7.27
1981	Sims & Redgrave (Maidenhead & Marlow)	2	Riddle & May (Dart & Staines)	E	8.16
1982	Clift & Redgrave (Marlow)	1	Staite & Spencer-Jones (Evesham & Bewdley)	$3\frac{1}{2}$	7.55
1983	Spencer-Jones & Baillieu (Bewdley & Leander Club)	1	Johnson & Staite (Tees & Evesham)	3	7.27
1984	Espersen & Kruse (Bagsv. & Kolding, DAN)	1	Crooks & Matheson (Notts. CRA & Kingston RC)	$1\frac{1}{4}$	7.25
1985	Eltang & Kruse (Kold. & Danske, DAN)	1	Lewis & Springer (Dirty Dozen, USA)	$3\frac{1}{4}$	7.14
1986	Parks & Chernoff (Charles River, USA)	1	Luke & Hancock (Llandaff & Derwent)	$3\frac{1}{2}$	7.32

66. The Chairman studies tomorrow's programme . . .

67. . . . and traditionally starts the first race of the day. If he does not turn up the officials at the start know there is trouble elsewhere.

68. Make do and mend.

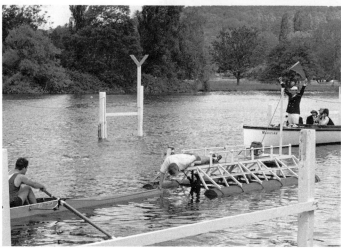

69. The start . . .

70. . . . bows level.

71. It was agony . . .

Double Sculls Challenge Cup

Year	Winner	Station	Loser	Lengths	Time
1987	Chouprina & Dosenko (Din., Moscow, USSR)	I	Scrivener & Henderson (Lea RC)	E	7.21
1988	Rudkin & Kittermaster (Tideway Sc. Sch. & Barclays Bank)	I	Scrivener & Henderson (Lea RC)	$\frac{1}{2}$	7.26

The Diamond Sculls

The Diamond Sculls was instituted in 1844 for a presentation prize thus described by *Bell's Life*:

> At the top of a long gold pin are a pair of well-executed sculls crossed, and from these are suspended a valuable drop diamond. On the guard pin, attached to the other by a neat gold chain, are green stones representative of a wreath of laurel.

In 1850, at the request of competitors, the presentation diamond scarf pins were discontinued in favour of presentation silver-gilt 'pineapple' pattern cups. At the same time the Stewards provided a challenge prize described by *Bell's* as '... sculls ... of about six inches in length, formed of frosted and bright silver, the handles of fillet gold, the sculls crossed and corded gold, the cord appearing in the centre of a wreath of green enamel set with rubies and brilliants and tied with gold, the ends of the tie sustaining a brilliant drop'.

The Pineapple Cup, certainly one of the most handsome prizes awarded in any amateur sport, became so valuable in later years that Henley had to obtain special dispensation from FISA for its continued presentation. Unfortunately inflation in the 1970s finally made the cost prohibitive. The last Pineapple Cup was made in 1975 and donated to the Regatta by De Beers Industrial Diamond Division Ltd as a permanent addition to the Challenge Trophy. De Beers also donate a miniature replica of the silver sculls which are presented to the winner instead of the cup.

The Diamond Sculls is open to all amateurs.

Year	Winner	Station	Loser	Lengths	Time
1844	T. B. Bumpsted (London Am. Sc.)		H. Morgan (Christ Church, Oxf.)	1	10.32
1845	S. Wallace (Leander Club)		J. W. Conant (St John's, Oxf.)		11.30
1846	E. G. Moon (Magdalen College, Oxf.)		T. H. Fellows (Leander Club)	E	—
1847	W. Maule (First Trinity, Cam.)	1	E. G. Moon (Magdalen College, Oxf.)	2	10.45
1848	W. L. Bagshawe (Third Trinity, Cam.)		W. Wilberforce (Oxford Univ. BC)	E	—
1849	T. R. Bone (London)		C. S. Bagot (Trinity College, Cam.)	E	—
1850	T. R. Bone (Meteor Club, London)		J. E. Clarke (Wadham College, Oxf.)	E	—
1851	E. G. Peacock (Thames Club)		E. Macnaghten (Trinity Coll., Cam.)		—
1852	E. Macnaghten (First Trinity, Cam.)		E. G. Peacock (London)	5–6	—
1853	S. R. Rippingall (Peterhouse, Cam.)	1	M. H. Irving (Balliol College, Oxf.)		10.02
1854	H. H. Playford (Wandle Club, Lon.)	1	R. C. Galton (Trinity College, Cam.)	Disq.	—
1855	A. A. Casamajor (Wandle Club, Lon.)		H. H. Playford (Wandle Club, Lon.)	$1\frac{1}{2}$	9.27
1856	A. A. Casamajor (Argonaut, Lon.)	2	C. Stephens (Reading BC)	E	—
1857	A. A. Casamajor (London RC)	1	J. Paine (London RC)	4 L	—
1858	A. A. Casamajor (London RC)				RO
1859	E. D. Brickwood (Richmond)	2	R. Beaumont (Third Trinity, Cam.)		10.00
1860	H. H. Playford (London RC)	1	E. D. Brickwood (London)		12.08
1861	A. A. Casamajor (London RC)	C	E. D. Brickwood (London)	3	10.04
1862	E. D. Brickwood (London RC)	2	W. B. Woodgate (BNC, Oxf.)	E	10.40

The Diamond Sculls

Year	Winner	Station	Loser	Lengths	Time
1863	C. B. Lawes (Third Trinity, Cam.)	2	E. D. Brickwood (London)	E	9.43
1864	W. B. Woodgate (BNC, Oxf.)	2	E. B. Michell (Magdalen Coll., Oxf.)		10.10
1865	E. B. Michell (Magdalen Coll., Oxf.)	2	C. B. Lawes (Third Trinity, Cam.)	4	9.11
1866	E. B. Michell (Magdalen Coll., Oxf.)	1	W. B. Woodgate (Kingston RC)	$2\frac{1}{2}$	9.55
1867	W. C. Crofts (BNC, Oxf.)	C	F. Willan (Exeter College, Oxf.)	2	10.02
1868	W. Stout (London RC)	2	W. C. Crofts (BNC, Oxf.)	2	9.06
1869	W. C. Crofts (BNC, Oxf.)	1	A. C. Yarborough (Lincoln, Oxf.)	3	9.56
1870	John B. Close (First Trinity, Cam.)	2	R. J. Waldie-Griffith (Jesus, Cam.)	E	9.43
1871	W. Fawcus (Tynemouth RC)	2	J. H. D. Goldie (LMBC, Cam.)	4	10.09
1872	C. C. Knollys (Magdalen Coll., Oxf.)	C	C. H. Lawton (York)	E	10.48
1873	A. C. Dicker (LMBC, Cam.)	1	W. Chillingworth (Twickenham RC)	E	9.50
1874	A. C. Dicker (LMBC, Cam.)	2	W. Fawcus (Tynemouth)	3	10.50
1875	A. C. Dicker (LMBC, Cam.)	1	W. B. Close (Cambridge Univ. BC)	E	9.15
1876	F. L. Playford (London RC)	1	R. H. Labat (London RC)	4	9.28
1877	T. C. Edwards-Moss (BNC, Oxf.)	1	A. V. Frere (Kingston RC)	E	10.20
1878	T. C. Edwards-Moss (BNC, Oxf.)	C	J. Lowndes (Hertford College, Oxf.)	E	9.37
1879	J. Lowndes (Hertford Coll., Oxf.)	C	F. L. Playford (London RC)	NRO	12.30
1880	J. Lowndes (Derby RC)	1	C. E. Adam (Oxford Univ. BC)	E	9.10
1881	J. Lowndes (Derby RC)	2	A. Wild (Germania, Frankfurt, GER)	4	9.28
1882	J. Lowndes (Derby RC)	C	A. Lein (Paris, FRA)	NRO	11.43
1883	J. Lowndes (Twickenham RC)	C	A. Wild (Germania, Frankfurt, GER)	6	10.02
1884	W. S. Unwin (Magdalen Coll., Oxf.)	2	R. H. Smith (Thames RC)	1	9.44
1885	W. S. Unwin (Magdalen Coll., Oxf.)	2	F. I. Pitman (Third Trinity, Cam.)	E	9.22
1886	F. I. Pitman (Third Trinity, Cam.)	2	W. S. Unwin (Magdalen Coll., Oxf.)	NRO	9.05
1887	J. C. Gardner (Emmanuel, Cam.)	2	G. Nickalls (Magdalen Coll., Oxf.)	2	8.51
1888	G. Nickalls (Magdalen College, Oxf.)	2	J. C. Gardner (Emmanuel Coll., Cam.)	$1\frac{1}{2}$	8.36
1889	G. Nickalls (Magdalen College, Oxf.)	2	C. J. Psotta (NY Athletic Club, USA)	E	8.56
1890	G. Nickalls (Magdalen College, Oxf.)	2	G. E. B. Kennedy (Kingston RC)	$\frac{1}{2}$	$8.57\frac{1}{2}$
1881	V. Nickalls (Magdalen College, Oxf.)			RO	
1892	J. J. K. Ooms (Nept., A'dam, HOL)	2	S. M. Boyd (Trinity College, Dublin)	E	10.09
1893	G. Nickalls (Magdalen College, Oxf.)	2	G. E. B. Kennedy (Kingston RC)	3	9.12
1894	G. Nickalls (Formosa BC)	1	V. Nickalls (Magdalen College, Oxf.)	$1\frac{3}{4}$	9.32
1895	Hon. R. Guinness (Leander Club)	2	G. Nickalls	$1\frac{1}{2}$	9.11
1896	Hon. R. Guinness (Leander Club)	2	R. K. Beaumont (Burton RC)	2	9.35
1897	E. H. Ten Eyck (Wachusett, USA)	1	H. T. Blackstaff (Vesta RC)	$1\frac{1}{2}$	8.35
1898	B. H. Howell (Trinity Hall, Cam.)	1	H. T. Blackstaffe (Vesta RC)	$3\frac{1}{2}$	8.29
1899	B. H. Howell (Thames RC)	2	H. T. Blackstaffe (Vesta RC)	4	8.38
1900	E. G. Hemmerde (Univ. Coll., Oxf.)	2	B. H. Howell (Thames RC)	$\frac{3}{4}$	8.42
1901	C. V. Fox (Guards Brigade RC)	2	St G. Ashe (Thames RC)	E	8.52
1902	F. S. Kelly (Balliol College, Oxf.)	1	R. B. Etherington-Smith (Leander)	$2\frac{1}{2}$	8.59
1903	F. S. Kelly (Leander Club)	2	J. Beresford Sr (Kensington RC)	E	8.41
1904	L. F. Scholes (Toronto RC, CAN)	2	A. H. Cloutte (London RC)	$1\frac{1}{4}$	8.23

The Diamond Sculls

Year	Winner	Station	Loser	Lengths	Time
1905	F. S. Kelly (Leander Club)	2	H. T. Blackstaffe (Vesta RC)	E	8.10
1906	H. T. Blackstaffe (Vesta RC)	2	W. H. Darell (Household Brigade)	E	8.35
1907	W. H. Darell (Household Brigade)	2	A. McCullock (Univ. Coll., Oxf.)	$1\frac{1}{4}$	9.24
1908	A. McCullock (Leander Club)	2	A. A. Stuart (Kingston RC)	E	8.25
1909	A. A. Stuart (Kingston RC)	2	R. Lucas (Mayence RC, GER)	E	8.30
1910	W. D. Kinnear (Kingston RC)	2	R. Lucas (Mainzer RC, GER)	E	8.51
1911	W. D. Kinnear (Kensington RC)	1	E. W. Powell (Eton Vikings)	$1\frac{1}{2}$	8.14
1912	E. W. Powell (Eton Vikings)	2	A. McCullock (Leander Club)	NRO	8.49
1913	C. McVilly (Derwent RC, Tasmania)	2	E. D. P. Pinks (London RC)	1	8.49
1914	G. Sinigaglia (Lario Club, Como, ITA)	1	C. M. Stuart (Trinity Hall, Cam.)	NRO	9.00
1920	J. Beresford Jr (Thames RC)	2	D. H. L. Gollan (First Trinity, Cam.)	3	8.57
1921	F. E. Eyken (Delft Univ., Laga, HOL)	2	J. Beresford Jr. (Thames RC)	$1\frac{1}{2}$	8.26
1922	W. M. Hoover (Duluth, Minn., USA)	2	J. Beresford Jr. (Thames RC)	E	9.32
1923	M. K. Morris (London RC)	1	D. H. L. Gollan (Leander Club)	1	8.23†
1924	J. Beresford Jr (Thames RC)	1	K. N. Craig (Pembroke Coll., Cam.)	E	10.32
1925	J. Beresford Jr (Thames RC)	2	D. H. L. Gollan (Leander Club)	E	8.28
1926	J. Beresford Jr (Thames RC)	1	G. E. G. Goddard (Jesus Coll., Cam.)	E	8.45
1927	R. T. Lee (Worcester College, Oxf.)	1	J. Wright (Argonaut RC, Tor., CAN)	NRO	9.06
1928	J. Wright (Argonaut RC, Tor., CAN)	2	R. T. Lee (Worcester College, Oxf.)	1	8.24
1929	L. H. F. Gunther (de Amstel, HOL)	2	J. Wright (Argonaut RC, Tor., CAN)	3 ft	8.42
1930	J. S. Guest (Don RC, CAN)	2	G. Boetzelen (Berliner RC, GER)	E	8.29
1931	R. Pearce (Leander, Hamilton, CAN)	2	F. Bradley (Pembroke Coll., Cam.)	E	10.03
1932	H. Buhtz (Berliner RC, GER)	1	G. Boetzelen (Berliner RC, GER)	E	9.15
1933	T. G. Askwith (Peterhouse, Cam.)	2	H. L. Warren (Trinity Hall, Cam.)	2	9.07
1934	H. Buhtz (Berliner RC, GER)	2	W. Rutherford (Princeton Univ., USA)	$3\frac{1}{2}$	8.10
1935	E. Rufli (FC Zurich RC, SUI)	1	J. Zavrel (FC Zurich RC, SUI)	$3\frac{1}{2}$	8.15
1936	E. Rufli (FC Zurich RC, SUI)	1	T. H. Tyler (Thames RC)	3	9.22
1937	J. Hasenohrl (RV Ellida, AUT)	2	J. F. Coulson (Arnaut, Toronto., CAN)	E	9.12
1938	J. W. Burk (Penn Athletic Club, USA)	1	L. D. Habbits (Reading RC)	E	8.02
1939	J. W. Burk (Penn Athletic Club, USA)	1	R. Verey (AKZ Sportowy, POL)	$1\frac{1}{4}$	9.13
1946	J. Séphériades (SN Basse Seine, FRA)	2	J. B. Kelly Jr (US Navy, USA)	3	8.21
1947	J. B. Kelly Jr. (Univ. of Penn., USA)	2	C. H. Frosdal (Bergens RK, NOR)	E	8.49
1948	M. T. Wood (NSW Police RC, AUS)	1	B. H. T. Bushnell (Maidenhead RC)	5	8.24
1949	J. B. Kelly Jr. (Univ. of Penn., USA)	2	J. H. Tinsey (Notre Dame, Phil., USA)	E	8.12
1950	A. D. Rowe (Leander Club)	2	R. H. Van Mesdag (Trinity, Dublin)	3	9.11
1951	T. A. Fox (Pembroke College, Cam.)	1	E. Larsen (Koge RK., DAN)	$4\frac{1}{2}$	8.59
1952	M. T. Wood (Sydney RC, AUS)	2	T. A. Fox (London RC)	$2\frac{1}{2}$	8.12
1953	T. A. Fox (London RC)	2	R. M. A. George (UN de Liège, BEL)	4	8.12
1954	P. Vlasic (Mornar Club, YOU)	2	A. Colomb (Aviron Romand, SUI)	6 ft	8.42
1955	T. Kocerka (AZS Bydgoszcz, POL)	2	S. C. Rand (Royal Air Force)	$1\frac{1}{4}$	8.33
1956	T. Kocerka (AZS Bydgoszcz, POL)	2	T. A. Fox (London RC)	4	8.37
1957	S. A. Mackenzie (Sydney RC, AUS)	2	V. Ivanov (Krasnoe Znamia, USSR)	4 ft	8.25

The Diamond Sculls

Year	Winner	Station	Loser	Lengths	Time
1958	S. A. Mackenzie (Sydney RC, AUS)	2	V. Ivanov (Central Army Club, USSR)	E	8.08
1959	S. A. Mackenzie (Sydney RC, AUS)	2	H. L. Parker (Vesper BC, USA)	E	8.39
1960	S. A. Mackenzie (Leander Club)	2	T. Kocerka (AZS Szczecin, POL)	$\frac{1}{2}$	8.03
1961	S. A. Mackenzie (Mosman RC, AUS)	2	U. Tjurin (Trud Club, L'grad, USSR)	$2\frac{3}{4}$	8.34
1962	S. A. Mackenzie (Leander Club)	1	W. L. Barry (Quintin BC)	3	8.38
1963	G. Kottmann (Belvoir RC, SUI)	2	W. L. Barry (Quintin BC)	2 ft	8.09
1964	S. Cromwell (Nonpareil RC, USA)	1	A. Demiddi (Rosario, ARG)	$2\frac{3}{4}$	8.6
1965	D. M. Spero (NY Athletic Club, USA)	2	H. A. Wardell-Yerburgh (Bristol RC)	$\frac{3}{4}$	7.42
1966	A. Hill (BSGM Baumschuleneweg, GER)	2	H. L. Wienese (de Amstel, HOL)	E	8.15
1967	M. Studach (G'hopper, Zurich, SUI)	2	J. Meissner (Mann. RV Amicitia, GER)	4	8.27
1968	H. A. Wardell-Yerburgh (Eton Vikings)	1	K. V. Dwan (PBD)	4	10.25
1969	H-J. Bohmer (Dynamo, Berlin, GER)	1	W. B. Tytus (Seattle Tennis Club, USA)	E	8.06
1970	J. Meissner (Mann. RV Amicitia, GFR)	2	P. G. R. Delafield (Tideway Sc. Sch.)	E	8.18
1971	A. Demiddi (Rosario, ARG)	2	J. W. Dietz (NY Athletic Club, USA)	$2\frac{1}{3}$	8.08
1972	A. Timoschinin (WMF Mos., USSR)	1	S. Drea (Vesper BC, USA)	$3\frac{3}{4}$	8.10
1973	S. Drea (Neptune RC, IRL)	2	D. P. Sturge (LMBC, Cam.)	$2\frac{1}{3}$	7.53
1974	S. Drea (Neptune RC, IRL)	2	K. V. Dwan (PBD)	E	8.20
1975	S. Drea (Neptune, RC, IRL)	2	J. W. Dietz (NY Athletic Club, USA)	$2\frac{1}{3}$	7.56
1976	E. O. Hale (Sydney RC, AUS)	2	P. Zeun (Peterborough City RC)	E	7.47
1977	T. J. Crooks (Leander Club)	1	J. W. Dietz (NY Athletic Club, USA)	$3\frac{2}{3}$	8.11
1978	T. J. Crooks (Leander Club)	1	H. P. Matheson (Thames T'men)	E	8.25
1979	H. P. Matheson (Nottingham RC)	2	J. T. Ghoos (Antwerpse RV., BEL)	E	8.36
1980	R. D. Ibarra (Mar del Plata, ARG)	1	R. Thorsen (Horten RK., NOR)	$1\frac{2}{3}$	8.14
1981	C. L. Baillieu (Leander Club)	2	S. C. Howell (University of London)	E	9.38
1982	C. L. Baillieu (Leander Club)	1	A. Whitwell (Thames Tradesmen)	E	8.18
1983	S. G. Redgrave (Marlow)	2	T. J. Crooks (Kingston RC)	2	8.23
1984	C. L. Baillieu (Leander Club)	1	B. Eltang (Danske Stud. RK, DAN)	4	7.57
1985	S. G. Redgrave (Marlow RC)	1	B. A. Lewis (Dirty Dozen RC, USA)	4	8.28
1986	B. Eltang (Danske Stud. RK, DAN)	2	S. G. Redgrave (Marlow)	NRO	8.08
1987	P-M. Kolbe (RC Hamburg, GFR)	1	V. Jakusha (Soviet Army, USSR)	$2\frac{3}{4}$	7.52
1988	G. H. McGlashan (Melb. Univ., AUS)	1	A. H. Sudduth (Harvard Univ., USA)	$3\frac{3}{4}$	7.43

The Silver Goblets and Nickalls' Challenge Cup

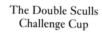

The Double Sculls
Challenge Cup

Special Race
for Schools

The Special Race for Schools 1974

The Special Race for Schools was introduced in 1974 to cater for schools whose training for, or competition in, the Regatta had been seriously interfered with by examination dates. It is raced on Saturday and Sunday only, over a shortened course from the Barrier. It is not recognized as an official Henley event, and until 1985 only medals were presented. In that year a trophy was added, presented by the Young family in memory of their son Nicholas.

Year	Winner	Station	Time	Year	Winner	Station	Time
1974	Radley College	2	4.47	1982	Shrewsbury School	1	4.46
1975	Shrewsbury School	1	4.33	1983	St Edward's School	1	4.32
1976	Shrewsbury School	2	4.44	1984	Shrewsbury School	2	4.37
1977	St Edward's School	2	4.38	1985	Shrewsbury School	2	4.36
1978	Bedford School	2	4.57	1986	St Edward's School	2	4.33
1979	St Paul's School	1	4.47	1987	Radley College	2	4.32
1980	Shrewsbury School	1	4.34	1988	Radley College	2	4.35
1981	Shrewsbury School	1	5.13				

Appendix 4 Discontinued Events

The Town Challenge Cup 1839–1883

This was founded, with the Grand Challenge Cup, in 1839, as a four-oar event for local crews, originally living within a five-mile radius of Henley. In 1852 the radius was extended to admit all clubs on the Thames between Windsor and Oxford (but excluding crews from Oxford University). Various alterations were made in attempts to attract a realistic entry whilst retaining the principle that this was an event for local crews, but there were never enough clubs to achieve this. Crews from Henley Town rowed over without opposition on eleven occasions, and on three occasions there were no entries at all.

In 1884 the Town Challenge Cup was withdrawn from competition and given in trust to the Henley Town and Visitors' Regatta.

Year	Winner	Station	Time
1839	The Wave, Henley	c	—
1840	Dreadnought, Henley		10.15
1841	Dreadnought, Henley		RO
1842	Dreadnought, Henley		RO
1843	Albion Club, Henley	1	10.45
1844	Henley Aquatic Club	2	10.05
1845	Henley Aquatic Club		RO
1846	Dreadnought, Henley		RO
1847	Dreadnought, Henley		RO
1848	Dreadnought, Henley		—
1849	Albion Club, Henley		RO
1850	1 Albion, Henley		—
1851	No entry		
1852	No entry		
1853	No entry		
1854	Defiance, Wargrave		9.05
1855	Henley BC		—
1856	Henley BC		—
1857	Henley BC		RO
1858	Henley BC		RO
1859	Henley BC		RO
1860	Dreadnought, Henley	2	11.00
1861	Henley BC		RO

Year	Winner	Station	Time
1862	Oxford Staff RC		9.56
1863	Henley BC	1	9.15
1864	Henley BC		10.32
1865	Henley BC	2	9.07
1866	Eton Excelsior RC	1	9.28
1867	Eton Excelsior RC	1	NRO
1868	Henley RC		RO
1869	Eton Excelsior RC		—
1870	Eton Excelsior RC	1	—
1871	Reading RC		—
1872	Marlow RC	2	—
1873	Henley RC	2	—
1874	Marlow RC	2	9.34
1875	Marlow RC		RO
1876	Marlow RC	2	—
1877	Marlow RC	1	10.16
1878	Henley RC	1	—
1879	Greenwood Lodge, Wargrave	1	—
1880	Reading RC	1	8.32
1881	Reading RC	2	8.45
1882	Reading RC	1	—
1883	Marlow RC	1	—

The District Challenge Cup for Fours 1840–1847

The District Challenge Cup was the third event introduced at Henley for four-oars 'limited to amateur crews or clubs belonging to the towns of Maidenhead, Marlow, Reading, Wallingford and Henley'. Members had to reside within four miles of the town in question. In 1842 the limit was extended to include Windsor and Oxford (but excluding University members).

There were no entries in 1846 and 1847 and the event was discontinued (see also the Visitors' Cup).

The winners of the District Challenge Cup between 1840 and 1845 were:

Year	Winner	Station	Time
1840	Dreadnought, Henley	2	11.11
1841	Dreadnought, Henley	2	RO
1842	Windsor and Eton Club	2	—
1843	Albion Club, Henley		RO
1844	Windsor and Eton Club		—
1845	Henley Aquatic Club		10.12

The Local Amateur Scullers' Race 1846–1857

In 1846 a Mr Makepeace gave a 'Silver Wherry' as a presentation prize for Henley amateur scullers, and this event was sometimes referred to as the 'Silver Wherry'. In 1848 the qualification was extended to residents within twelve miles of Henley.

Year	Winner	Lengths
1846	Sergeant	E
1847	Sergeant	
1848	Sergeant	E
1849	Giles	E
1850	Williams	3
1851	Ive	E
1852	Piper	Disq.
1853	Popjoy	Disq.
1854	Piper	E
1855	Giles	
1856	Giles	
1857	Giles	

The photographs overleaf are all of 'Silver Wherries' presented for this event which show the development of sculling boats from the earliest 'Makepeace' of 1846 or 1847 (2), clearly descended from the Wherry originally presented for the Pair-Oars event (1) (itself developed from the 'skiffs' used by London Watermen to convey passengers), via the 1848 model (3), to the 1856 'Walford' Wherry (4), which is recognizable as a 'modern' sculling boat.

The years 1841–72 saw most of the important developments in boat design. The first recorded carvel built boat (smooth skin as opposed to overlapping planks) was used by Oxford University in 1841. In 1844 Clasper's of Newcastle built the first outrigged four, with rowlocks carried on 8-inch iron rods.

In 1847 Henry Clasper built a keelless four in which Oxford University subsequently won the Stewards' Cup in 1852. The first keelless eight, built by Mat Taylor of Newcastle, followed in 1856, and in her Royal Chester Rowing Club won both the Grand and the Ladies'. Sliding seats, first credited to J. C. Babcock of New York, reached Henley in 1872.

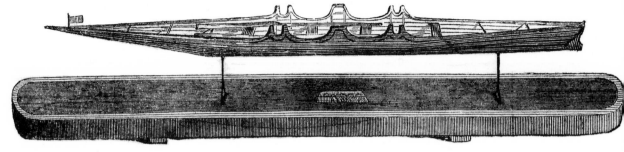

1. Silver Wherry.

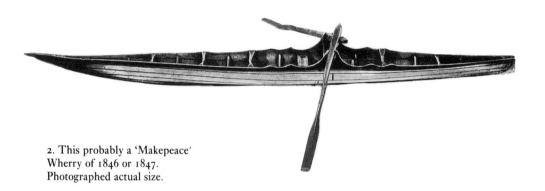

2. This probably a 'Makepeace'
Wherry of 1846 or 1847.
Photographed actual size.

3. Silver Wherry. 1848. Presented by
Mr Makepeace for any Amateur
Sculler residing within 12 miles of
Henley-on-Thames. Photographed
actual size.

4. 1856–Silver Wherry presented by
Mr Walford for any Amateur Sculler
residing within 12 miles of Henley.
Photographed actual size.

The District Goblets for Pair Oars 1858–1867

This was a race for amateurs residing within twenty-five miles of Henley, but excluding the universities and public schools. The restriction on university and public school oarsmen was removed in 1861.

In 1858 a protest was lodged against the winners, Messrs Chapman and Pyle, on the grounds that they did not live within the prescribed distance of Henley. This was rejected, surprisingly, since Mr Chapman lived in Richmond and was staying with Mr Pyle in Staines when they entered under the assumed names of Foster and Morton, Staines.

The winners of the eight races that took place between 1858–67 were:

Year	Winner	Station	Time
1858	Chapman and Pyle (Staines)		–
1859	Giles and Sergeant (Henley)		–
1860	Dolly and Dolly (Oxford)		–
1861	Hopkins and Norsworthy	2	11.00
1862 and 63	No entries		
1864	Hunt and Pescud (Henley)		10.30

Year	Winner	Station	Time
1865	Carter and Cripps (Eton & Parmoor)		–
1866	Morrell and Willan (Oxford)	1	10.11
1867	Prickett and Plowman (Oxford City)		RO

The Presentation Cup for Fours Without Coxswain 1869–1872

Until 1868 coxswainless fours were unknown at Henley. In that year Brasenose College, competing in the Stewards' Challenge Cup, made their coxswain jump overboard at the start, for which they were duly disqualified. But their point was successfully made and in 1869 the 'Presentation Cup for Fours without Coxswain' was advertised under the same qualifications as the Stewards' Cup. It was contested only twice, and in 1873 the Stewards' Challenge Cup became an event for coxswainless fours.

Year	Winner	Time
1869	Oxford Radleian Club	8.40

Year	Winner	Time
1872	London RC	RO

The Public Schools Challenge Cup for Fours 1879–1884

This event was for public schools which could not at that time aspire to enter for the Ladies' Plate. From H. T. Steward's records it appears to have been well supported, but was discontinued in 1885 when the trophy was acquired by Marlow Regatta where it is still contested.

Year	Winner	Station	Time
1879	Cheltenham College	I	11.06
1880	Bedford School	C	8.42
1881	Bedford School	I	9.22

Year	Winner	Station	Time
1882	Magdalen College School	2	–
1883	Hereford School	2	–
1884	Derby School	I	–

Women's Events

Invitation events for women were introduced in 1981, over a course from the Special Schools Race start near the Barrier. In 1982 the distance was reduced to about 1,000 metres. The events were discontinued after 1982 because it was considered that the Regatta programme was so full that it would not be possible to stage open events for women without drastically curtailing, or withdrawing, some existing event.

Women's Invitation Coxed Fours

1981	1980 RC, USA	5.44
1982	Boston University, USA	3.36

Women's Invitation Double Sculls

1981	L. Roy and J. Mason (Adanac BC, CAN)	6.21
1982	R. Clugston and A. Ayling (Borough Road College RC and Kingston RC)	3.56

Women's Invitation Single Sculls

1982	B. Mitchell (Thames Tradesmen)	3.56

Appendix 5 Stewards and Committee

The earliest minute book for the Henley Royal Regatta dates from 1867. For the names of Stewards and Committee before that date we rely on Regatta Notices, correspondence and press reports. The lists of names in this Appendix in the earlier years, and the relationships between various Stewards and Committee members, are mainly the result of researches by the late President, Harold Rickett. The dates in some cases were established by a process of elimination. Thus, for example, W. P. Williams-Freeman was still serving as a Steward in 1870, but not in 1874. In such cases a middle date is shown with the prefix 'c'. The numerals in square brackets refer to the notes on page 214.

Stewards

The Mayor of Henley (*ex officio*)		J. Wheble	1845–c1863
Thomas Stonor [1]	1839– 1881	The Marquis of Downshire	1847–c1863
W. P. Williams-Freeman [2]	1839–c1872	The Earl of Falmouth	1847– 1852
W. F. Maitland	1839– 1858	The Earl of Kilmorey	1847–c1858
C. Lane	1839–c1877	The Hon. T. E. Stonor [1]	1847– 1865
E. Gardiner [3]	1839–c1841	H. Baskerville [8]	1847– 1875
E. F. Maitland	1839– 1842	G. East [5]	1849–c1862
Charles Stonor [1]	1839– 1840	R. Palmer	c1851–c1872
C. R. Scott Murray [4]	1839–c1866	J. F. Hodges	c1851– 1894
Sir William R. Clayton, Bt [5]	1839– 1866	T. Hall	c1851–c1858
Sir E. G. Clayton East, Bt [5]	1839– 1851	J. Silverwright	c1851–c1858
J. Fane	1839– 1850	W. B. Reade	c1851–c1858
The Rev. C. E. Keene	1839– 1850	The Hon. Spencer D. Montagu	c1857–c1878
Lord Parker [6]	c1842– 1895	H. P. Malet	c1857–c1872
W. H. Vanderstegen	c1842–c1887	W. H. Stone	c1857–c1866
J. W. N. Birch	c1842–c1866	A. C. Forbes	c1857–c1901
Col. Bourchier	c1842– 1846	S. H. Vansittart	c1858–c1878
Major M. L. Cooper	c1842– 1846	G. Barker	c1858–c1866
H. P. Powys	c1842– 1848	Edward Mackenzie [9]	c1858– 1881
G. J. Donkin [7]	c1842–c1857	H. Knox	c1858– 1908
J. Phillimore	c1842– 1848	C. G. Richardson	c1858–c1866
The Earl of Orkney	1844–c1860	Col. Fane, MP [10]	c1858– 1871
G. Jackson	1844– 1875	Admiral The Hon. G. Grey	c1858–c1875
S. W. Gardiner [3]	1844–c1866	W. Scott	c1858–c1866
Col. Knollys	1845– 1883	The Hon. F. Stonor [1]	c1865– 1881

J. W. Rhodes	c1865– 1910	Lord Ampthill	1894– 1935
W. D. Mackenzie [9]	c1865– 1928	W. F. Holt-Beever	1894– 1945
C. Scholefield	c1865– 1874	R. Ovey	1894–c1901
J. H. Wilson	c1865–c1872	F. I. Pitman [22] [38]	1896– 1942
The Revd A. H. Fairbairn	c1865–c1872	Leonard Noble [14]	1897– 1943
C. H. Ames	1868–c1877	R. C. Lehmann	1898– 1929
G. G. Elger	1868–c1873	W. A. L. Fletcher	1899– 1919
Sir William R. Clayton, Bt [5]	1868 and	W. H. Eyre	1901– 1939
	1871– 1914	C. Gurdon	1901– 1931
H. Hodges	1868–c1902	R. C. M. G. Gridley	1901– 1916
R. R. Robinson	1868–c1877	W. F. C. Holland	1901– 1917
H. H. Playford [11]	1868–c1873	R. T. Hermon-Hodge [23]	1901– 1937
The Revd E. Warre [12]	1868– 1920	H. F. Nicholl	1901– 1918
F. Willan	1870– 1931	R. S. de Haviland	1905– 1921
C. Stevens	1870–c1890	G. D. Rowe	1905– 1934
The Revd R. W. Risley [13]	1872– 1884	R. S. Bradshaw	1905– 1946
J. G. Chambers [13]	1872– 1883	The Lord Camoys [1]	1905– 1963
J. Noble [14]	1874–c1889	C. M. Pitman [22]	1907– 1948
W. H. Smith [15]	1874– 1891	Col. Sir Douglas Dawson	1907– 1933
F. Fenner [16]	1879– 1903	Sir Frank Crisp	1907– 1919
H. T. Steward [17]	1879– 1915	V. Fleming	1907– 1917
Major J. Baskerville [8]	1979– 1927	H. G. Gold [24]	1909– 1952
H. Mair	1879–c1901	S. D. Muttlebury	1909– 1933
Sir Francis G. Stapleton, Bt	1880– 1899	C. T. Steward [17]	1909– 1943
Col. Fane MP [10]	1880– 1884	R. B. Etherington-Smith	1909– 1912
W. P. W. Freeman [2]	1880–c1884	W. R. D. Mackenzie [9]	1909– 1952
The Lord Camoys [1]	1881– 1897	Hon. E. A. Stonor	1909– 1911
W. H. Grenfell [18]	1882– 1945	C. W. Kent	1910– 1959
J. H. D. Goldie [13]	1883– 1896	H. W. M. Willis	1910– 1936
Lord Londesborough [19]	1884– 1895	H. A. Steward [17]	1913– 1948
T. C. Edwards-Moss	1885– 1893	G. S. Maclagan	1914– 1914
J. Cooper [20]	1885– 1905	W. Noble	1914– 1916
J. Page	1885– 1910	Lt. Col. C. D. Burnell [25]	1919– 1969
A. Brakspear [21]	1885– 1909	J. F. Cooper [20]	1919– 1928
The Earl of Antrim	1885– 1911	E. Noble [14]	1919– 1961
J. Foster	1887– 1910	R. W. M. Arbuthnot	1922– 1962
H. E. Rhodes	1888– 1889	Sir W. Anker Simmons	1923– 1927
Col. Makins	1888– 1906	Brigadier J. H. Gibbon	1924– 1960
W. R. Griffiths	1888– 1910	F. J. Escombe	1926– 1938
The Revd S. A. Donaldson	1889– 1915	A. S. Garton [26]	1926– 1948
C. A. Scott Murray [4]	1891– 1909	Viscount Hambleden [15]	1928– 1948
The Hon. W. F. D. Smith [15]	1892– 1928	S. Fairbairn [27]	1928– 1938
D. H. McLean	1894– 1901	W. Dudley Ward	1928– 1946
J. A. Drake-Smith	1894– 1899	A. F. R. Wiggins	1928– 1961

H. A. Game	1930– 1949	Rt. Hon. Sir R. Nugent, Bt [33]	1962–
F. W. Warre [12]	1930– 1953	D. H. Mays-Smith	1962– 1969
P. Haig Thomas	1935– 1950	Dr. D. M. Jennens	1962–
C. W. Wise	1935– 1971	R. L. Howard	1962–
G. O. Nickalls	1935– 1973	R. D. Burnell [25] [26]	1965–
H. R. N. Rickett [28]	1935– 1968	C. G. V. Davidge	1966–
K. M. Payne	1938– 1988	J. A. Macnabb	1966–
Lord Lloyd of Dolobran	1939– 1941	T. B. Langton	1966– 1986
J. Beresford	1945– 1974	E. G. H. Moody	1966–
Sir Clive Baillieu [29]	1945– 1966	The Lord Elworthy	1968–
The Revd H. B. Playford [11]	1946– 1981	J. D. Cazes	1968–
C. Luker [30]	1946– 1968	A. B. Hodgson	1969–
C. W. H. Taylor	1947– 1960	Sir Adrian Cadbury	1969–
E. D. Horsfall	1947– 1973	G. H. Brown	1969–
The Hon. J. W. H. Fremantle [31]	1947–	I. L. Elliott	1969–
Col. D. T. Raikes	1947– 1966	Dr E. V. Bevan	1971– 1988
The Viscount Bruce of Melbourne	1948– 1967	H. R. P. Steward [17]	1971– 1981
S. I. Fairbairn [27]	1948– 1968	P. R. C. Coni	1974–
J. B. Rosher	1948– 1965	M. A. Sweeney	1974–
G. W. F. Fraser	1949– 1950	D. A. Chipp	1974–
A. Whitworth	1949– 1960	W. H. Perry [34]	1974–
F. E. Hellyer	1949– 1950	R. H. Brakston	1974– 1976
P. H. G. H-S. Hartley	1949– 1976	T. Keller [35]	1975–
A. D. B. Pearson	1949– 1981	A. A. M. Mays-Smith	1975–
W. P. Mellen	1949– 1953	J. A. Stephenson	1975–
R. E. Eason	1949– 1976	A. G. Robertson	1975–
T. A. Brocklebank	1949– 1983	P. G. R. Delafield	1976–
Viscount Nuffield	1951– 1963	D. W. Parry	1976–
Dr W. G. R. M. Laurie	1951–	J. Carson-Bury	1976–
T. R. B. Sanders	1951– 1985	The Lord Camoys [1]	1978–
A. Burrough	1951–	C. M. Davis	1978–
P. N. Carpmael	1953– 1988	M. J. Langton	1978–
Rt. Revd. G. A. Ellison [32]	1953–	R. C. Lester	1978–
J. H. T. Wilson	1953–	A. R. Watson	1980–
W. A. D. Windham	1953–	J. A. Veats	1981–
G. D. Clapperton	1953– 1971	I. Reid	1983–
C. G. Rickett [28]	1953–	C. L. Baillieu [29]	1984–
W. Rathbone	1959–	D. C. Christie	1984–
Dr J. R. Owen	1959– 1985	J. K. Mullard	1985–
J. L. Garton [26]	1959–	J. C. Luker [30]	1984–
M. Buxton	1959–	C. P. Etherington	1985–
R. M. A. Bourne	1959–	The Very Revd. J. M. Jabale	1985–
J. G. P. Crowden	1959–	J. D. J. Howard	1988–
J. H. Page	1961– 1977		

Committee

Names and dates of the early Committee members are less well documented than those of the Stewards. Members of the original Committee, elected at the public meeting on 26 March 1839, were:

S. B. Cooper [36]	J. S. Plumbe	C. Kinch	P. B. Cooper (Treasurer) [20]
W. H. Brakspear [21]	W. Plumbe	H. Stubbs	J. Nash (Joint Hon. Secretary)
E. Young	R. Owthwaite	J. H. Brooks	C. Towsey (Joint Hon. Secretary).
E. Elsee	H. N. Byles		

The following are known to have served subsequently on the Committee:

J. Cooper [20]	J. D'o Brooks	Mr Partridge	R. P. Jeston
H. Clements	C. Lucey	J. Page	N. Mercer
T. Jeston	Mr Hews	Mr Copeland	Mr Stubbs
T. N. Watts	Mr Ive		

In 1881 a Standing Committee was set up, later to be known as the Committee of Management. Originally with six representatives from the Town, and six rowing men, power soon swayed towards the oarsmen. In 1885 the new Constitution abolished the original Committee, the remaining members either becoming Stewards or resigning.

The following have served on the Committee since 1881:

*Representing the Town**		*Representing Rowing**	
J. F. Hodges [37]	1881–1894	Revd. E. Warre [12]	1881–1889
W. D. Mackenzie [9]	1881–1922	F. Willan	1881–1908
J. Cooper	1881–1893	Revd. R. W. Risley	1881–1884
J. Page	1881–1901	J. G. Chambers	1881–1883
J. D'o Brooks	1881–1883	F. Fenner [17]	1881–1903
W. H. Brakspear [21]	1881–1882	H. T. Steward [38]	1881–1915

*The differentiation ceased after 1881.

A. Brakspear [21]	1882–1909
J. H. D. Goldie	1883–1896
W. H. Grenfell [18]	1883–1886
	and 1909–1945
A. C. Forbes	1885–1895
The Earl of Antrim	1887–1892
T. C. Edwards-Moss	1890–1893
W. R. Griffiths	1893–1910
The Hon. W. F. D. Smith [15]	1894–1928
D. H. McLean	1894–1901
J. A. Drake-Smith	1894–1898
Lord Ampthill	1896–1900
	and 1910–1927
F. I. Pitman [22] [41]	1896–1942
R. C. Lehmann	1899–1920
W. A. L. Fletcher [40]	1901–1919
W. H. Eyre	1901–1927
C. Gurdon [39]	1902–1931
R. C. M. G. Gridley	1904–1916
W. F. C. Holland	1911–1917
C. T. Steward [17]	1916–1943
H. G. Gold [24] [42]	1919–1951
R. S. Bradshaw	1919–1946
G. D. Rowe	1919–1930
Lt. Col. C. D. Burnell [25]	1920–1969
R. W. M. Arbuthnot	1923–1928
F. J. Escombe	1928–1938
A. S. Garton [23] [26]	1928–1948
W. R. D. Mackenzie [9]	1929–1951
Brig. J. H. Gibbon	1929–1959
C. M. Pitman [22]	1931–1948
H. A. Game	1932–1949
K. M. Payne	1939–1988

H. A. Steward [17]	1945–1948
G. O. Nickalls	1945–1973
J. Beresford	1945–1974
Viscount Hambleden	1946–1948
H. R. N. Rickett [28] [43]	1948–1965
Revd. H. B. Playford [11]	1948–1981
C. W. H. Taylor	1948–1960
E. D. Horsfall	1948–1959
The Hon. J. W. H. Fremantle [31]	1949–1977
J. B. Rosher	1952–1964
W. P. Mellen	1952–1953
C. W. Wise	1953–1964
S. I. Fairbairn [27]	1960–1968
A. Burrough	1960–1985
J. L. Garton [26] [44]	1961–1978
Dr W. G. R. M. Laurie	1964–1986
J. G. P. Crowden	1964–
Dr D. M. Jennens	1965–1986
Dr J. R. Owen	1968–1978
W. A. D. Windham	1973–
C. G. V. Davidge	1973–
R. H. Brakston	1974–1976
P. R. C. Coni [45]	1976–
J. Carson-Bury	1977–1986
J. A. Stephenson	1978–1986
A. G. Robertson	1978–
M. A. Sweeney	1979–
I. Reid	1986–
R. C. Lester	1987–
J. A. Veats	1987–
C. L. Baillieu [29]	1987–
J. D. J. Howard	1988–

Notes

[1] Thomas Stonor was created 3rd Baron Camoys in 1839. Described as 'acting Steward of the Regatta' in 1843, Patron in 1844, and Vice-Patron in 1851 (when Prince Albert became Patron), he became the first President c. 1865.
Relationship of other members of the Stonor family is shown below with the date of their election as Stewards, where applicable, shown in parentheses.

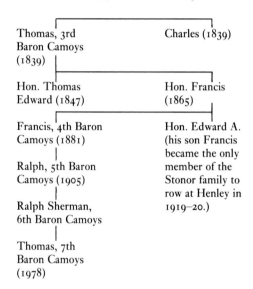

Thomas, 3rd Baron Camoys (1839)　　　　　Charles (1839)

Hon. Thomas Edward (1847)　　　　　Hon. Francis (1865)

Francis, 4th Baron Camoys (1881)　　　　　Hon. Edward A. (his son Francis became the only member of the Stonor family to row at Henley in 1919–20.)

Ralph, 5th Baron Camoys (1905)

Ralph Sherman, 6th Baron Camoys

Thomas, 7th Baron Camoys (1978)

[2] Father of W. P. W. F. (1880): 'opened grounds of Phyllis Court to Regatta' in 1844.
[3] Father of S. W. G. (1844).
[4] C. R. S. M. was father of C. A. S. M. (1891)
[5] General Sir W. R. C. was grandfather of Sir W. R. C. (1868). Sir E. G. Clayton East (1839) was father of G. East (1849) who changed his name from Clayton East by Royal licence in 1839, and became Sir George East in 1851.
[6] Succeeded as Lord Macclesfield in 1850.
[7] Of Wyfold Court, Reading, donor of Wyfold Cup, 1847.
[8] Father of Major J. B. (1879).
[9] Father of W. D. M. (c. 1865), grandfather of W. R. D. M. (1909).
[10] May be same as 'Major' Fane who resigned in 1871, being four years in arrears with his subscription. But either he was re-elected in 1880, or his son was elected in that year.
[11] Great uncle of H. B. P. (1946). Playford and Warre

(below) were the first two rowing men to be elected as Stewards.
[12] Father of F. W. W. (1930). Revd Edmund Warre was later Head Master and Provost of Eton College.
[13] Risley and Chambers were elected Stewards on their appointment as umpires in 1872, J. H. D. Goldie was similarly elected in 1883.
[14] Father of L. N. (1897), and E. N. (1919).
[15] Father of Hon. W. F. D. S. (1892) who became 2nd Viscount Hambleden and grandfather of 3rd Viscount Hambleden (1928).
[16] Judge at Regatta from 1889–1909 and presented the prizes in 1931 at age 91, dying in 1937 aged 98.
[17] Father of C. T. S. (1909) and H. A. S. (1913) and grandfather of H. R. P. S. (1971).
[18] Created Lord Desborough in 1905.
[19] Created Earl of Londesborough in 1887.
[20] Father of J. F. C. and son of P. B. C. (first Treasurer of the Regatta).
[21] Son of W. H. Brakspear.
[22] Brother of C. M. P.
[23] Created Baronet in 1902 and Lord Wyfold in 1919.
[24] Knighted for services to rowing in 1949.
[25] Father of R. D. B. (1965).
[26] Uncle of J. L. G. (1959) and father-in-law of R. D. B. (1965).
[27] Father of S. I. F. (1948).
[28] Elder brother of C. G. R. (1953).
[29] Created Lord Baillieu in 1953. Father of C. L. B. (1984).
[30] Father of J. C. L. (1984).
[31] Succeeded as Lord Cottesloe in 1956.
[32] Bishop of Willesden, later Bishop of Chester (1957) and Rt. Revd and Rt. Hon. Bishop of London (1973).
[33] Created Lord Nugent of Guildford in 1966.
[34] First American to be elected as Steward.
[35] The Swiss President of the Fédération Internationale des Sociétés d'Aviron.
[36] Relationship to P. B. C., J. C., and J. F. C., not known but probably brother to P. B. C.
[37] Chairman 1881–1894.
[38] Chairman 1894–1915.
[39] Chairman 1915–1919.
[40] Chairman 1919 (four days).
[41] Chairman 1919–1942.
[42] Chairman 1945–1951.
[43] Chairman 1952–1965.
[44] Chairman 1965–1978.
[45] Chairman 1978–.

Appendix 6 Chronology

1839 Inaugural Meeting announced in *Jackson's Journal* on March 21.

Inaugural Meeting in Town Hall on March 26.

Rules for the Grand Challenge Cup and Town Cup published on May 1.

First Henley Regatta held on June 14.

1840 Finish moved downstream from Bridge to Red Lion lawn.

District Fours instituted.

1841 Stewards' Challenge Cup instituted.

1842 Umpire's crew joins in final of Grand.

1843 Rule limiting substitutions.

Great Western Railway reaches Twyford.

Oxford University win Grand with seven men.

1844 First accounts published.

Omnibus connection between Twyford station and Henley.

Spectator stands erected on Berkshire bank.

Diamond Sculls instituted.

1845 Outrigged boat first used at Henley.

Ladies' Plate and Silver Wherries instituted.

1846 Local Sculls instituted.

1847 Visitors' Cup instituted.

Wyfold Cup instituted as trophy for winners of Challenge Heats in Grand Challenge Cup.

1849 Laws of Boat Racing formulated.

Henley townspeople send Address to Stewards.

1850 Henley adopt Laws of Boat Racing.

Silver Wherries replaced by Silver Goblets.

Regatta cut to one day with only six races.

1851 Prince Albert becomes Patron, and Henley Regatta 'Royal'.

1855 Wyfold Cup allocated as trophy for four-oared event.

1856 Royal Chester bring first keelless boat to Henley.

1857 Draw replaces tossing for Station.

Great Western branch line to Henley opened.

Regatta days changed from Monday and Tuesday to Friday and Saturday.

1858 District Goblets instituted.

1861 First entries by Eton and Radley.

1862 Woodgate races five times in one day.

Introduction of stakeboats.

1866 Thames Conservancy assume control of the river.

1868 Coxswain Fred Weatherly jumps out of Brasenose four.

Thames Cup instituted.

1869 Presentation Cup for Coxless Fours instituted.

1870 Beginning of houseboat era.

1872 Rule defining a boat's 'proper course' introduced.

'Challenge Heats' abolished.

First foreign entry from E. Smith (USA) in Diamond Sculls.

Sliding seats first used in Regatta.

1873 Stewards' Challenge Cup becomes event for coxless fours.

Tents provided for boat storage.

1874 Visitors' Cup becomes event for coxless fours.

1878 Amateur status of G. W. Lee and G. Lee and Shoe-wae-cae-mette BC questioned.

1879 First formal definition of an amateur.

Foreign entries to be made by 31 March.

Foundation of Metropolitan Rowing Association.

Public Schools Cup instituted.

1880 First Continental entry from Germania, Frankfurt.

Sub-committee set up to report on organization and finance.

1881 Standing Management Committee set up.

1882 Metropolitan Rowing Association becomes Amateur Rowing Association and assumes control of rowing.

1884 Stewards reject plan to cut off Poplar Point.

1885 First formal Constitution published, abolishing old Committee and establishing Committee of Management.

1886 ARA General Rules for Regattas adopted.
New Course introduced with finish at Poplar Point.
Regatta extended to three days.

1887 First visit by members of Royal Family.

1890 Foundation of National Amateur Rowing Association.

1891 Boats measured for bows-level starts.

1893 First foreign Agreement signed with French Rowing Union.

1894 Swans 'upped' for first time.

1895 Nereus, Amsterdam, becomes first foreign winner of Thames Cup.
Nickalls Challenge Cup added to Silver Goblets.

1896 Stewards reject ARA call for ban on all foreign entries.
Leander clubhouse built at Henley.

1898 Tom Eyck's entry for Diamonds rejected.

1899 Booms first installed.
Eliminating heats before Regatta introduced.

1901 Proposal to ban foreign entries again rejected.
Pennsylvania first foreign finalists in Grand.

1902 Great Western Railway run twenty-six trains from Paddington to Henley on Tuesday and Wednesday and twenty-eight for finals on Thursday.

1903 Professional coaches banned except for scullers.
Fawley signal introduced.
Boathouse site above Bridge becomes Henley's first land acquisition.

1905 F. S. Kelly sets Diamond Sculls record of 8 min. 10 sec.
Dispute over amateur status of Vesper BC.

1906 Resolution banning future entries from Vesper.

Club Nautique de Gand first foreign winners of Grand Challenge Cup.
GWR transports 17,727 visitors to Henley in one day.
Regatta seeks to purchase Phyllis Court Club.

1908 Olympic Regatta at Henley.

1911 Finals moved to Saturday.
Remenham Club opens.

1912 Visit by King George V and Queen Mary.

1919 Peace Regatta with special events.
NARA entry for King's Cup rejected.
Stewards' Enclosure Club founded.
Visit by Duke of Connaught.

1920 J. B. Kelly's entry for Diamonds refused.

1921 Visit by Prince of Wales.

1923 Experimental Straight Course.
Visit by Prince Henry.

1924 Straight Course introduced.

1926 Purchase of Boat Tents' site adjacent to Leander Club.

1928 Visit by Duke of Kent.
First Elimination Races.

1929 Browne and Nichols School the first American winners of Thames Cup.
First official times taken at Barrier.

1931 Visit by Duke and Duchess of York.
H.R.A. Edwards wins Grand, Stewards', and Goblets.

1936 Australian entry for Grand Challenge Cup refused.

1937 Amateur Status rule revised.
Ban on professional coaches rescinded.
Purchase of remainder of Lion and Blandy Meadows.

1938 Purchase of competitors' car park field.
F. S. Kelly's Diamonds record falls to J. W. Burk after thirty-three years.

1939 Centenary Regatta.
Visit by Duke of Kent.
First invitations to foreign crews.
Centenary Double Sculls event.

1939 Regatta land requisitioned as timber yard.

−45 Some wartime school races.

1945 One-day Peace Regatta.

1946 Visit by Princesses Elizabeth and Margaret.
Princess Elizabeth Cup instituted.
Double Sculls instituted.

Ladies admitted to membership of Stewards' Enclosure.

First membership list published.

First BBC radio commentary.

1947 Amateur Rowing Association affiliated to Fédération Internationale des Sociétés d'Aviron.

1948 Olympic Regatta at Henley.

Proposal to introduce Coxed Fours rejected.

Purchase of Selwyn's Field.

1949 Amateur Status rule again amended.

1952 *Times* article on Henley qualifications.

First land acquisition on Fawley Meadows.

Death of Sir Harcourt Gold.

1954 Stewards reject FISA request to introduce Interference Rule.

First entries from Soviet Union.

1955 Purchase of Park Farm land.

Arrival of foreign boats delayed by dock strike.

USSR crews scratch and are re-instated.

1957 Attempt by Berkshire County Council to claim towpath as unrestricted right of way defeated.

Interference Rule introduced.

Unsuccessful attempt to purchase Remenham Lodge.

1958 Purchase of Green's Field.

1960 Oxford and Cambridge Presidents request open Ladies' Plate.

Ladies' Plate opened to non-collegiate boat clubs of Oxford, Cambridge and London Universities.

1962 Purchase of Bridge House.

Entries exceed 200.

1963 Prince Philip Cup instituted.

1964 125th Anniversary of foundation.

Visit by Queen Mother, Princess Margaret and Lord Snowdon.

Harvard crew of 1914 return to process on course and present new Grand Challenge Cup.

1966 Federal and Democratic Republics of Germany recognized as separate countries for Henley entries.

Foreign student crews admitted to Ladies' Plate.

Fairground contract terminated and fairground becomes car park.

1967 'Bows Level' starting installation first used.

1968 Visit by Prince Philip, Duke of Edinburgh.

Regatta postponed one week due to school examinations.

Strongest stream since records first kept in 1883.

Britannia Cup instituted.

1969 Selective Draw system introduced.

Chairman Garton expresses 'deep concern about the trend of the finances'.

1970 Composite crews admitted to open events.

1972 Anti-doping tests introduced.

Ridley College disqualified after losing a man overboard.

1973 First Nottingham International Regatta over weekend of Henley draw.

1974 Sunday finals introduced.

Special Race for Schools instituted.

1975 Cost of staging Regatta exceeds £100,000.

Regatta House (Bridge House) sold.

1976 Visit by Princess Alexandra.

First year of corporate entertainment tents.

Heatwave.

1977 Visit by Princess Anne.

1980 Visit by Prince Michael.

Membership of Stewards' Enclosure limited to 5,000.

1981 Visit by Princess Grace of Monaco.

Invitation Events for Women introduced experimentally.

Queen Mother Cup instituted.

1983 Sliding rigger banned.

Purchase of Carpenter's Arms site.

1984 Visit by Prince Michael.

Entries top 300.

1985 Visit by Prince Andrew.

Ladies' Plate opened to non-student crews.

1986 HM The Queen opens new Headquarters.

Regatta extended to five days.

1987 Henley takings top £1 million. Profits exceed £300,000.

Purchase of Temple Island.

Private visit by Prince Michael.

1988 Visit by The Princess Royal.

Index

This index covers the text in Parts 1 and 2 and the captions to the illustrated material throughout the book. It does not include the names of Stewards and members of the Committee listed separately in Appendix 5 nor the names set out in the many tables in Part 3. Page numbers in *italic* refer to the illustrations in the text.

BY APPOINTMENT
TO HER MAJESTY THE QUEEN
LIVERY & MILITARY TAILORS
GIEVES & HAWKES, LONDON

BY APPOINTMENT
TO HIS ROYAL HIGHNESS
THE DUKE OF EDINBURGH
NAVAL TAILORS & OUTFITTERS
GIEVES & HAWKES, LONDON

BY APPOINTMENT
TO HIS ROYAL HIGHNESS
THE PRINCE OF WALES
TAILORS & OUTFITTERS
GIEVES & HAWKES, LONDON

GIEVES & HAWKES
No. 1 Savile Row, London

William Heinemann acknowledge with pleasure the generous help
given them by Gieves & Hawkes in the publication of this book.